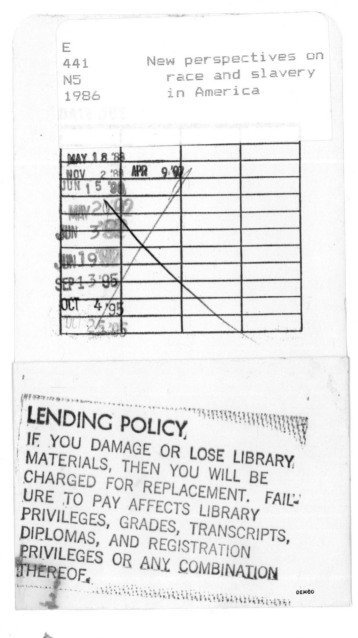

NEW PERSPECTIVES ON

Race and Slavery
in America

NEW PERSPECTIVES ON
Race and Slavery in America

ESSAYS IN HONOR OF
Kenneth M. Stampp

Robert H. Abzug and Stephen E. Maizlish, Editors

THE UNIVERSITY PRESS OF KENTUCKY

Publication of this book has been assisted by a grant from the Organized Research Fund of the University of Texas at Arlington.

Scholarly publisher for the Commonwealth, serving Bellarmine College, Berea College, Centre College of Kentucky, Eastern Kentucky University, The Filson Club, Georgetown College, Kentucky Historical Society, Kentucky State University, Morehead State University, Murray State University, Northern Kentucky University, Transylvania University, University of Kentucky, University of Louisville, and Western Kentucky University.

Editorial and Sales Offices: Lexington, Kentucky 40506-0024

Library of Congress Cataloging-in-Publication Data
Main entry under title:

New perspectives on race and slavery in America.

Includes bibliographies and index.
1. Slavery—United States—Addresses, essays, lectures. 2. Afro-Americans—History—Addresses, essays, lectures. 3. United States—Race relations—Addresses, essays, lectures. 4. Stampp, Kenneth M. (Kenneth Milton) I. Stampp, Kenneth M. (Kenneth Milton) II. Abzug, Robert H. III. Maizlish, Stephen E., 1945-
E441.N5   1986   973'.0496073   85-22569
ISBN 0-8131-1571-X

In Memory of
Arthur Pettit and Robert Starobin

Contents

Acknowledgments

Numerous friends and colleagues helped make this book possible. We particularly wish to thank Bob Perkins, Dean of the Graduate School of the University of Texas at Arlington, for his kind generosity; and the Organized Research Fund of the University of Texas at Arlington for its financial assistance. We also appreciate the advice and support of the staff at the University Press of Kentucky and the expert indexing of Nancy Stevens. Patrick Riddleberger, a Stampp student himself, deserves special thanks for his aid and encouragement. Finally, our deepest appreciation goes to Kenneth Stampp, whose example of excellence and integrity we honor in this volume.

Robert H. Abzug
Austin, Texas

Stephen E. Maizlish
Fort Worth, Texas

Introduction

ROBERT H. ABZUG

The title *New Perspectives on Race and Slavery in America* accurately reflects the breadth and limits of the essays presented in this volume, but certainly not of the historian they honor. Kenneth M. Stampp, it is true, remains best known as one of the great historians of slavery. The publication in 1956 of *The Peculiar Institution: Slavery in the Ante-Bellum South* has been justly credited as a landmark in the rewriting of Afro-American and race relations history. Yet in over forty years of contributions to scholarship, Stampp has ranged over the entire Civil War era. Only by considering the broad vision of his endeavors can one come to appreciate the power and resiliency of his work, as well as the profoundly humane influence he has had on his students and colleagues.

Kenneth Stampp's first and central fascination has always been with the Civil War—its causes, its consequences, its mixture of high idealism and grim reality. Writing his doctoral dissertation under William B. Hesseltine at University of Wisconsin, he charted wartime politics in a key northern state in what would later be published as *Indiana Politics during the Civil War* (1949). Even as his dissertation awaited publication, he was hard at work on a study of Lincoln and the North during the secession crisis. *And the War Came* (1950) answered those historians who believed that blundering and irresponsible agitators had caused the war. Stampp argued that crucial issues, mostly raised by the existence of slavery, made war probable if not inevitable. He drew a sensitive portrait of Lincoln as he faced the growing crisis, abhorring war but knowing that it might be necessary; at the same time, Stampp demonstrated that the various compromises offered by "peacemakers" of the secession winter were unrealistic because they left untouched the basic issues dividing the sections.

In neither *Indiana Politics during the Civil War* nor *And the War Came* did Stampp pay much attention to issues of race or even to the importance of the antislavery movement, omissions which in retrospect he readily admits. However, the institution of slavery loomed large in his sense of Civil War causation. "Without the 'peculiar institution,'" he wrote in *And the War Came,* "there could have been no proslavery or antislavery agitators, no division on the issue (whether real or fictitious) of slave territory."[1] And it was to the slave institution that he turned next. Ulrich Phillips's *American Negro Slavery* (1918) and *Life and Labor in the Old South* (1929) had long been standards in the field. Phillips envisioned slavery as something of a glorious burden for the master, not always showing much monetary reward but encouraging the finer moral instincts of paternalism and allowing the growth of aristocratic sensibilities. In many ways his work, though meeting high standards of scholarship, reflected the values and assumptions of the slaveowners whose lives he painted. He paid relatively little attention to the slaves, caricaturing them as mostly contented and childlike exotics in need of the master's care and control.

Since the 1930s a number of historians—Herbert Aptheker, Richard Hofstadter, and to some extent black scholars W.E.B. Du Bois and John Hope Franklin—had challenged this picture of slavery, but none had provided a thoroughly researched, full-scale reinterpretation. The need for such a work was only underlined by the resurgence of the civil rights struggle after World War II; Phillips's view of the slave seemed at best antiquated and at worst malevolent. *The Peculiar Institution* more than filled the void. Researched mostly in segregated archives and published two years after *Brown* v. *Topeka Board of Education,* it was not only superb history but also a book of and for its time. Stampp forthrightly rejected Phillips's racist tone; instead he assumed "the basic irrelevance of race" and that "slaves were merely ordinary human beings."[2]

Building upon an egalitarian view of the slave and an unsentimental vision of the master, Stampp produced a comprehensive and radically different picture of the institution. He thoroughly documented the cruelty of the system to the slave, describing the work day, punishments, discontent, limitations on family life and cultural expression, as well as diet and health. As for the masters, Stampp stripped them of their paternalistic trappings and saw them basically as owners and managers of a rather profitable system of labor exploitation. In all, *The Peculiar Institution* reset the terms of historical inquiry into slavery and also inspired a new generation of scholars to seek a more two-sided perspective on the history of American race relations.

Having explored the institution whose existence had caused the Civil War, Stampp turned to the aftermath of that conflict—Reconstruction. *The Era of Reconstruction* (1966) synthesized a growing body of scholarship that rejected the old, simplistic notion of Reconstruction as a "tragic era." Tradition had it that Radical Reconstruction was fraught with corruption, unscrupulous politicking, and cynical use of ignorant freedmen as voters and officeholders to further the aims of the Republican party. The net result was that the (white) South was cruelly abused socially and politically, a condition relieved only by the appearance of Redeemer governments in the various southern states. Stampp argued, along with other revisionist historians, that compared to similar situations in history the South endured relatively mild punishment; that corruption among Republicans in the South only typified a nationwide failing in both parties; that underlying much of the Radical program was an important strain of idealism aimed at bettering the lives of the freedmen; and that, in fact, the tragedy of Reconstruction lay less in the fate of southern whites than in its failure to offer complete freedom and equality to blacks.

Since 1966 Stampp has embarked upon some of the most interesting interpretive forays of his career. In articles and conference papers eventually collected and published as *The Imperiled Union* (1980), he approached the Civil War and slavery from psychological, legal, and historiographical perspectives. He joined the debate over the psychological effects of slavery in "Rebels and Sambos: The Search for the Negro's Personality in Slavery" (1970-71), and added his own distinctly devastating appraisal of Robert Fogel and Stanley Engerman's controversial book on slavery in *"Time on the Cross:* A Humanistic Perspective" (1976). He also raised hackles with "The Southern Road to Appomattox" (1968-69), a psychological interpretation of why the South lost the Civil War. Stampp argued that Confederates themselves contributed to defeat because of an incomplete commitment to the war rooted in qualms over slavery and a never quite vanquished strain of unionism.

More recent essays in *The Imperiled Union* returned to the old question of the Civil War's coming. Stampp scrutinized the growth of constitutional and historical traditions concerning secession in his presidential address to the Organization of American Historians, "The Concept of Perpetual Union" (1978). He also reviewed the massive but inconclusive literature on the question of the Civil War's inevitability in "The Irrepressible Conflict." And Stampp continues to explore new ways of understanding the coming of the war. Currently he is researching a major work that will depict American society in 1857, the year Stampp has come to see as the last before conflict between the sections became inevitable.

Stampp's long record of scholarship represents both a series of important individual contributions and the elaboration of a compelling historical vision. He assumes the existence of a unity known as American history and tells his story within that continuum. Thus *The Peculiar Institution* treats slavery not simply as balkanized ethnic or regional history but as part of an ongoing drama of American democratic ideals facing unvarnished historical reality. Its almost epic quality comes from depicting slavery as a southern tragedy within the broader national history, a sense one gets from the very first paragraph: "To understand the South is to feel the pathos in its history. This aura of pathos is more than a delusion of historians, more than the vague sensation one gets when looking down an avenue of somber, moss-draped live oaks leading to stately ruins or to nothing at all. For southerners live in the shadow of a real tragedy; they know, better than most other Americans, that little ironies fill the history of mankind and that large disasters from time to time unexpectedly help to shape its course."[3]

This sense of the tragic binds most of Stampp's major works. For instance

And the War Came, mostly a book about political maneuvering and the growth of public opinion, gains depth and meaning from knowledge of the war to come. Stampp brings this into final focus on the last page of the book: "[W]hat the Yankees achieved . . . was a triumph not of middle-class ideals but of middle-class vices. The most striking products of their crusade were the shoddy aristocracy of the North and the ragged children of the South. Among the masses of Americans there were no victors, only the vanquished."[4]

The epic and tragic senses of Stampp's vision are complemented by the all-too-human qualities of his principal actors. He has rarely been concerned with heroes and villains; rather he writes of individuals of ordinary dimension, caught in historical circumstances demanding extraordinary talent, wisdom, and courage. Thus slavery grew from small beginnings to intractable dimensions on a path taken step-by-step by individuals "more or less blind to the ultimate consequences of the choices they were making." As for the Civil War, it came as a result of ordinary politicians acting in typical ways, responding to crisis as statesmen always have. "The choice they actually made was the usual one," wrote Stampp. "It was nevertheless tragic." His injunction not to deal "too harshly" with those who could not prevent war in 1861 applied to most of those whom Stampp found wanting. Even the master was due "compassion" for "the moral dilemma in which he was trapped." Yet Stampp always affirmed that it was the victim who deserved the most consideration, whether in the case of the slave or one of the Civil War's anonymous crushed souls.[5]

Finally, Stampp assumes a basic psychological and cultural unity among Americans that transcends the differences which divide them. They are all party to a single and stormy national drama. In *The Peculiar Institution,* then, he emphasized the commonalities of the races—"that innately Negroes *are,* after all, only white men with black skins."[6] The tragedy of slaveholding was that the masters, good Lockeians and Christians and therefore a part of the American mainstream, tolerated the guilt engendered by slavery's evils and rationalized away their doubts because of the system's social and economic rewards. Stampp's hard-nosed, common sense assessments of slavery, the coming of the Civil War, and Reconstruction, gain much of their verve and depth from their being made within the context of a national ethos.

This aspect of Stampp's work stands in marked contrast to a more particularist perspective common in some recent scholarship, works that in a number of areas have offered alternatives to Stampp's approach. For instance, some political demographers have disputed the centrality of slavery to the political drama of the coming of the Civil War. They have produced numerous local and state studies that argue for the primacy of voter religion and ethnicity, as well as a miscellany of local issues, in the explanation of election results in the 1840s and 1850s. In these renderings, big issues such as slavery and freedom often become mere rhetoric.

Most of all, *The Peculiar Institution* has seen its vision of slavery challenged in various ways. Afro-Americanists have emphasized the more distinctive elements of black culture in slavery and freedom. The works of John Blassingame, George Rawick, Herbert Gutman, Eugene D. Genovese, and Lawrence Levine, among others, have provided a useful corrective to what they have seen as an underestimation of the vitality of black culture in Stampp's chapters on slave life. And scholars of southern society have argued for that section's social and cultural uniqueness. Eugene D. Genovese has attacked Stampp's vision of the South directly, positing instead a picture of the region as a preindustrial society whose slave institution engendered a distinct and integral set of values and norms. Most recently Bertram Wyatt-Brown, taking issue with both Stampp and Genovese, has argued for a distinctive antebellum southern culture based more on the idea of honor than on its peculiar institution.

These approaches and other recent particularist strains—women's history and the various ethnic histories—have greatly enriched our sense of the past. However, the proliferation of so many topical and methodological specializations, all too often with extremely parochial agenda, has tended to blunt our sense of a national history. Indeed, some may argue that the national synthesis is no longer either a possibility or the preferred way to envision the past, that the story of the United States lies in a collection of discrete local, sectional, gender, and ethnic histories. If that view prevails, its triumph will have less to do with historical verisimilitude than with the disintegration of the humanistic historical imagination which Stampp so well represents. Despite differences of section, race, class, or philosophy, his historical figures remain human beings, nothing more, nothing less. If recent scholarship has sometimes been more successful in describing the outer garment of those who lived in the past, Stampp and those who write in the same vein have been there to remind us of a common humanity and national tradition and of the sometimes profoundly tragic brotherhood of the human condition.

It is a happy coincidence when a great scholar is also a consummate teacher. Kenneth Stampp is surely both. Since his arrival at the University of California, Berkeley in 1946, he has directed the doctoral work of a veritable family of scholars and continues to do so today. His students have always been encouraged to seek their own topics and their own interpretations. Stampp has wished to promulgate no "school" of history, only high standards of research, writing, and spirited inquiry. The long list of significant books that began as Stampp dissertations, many of which treat subject areas that he never addressed and others which modify or dispute Stampp's own work, testifies to the success of his philosophy of mentorship.

The essays in this volume represent some of the latest work of a number of Stampp's students. Topics range in period from the seventeenth century to the early 1960s. Subjects include the psychology of race relations, black responses to freedom, race as an issue in local and national politics, and the ongoing impact of slavery and its abolition on southern identity. Despite their diversity, they share with Stampp's own work a commitment to the spirit of humanistic inquiry and a sense of relation to the larger drama of race in American history.

The book begins with Robert McColley's careful reconsideration of the origins of Virginia slavery, a question that has sparked historical controversy for decades. McColley concentrates on the language used to describe black and white servitude in order to sharpen our sense of how quickly slavery became the enforced status of Africans in the colony. In doing so, he moves beyond the old chicken-and-egg argument over which came first, racism or slavery. Moving to the nineteenth century, William W. Freehling investigates the master-slave nexus through the Denmark Vesey slave plot of 1822. Freehling elucidates the tangle of motives, self-deception, and contradiction that linked the key actors, black and white, and shows how the violent world surrounding Vesey was a microcosm *in extremis* of the American slave system.

Recent scholarship has been notable for its discovery and assessment of racism in northern society and politics. For instance, it has become a commonplace that race baiting was a key theme in northern Democratic party campaigns in the 1850s. Stephen Maizlish argues that historians have much exaggerated the Democrats' use of race. While not denying its presence, he shows that the race issue became important only at particular moments in the 1850s and that any number of other themes might better define the heart of Democratic ideology. It was only during and after the Civil War, Maizlish demonstrates, that race became a central Democratic concern.

At the same time, historians have carefully examined the Republicans' reputation for racial tolerance and have found it wanting. Not only have they found evidence of Republican racism; various scholars have also argued that the rise of the Republican party was due more to ethnic and religious issues, as well as the vicissitudes of the party system, than to anything related to the sectional conflict. William E. Gienapp, while agreeing with those who find little abolitionism in Republican ranks and accepting the findings of demographers concerning religious and ethnic issues, reasserts the importance of sectional issues in the new party by demonstrating the appeal of the "slave power conspiracy" argument. He makes the case that concern over the slave power was neither mere rhetoric nor based on irrational fears but was rather a reasonable response to events.

Turning to the Civil War and Reconstruction, Reid Mitchell, Leon F. Litwack, and Arthur Zilversmit all cast light on very different aspects of this most turbulent era of American life. Mitchell investigates the consciousness and culture of the Confederate soldier and, in doing so, illuminates loyalties and motivations that help explain not only the course of the war but also southern life after Appomattox. Litwack assesses the gains of newly freed blacks and points out continuities in the limits on black freedom from Reconstruction to the present. Turning to the venerable topic of the Grant presidency, Zilversmit finds the former general to have been more a friend of the freedman than has been assumed.

In a final section, James Oakes, John G. Sproat, and Joel Williamson complete the sweep of history from early Virginia to our own era. Oakes points out an irony of emancipation for southern politics in the late nineteenth and early twentieth century—abolition of slavery actually strengthened the political hand of the planters vis-à-vis their traditional yeoman rivals. John G. Sproat contributes a pioneering interpretation of the impact of desegregation efforts of the 1950s and 1960s on white southerners; he emphasizes the precarious position of white "moderates." Joel Williamson concludes the volume by meditating upon poignant and tragic themes in modern southern culture. By no means an apology for either slavery or racial discrimination, Williamson's essay ponders the nature of a society that has lost its formative institution and moral legitimacy for its distinctive racial system. In a sense Williamson engages in the remythologizing of southern history, but from an egalitarian perspective filled with mournful irony.

Kenneth Stampp once gently chided that "naive reviewer" who hails one or another work as "definitive," only to see its findings soon modified or rejected by the "endless and inevitable" process of revision.[7] We join Stampp in making a virtue of necessity by recognizing dialogue and change as the lifeblood of scholarship. We hope that these essays contribute significantly to a field whose hallmarks have been innovation and controversy and whose nagging questions will continue to provoke new perspectives for some time to come.

1. Kenneth M. Stampp, *And the War Came: The North and the Secession Crisis, 1860-61* (Chicago, 1964; originally published 1950), 2.

2. Kenneth M. Stampp, *The Peculiar Institution: Slavery in the Ante-Bellum South* (New York, 1956), vii.

3. Ibid., 3.

4. Stampp, *And the War Came*, 298.

5. Stampp, *The Peculiar Institution*, 6; Stampp, *And the War Came*, 3; Stampp, *The Peculiar Institution*, 430.

6. Stampp, *The Peculiar Institution*, vii-viii.

7. Kenneth M. Stampp, *"Time on the Cross:* A Humanistic Perspective," in Kenneth M. Stampp, *The Imperiled Union: Essays on the Background of the Civil War* (New York, 1980), 72.

PART I

The Peculiar Institution

1

Slavery in Virginia, 1619-1660: A Reexamination

ROBERT McCOLLEY

Most accounts of the beginnings of black servitude in Virginia (and therefore in British North America) are still remarkably like this one published in 1979: "The first 20 Negroes in the English mainland colonies arrived at Jamestown, Virginia in 1619 aboard a Dutch frigate and were sold to the colonists as indentured labor, not as slaves."[1] Such accounts then skip to 1660 or beyond, leaving the question vague as to when the institution of slavery started in Virginia. It will be maintained here that the familiar account just cited does not correspond to the known facts and that the records of early Virginia are reasonably clear about the status of the blacks who lived there before 1660.

The year 1660 marks a definite period in the history of black Virginians for several reasons. The older and still influential literature on the subject unfailingly recognizes that slavery existed in the colony by this time. Furthermore, this was the year of the restoration of the Stuart monarchy. Charles II established a government committed to the African slave trade and Negro slavery as integral parts of a scheme of imperial expansion. And most importantly, British planters of the West Indies had decisively turned to the cultivation of sugar and the use of slave labor.

Before 1660 and, indeed, for several years after, white labor under indentures lasting several years made up the bulk of the labor force in Virginia and Maryland. No one can argue that blacks played some sort of crucial or decisive role in the development of the Chesapeake economy until the last third of the seventeenth century. The position taken here is that, though few in numbers, the earliest blacks created a demand for more, when procuring more became possible. The population figures for the period are interesting. For the year 1625, the white population totalled 1,227 and the black population totalled 23, or 2 percent. By 1648 the white population had risen to 15,000 and the black to 300, still 2 percent. By 1670 there were 38,000 whites but the percentage of blacks had risen to 5 percent, or 2,000. These figures suggest that the proportion of blacks to whites did not rise significantly in the 1630s or 1640s, but began to increase at some point between 1648 and 1660. For reasons that will appear below, it seems likely that the number of blacks in Virginia more than doubled in the 1650s, and then doubled again in the 1660s.[2]

Perhaps the most important confusion concerning the period before 1660 is the one caused by a change in the meaning and use of the critical words *servant* and *slave*. The *Shorter Oxford Dictionary* reminds us of a fact so obvious it is indeed odd that we have failed to notice it: the typical word used by American slaveholders when referring to their blacks was *servant*, from the early seventeenth century until the end of the Civil War, and even later in memoirs, histories, and fiction. The term *slave* came also to be used, but in the South it was chiefly found as a technical term in the marketplace, the legislature, and economic treatises. Antislavery writers and publicists, not southern planters, insisted on using the term *slave* exclusively.[3]

In the early seventeenth century the word *servant* meant both servant and slave in our modern senses. One reason for this may have been that almost everyone who could then write English had also studied Latin, where *servus* normally means slave. During the seventeenth and eighteenth centuries the English had not yet fully differentiated *slave* from *sclave* or *sclav*, although many undoubtedly used *slave* in the modern sense, without any reference, conscious or otherwise, to the people of eastern Europe. Still, it is significant that *slave* (Latin *sclavus*) originally meant a race of white people from a certain region of the world; when such people were widely and commonly sold and bought as slaves, the word came to connote a status. The same thing later happened to the African when, for several centuries, *Negro* or *Noir* implied a condition of slavery unless otherwise specified.

To demonstrate the ways in which Englishmen used the words *servant* and *slave* in the early seventeenth century, we have three examples from the King James Bible of 1611, several lines from Shakespeare's *Tempest*, and three examples from the records of Virginia. In Gen. 39:17, Potiphar's wife complains about Joseph, "the Hebrew servant, which thou has brought unto us." In 1 Corinthians 7:22, Paul writes, "For he that is called in the Lord, being a servant, is the Lord's freeman: likewise also he that is called, being free, is Christ's servant." Modern translators, on the other hand, make Joseph a Hebrew slave, which is abundantly clear from the context. And it is equally clear that Paul meant to contrast slave and free as we now understand the words. But in 1 Sam. 18:22 we read in the King James version, "And Saul commanded his servants, saying, Commune with David secretly, and say Behold, the king hath delight in thee, and all his servants love thee," and here our modern translators quite properly retain the word *servants*, for these were people of importance at court.

Shakespeare's *Tempest* is even more suggestive, employing the words *servant* and *slave* in frequent and striking contrast. Shakespeare's protagonist, Prospero, by means of magic spells, is master of the alert and faithful sprite, Ariel, and the boorish Caliban. Even when Ariel complains of his servitude, he remains candid and respectful. Prospero, in turn, treats Ariel with civility and trusts him with matters of life and death. And he calls him "servant." By contrast, Prospero addresses Caliban in a manner shocking to modern readers, precisely because he has exhibited such unfailing refinement up to this point in the play:

> We'll visit Caliban, my slave, who never
> Yields us kind answer. . . .
> Thou poisonous slave, got by the devil himself
> Upon thy wicked dam, come forth! . . .
> Thou most lying slave,
> Whom stripes may move, not kindness![4]

Slave and *servant,* as Shakespeare is using them, do not signify a difference in status, for Ariel and Caliban are equally under the power of Prospero. But the servant is himself good; the slave is vile and wretched.

In Virginia an edict of 1618 proclaimed that men guilty of missing church should "lye neck and heels . . . the night following and be a Slave the week following." In 1623 young Richard Frethorne wrote an emotional account of the recent Indian massacre to his parents in England. He called the Indian attackers *slaves.* Finally, we have the complaint of Thomas Best, also in 1623, that "My Master Atkins hath sold me for a £150 sterling like a damned slave." In the first example what is called slavery is in fact a brief period of service, but it is as punishment for a crime and presumably must be performed without compensation. Frethorne uses *slave* as Prospero does, to convey his impression of savage brutes. Only Best approaches our idea of slavery, yet he was what Virginians were beginning to call an indentured servant.[5]

In the second half of the seventeenth century, Englishmen began to use the word *slave* regularly in commercial and legal language. To some this will seem evidence of the debasement of the African by a nation increasingly turning to the slave trade as a source of profit and exploitable labor. But it must again be recalled that those who actually owned slaves continued to call them servants, and the word *slave,* when used in law and trade, very largely lost the connotations of brutality, outrage, and debasement we have noted in the early years of the century. The slave trader, for instance, whatever his private thoughts about the people he offered for sale, always wished prospective buyers to think he was offering reliable Ariels and not doltish Calibans. Charles Verlinden, a Belgian authority on medieval European slavery, insists on continuity between the slavery of the Mediterranean world and that of the Atlantic commercial area that began to develop with the Portuguese expansion of the late fifteenth century. As sugar cultivation spread first to the Atlantic islands (Canaries, Madeiras, Azores, Cap Verdes, São Thomé) and then to the New World, the term *sclavus,* in regular use in the Mediterranean, where Slavs were in fact the most numerous slaves, now replaced the older *servus* in official and commercial language.[6]

It is not surprising, then, that the English began regularly to use the word *slave* in a practical, unemotional way during the years that they adopted the sugar industry and moved into the transatlantic slave trade. Virginia, though engaged in producing tobacco, was nevertheless connected to the same Atlantic trade which sugar, more than any other commodity, would dominate for a century and a half. For Virginians and many other colonials, a clear distinction between *servant* and *slave* (as legal terms, denoting status) became quite useful in the second half of the seventeenth century.

Once we understand that the earliest Virginians used the word *servant* where later they would use *slave*, we are in a good position to understand the early records. But another important point remains to be made about the English background: although the English had made only individual and isolated ventures into the slave trade before the first Royal Africa Company (1663), they had in fact regularly encountered black slaves in the seaports of the Mediterranean, the Atlantic, and along the coasts of Africa itself. James B. Walvin begins the first chapter of his valuable book, *Black and White: The Negro and English Society, 1555-1945,* with an arresting fact: "Early in 1555 John Lok returned from his second voyage to Guinea, carrying with him 'certain blacke slaves, whereof some were tall and strong men, and could wel agree with our meates and drinkes.'" The next year "Master William Towrson Marchant of London" was trading for gold and ivory along the Guinea Coast and took aboard an African who "could speak a little Portuguise." After trading for various items, "He demanded, why we had not brought againe their men, which the last yeere we tooke away, and could tell us that there were five taken away by Englishmen: we made him answere, that they were there kept till they could speake the language, and then they should be brought againe to be a helpe to Englishmen in this Countrey: and then he spake no more of the matter." Sure enough, when Towerson returned on his second voyage to Guinea he had several Negroes with him, and they were of considerable service in establishing cordial relations and initiating trade with chieftans who were inclined to be suspicious of strange Europeans.[7]

Whether by accident, compulsion, or choice, many of the blacks taken from the coasts of West Africa to English seaports either remained there or took up careers as sailors and joined the floating population engaged in Atlantic trade and warfare. Other blacks came to London with Spanish diplomats, churchmen, and merchants, especially after the accession of Queen Mary in 1553 and her marriage to Philip II of Spain. Others returned with English merchants and diplomats who had visited the bustling ports of Lisbon and Seville, centers of the slave trade in the sixteenth century. Modern historians of slavery have been so preoccupied with understanding the complex of interests, rationalizations, and neuroses which led Europeans to treat Africans first as inferiors and then as chattels, that they have rather neglected the many kinds of cooperation and admiration involved in their relations. Especially underplayed, though it receives good measure in Walvin's book, is the delight that wealthy and noble Europeans had in decorating their establishments with handsome and dignified Africans decked out in glittering livery.

Walvin shows that the merchants and imperial politicians of London had been involved off and on with the buying and selling of Negroes for fifty years before the founding of Virginia and that they were familiar with trading conditions in Africa, as well as the profitable uses of black slaves in various colonies of Spain and Portugal. Although slavery was never acknowledged by the statute law of England, it nevertheless happened that for over two hundred and fifty years various Englishmen, English colonials, and foreigners routinely brought blacks into England and retained them there. The Somerset case of 1772 would not have been possible, and certainly would not have attracted attention, had this not been the case. And the Somerset decision, however gratifying to the free blacks of London and the new abolitionists, no more put a stop to bringing slaves into England than *Brown* v. *Topeka Board of Education* put an end to racial segregation in the public schools of the United States.[8]

Unlike the plantation slavery which later developed in the Americas, however, the mercantile and domestic servitude of blacks in England often led to emancipation, for there was never a question of maintaining a large and disciplined black proletariate. Neither African nor Indian slavery figured in the plans of those Englishmen who first planted colonies in North America. They recognized an acute problem of overpopulation in their own nation and assumed optimistically that some combination of English and native workers would support their colonies. Yet while some of them censured the Spaniards for enslaving American Indians and black Africans, others observed that the Spanish Empire suffered from a severe shortage of labor and that great profits might be made in the Atlantic slave trade. It would be unfair to characterize the English as hypocritical, for the nation was not of one mind on this or any other question of politics, economics, or religion. It would be fair and accurate, on the other hand, to say that among the many Englishmen who concerned themselves with overseas trade and colonization were some who were quite willing to buy, sell, and employ Africans just as those pioneers of modern colonization, the Portuguese and Spaniards, did.

It is now proper to account for the several hundred blacks that appeared in Virginia between 1619 and 1650. The records of the colony tell us something of the background of two blacks who found themselves there. One of these was a sailor, "John Phillip, A negro Christened in *England* 12 yeeres since."[9] It appears from Phillip's testimony that he had been employed on an English ship which had captured a Spanish trading vessel and held it for ransom. He gave his testimony to the Council of Virginia in 1624, when that government was still bound by the wishes and decrees of James I to maintain peace with Spain and all her possessions, desisting both from piracy and smuggling. Having given his testimony, John Phillip disappears from the rather fragmentary records of his age. But his brief appearance gives us one good example of a black man who had lived in England before he came to Virginia. Of course he may soon thereafter have left, continuing his career as a sailor.

In 1625 the council took more extensive testimony of another illegal voyage by an English "frygott" which, because of its poor condition and short rations, put into Virginia. Having "lighted upon a *Spanish* frigott," the English relieved it of "some Raw hides and some Tobacco and a negro and a *ffrenchman* who were desirous to goe along with them, and a Portugall to be their Pilot out of the islands." Over the next several months the council made three remarkable decrees concerning the Negro, who had, in the last of them, acquired the name Brase. In the first of these, the Negro's labor was directed as compensation for some clothes to be given the Portuguese pilot. In the next, Brase was assigned as servant to Lady Yeardley, and she was directed to pay "monthly for his labor forty pound waight of good marchantable tobacco." But it was not clear who would be paid, unless it was the Captain Jones who had supplied clothes to the Portuguese. Finally, Governor Francis Wyatt and his fellow councillors decided to remove and void all previous arrangements concerning Brase and place him entirely in the service of Wyatt himself.[10]

With Brase, taken from a Spanish ship, and John Phillip, a black English sailor serving on a privateer, firmly in mind, we may turn back to the arrival in August 1619 of an armed Dutch ship which landed "twenty and odd [i.e., more than twenty] Negroes" in exchange for "nothing but victual." We have already noted the legend that there were twenty, that they landed in Jamestown, and that the ship was Dutch (and, presumably, quite unexpected). But our only witness, John Rolfe, testifies that there were more than twenty and that they landed at Point Comfort, many miles downstream from Jamestown, and, by comparison, a rather isolated place. Rolfe's letter says nothing about the status of these blacks, nor does any other surviving document. The practice of indentured servitude was itself just taking form in Virginia, and there is no good reason to suppose that the blacks had any claims or rights which the Virginians who took them recognized by contractual agreements.[11]

Where did the "twenty and odd" come from? W.F. Craven gives a detailed and fascinating account in *The Dissolution of the Virginia Company*. It turns out that our nameless Dutch ship, far from being in Virginia by accident, had an English pilot and had been sailing with the English ship *Treasurer,* a veteran of the run from London to Bermuda and Virginia. *Treasurer,* in turn, had been fitted in Virginia for a privateering voyage to the West Indies, for which purpose she even carried a commission by the Duke of Savoy who, unlike the King of England, was then at war with Spain. *Treasurer* arrived in Virginia a few days after the Dutchman and also carried a cargo of blacks, but carried them on to Bermuda. From these established facts, it is virtually certain that the earliest known blacks in Virginia had been taken by raiding a Spanish ship in the Caribbean. It is less certain but still likely that they were en route from Seville by way of the Azores to some destination on the Spanish Main. Like Brase and John Phillip, the blacks of 1619 were in Virginia because of the extensive but poorly documented business of commerce-raiding.[12]

The then governor of Virginia, Samuel Argall, had invested in the *Treasurer's* expedition, as had his friend Robert Rich, Earl of Warwick, in England. With the ascendancy of Sir Edwin Sandys, Virginia could no longer be a base from which to raid the Spanish Caribbean, for Sandys fully supported the peaceful foreign policy of James I. But even had the authorities in Virginia continued to connive at an anti-Spanish policy, the colony was simply too remote to serve as an efficient base for raiding the colonies and shipping of Spanish America. On the other hand, Virginia might still be a market for blacks taken by privateers based elsewhere. Thus, according to records kept in England, Captain Arthur Guy captured a Spanish slaver and exchanged Africans for tobacco in Virginia in 1627.[13]

Between 1630 and 1640 the English rushed to their new island colonies in the Caribbean. They now significantly increased their raids on Spanish ships and plantations, but at the same time they created Caribbean markets to absorb the slaves they were stealing. Meanwhile the Dutch were engaging in the slave trade in a comprehensive way, by replacing the Portuguese in West Africa and selling directly in American markets. But for almost twenty years the Dutch also attempted to take over Brazil and establish a great sugar industry there. Until the Portuguese drove them out in 1648, that was their favorite outlet for black slaves. Nevertheless, the Dutch also managed to increase the supply of blacks to the Caribbean in the 1640s and made that their primary area for retailing slaves in the 1650s. Such was the demand for them in the burgeoning sugar islands that there were few enough left over for North America. Still, there was now a regular trade (originating early in the 1640s) between New England, the other English colonies of North America, and the West Indies; until 1664 it also involved considerable trade with the colony of New Netherland, though the Puritan Navigation Act of 1651 tried to outlaw such trade. The coasting and West Indian trade was generally carried on in small ships that returned to their home bases in North America each year. It therefore became possible for Chesapeake planters to place orders for merchandise and for slaves in the tropics. They could also now purchase slaves from those captains who returned from the islands with a few blacks bought on speculation.[14]

The English, having imitated the Portuguese and Dutch in so much else, were obviously aware of the advantage of going directly to Africa for slaves, and evidently a number of private traders attempted this in the 1640s and 1650s. Besides the temporary inconveniences caused by their own civil war, however, the English faced the usual difficulties of the African slave trade: a climate very dangerous to the health of northern Europeans, uncertainty in finding cargoes, tough bargaining by African chieftans, and the effective hostility of those Europeans already on the scene. One of the first things the supporters of Charles II did after his restoration was to start a company under royal patronage for buying slaves in West Africa and selling them in the American colonies, from which the Dutch were barred by new navigation acts and the conquest of New Netherland. But after shipping some thousands of slaves this company faltered, largely because of the fierce opposition of the Dutch. The British did not have a regular supply of slaves until the reorganized Royal Africa Company of 1672 had established its position in Africa.[15]

At no time between 1619 and 1660 did the English have a regular part in the African slave trade, let alone a prominent one. During these years they largely exhausted the possibility of getting slaves by stealing them and became for a time the leading customers for Dutch slave traders—in their Caribbean sugar islands. The colonies of North America, including Virginia, were involved in this trade, though in a peripheral way. Their need for labor was less urgent than that of the rising class of sugar planters (English servants shied away from the islands after 1640 but were still willing to take indentures in Maryland and Virginia). Furthermore, after the price of tobacco collapsed in 1630, Virginia planters would always have less money to spend on labor than their Caribbean cousins. Yet, being farther from the African source, they would normally have to pay more for slaves than the sugar planters who could more easily afford them. It is therefore quite understandable that only a trickle of slave trading went on to the Chesapeake until the English sugar islands were fully stocked.[16]

Because it was relatively difficult to acquire blacks before 1660, one should not be surprised to discover that, generally speaking, those Virginians who owned them were among the wealthiest, the most powerful, and the most resourceful people in the colony. As we have seen, Governor Argall was personally involved in outfitting the expedition that sailed to the West Indies and returned with cargoes of blacks for both Virginia and Bermuda. His successor, George Yeardley, owned more of the 1619 group than anyone else. We have also noted how Governor Francis Wyatt decided to keep the Negro Brase for himself. Others in the first generation of Virginians who owned several blacks were Captain William Tucker, the leading man in Elizabeth City, and the merchant-planter Abraham Piersey, reputed to be the richest man in the colony. In the 1630s the enterprising and well-connected George Menefie was the largest importer of blacks of whom records survive. Edmund Scarburgh, the most powerful planter on the Eastern Shore in his heyday, imported forty-one blacks by way of New Netherland in 1656. Richard Lee, founder of Virginia's most famous family (as many judge such things), engaged to import eighty blacks in 1660, although it appears that the shipment never reached Virginia.[17]

These were men who were leaders in every aspect of the young colony's life.

They succeeded where so many others failed because of strong physical constitutions, enterprise, a shrewd sort of intelligence, and a certain amount of good fortune. If only one or two of these worthies had owned blacks, we might put it down as a chance circumstance. But in an era when blacks were scarce and usually available only by means of elaborate overseas transactions, these tough-minded pioneers must have had special reasons for buying them. We must rule out any idea that they might have been unable to get good white servants; these were the very Virginians who had the pick of each year's importation. The first thousand or so blacks came into Virginia not because white labor was scarce, or notably unruly, or, after 1630, dying off at too great a rate; far-sighted and imaginative planters bought them when they could for their precious quality of permanence.

An authentic voice of early Virginia addressed this very issue. The long passage quoted below is nominally concerned with the excellent character and estate of Captain Samuel Matthews. But it speaks more directly to the way in which a great planter could secure an independent estate by the judicious management of black labor. It is a commonplace of Virginia history that the first William Byrd, William Fitzhugh, "King" Carter, and others did this toward the end of the seventeenth century. But the following was written in 1648:

> Worthy Captaine Matthews, an old planter of above thirty years standing, one of the Counsell and a most deserving Commonwealthsman, I may not omit to let you know this gentleman's industry.
>
> He hath a fine house, and all things answerable to it, he sowes yeerly store of hempe and flax, and causes it to be spun; he keeps weavers and hath a tan-house, causes leather to be dressed, hath eight shoemakers employed in their trade, hath forty Negroe servants, brings them up to trades in his house: He yeerly sowes abundance of wheat, barley, &c. The wheat he selleth at four shillings the bushell; kills store of beeves, and sells them to victuall the ships which come thither: hath abundance of kine, a brave dairy, swine great store, and poltery; he married the daughter of Sir Thomas Hinton, and in a word, keeps a good house, lives bravely, and a true lover of Virginia; he is worthy of much honour.[18]

Every part of this is interesting, but our special concern is with the "forty Negroe servants," whom Captain Matthews brought up "to trades in his house," many of which are then handsomely detailed. We are indebted to the anonymous author of the pamphlet *A Perfect Description of Virginia . . . Being Sent from Virginia at the Request of a Gentleman of Worthy Note* both for this description of Captain Matthews and for the estimate of the black population of Virginia in 1648. If the figure of 300 is accurate, Matthews alone owned about 13 percent of the blacks in the colony. Since the daughter of Sir Thomas Hinton was also the widow of Abraham Piersey, she presumably contributed to this impressive total, and among the "Negroe servants" were some of the original importation of 1619.

By March 1660 the desire of the leading planters of Virginia for more black slaves was clearly set forth in a law which offered special inducements to the Dutch to bring them Negroes. This enactment came at a time when the Puritan Navigation Act could be presumed void and before the new navigation acts of Charles II had reached Virginia. In the end it represented wishful thinking, for the era of more or less free trade with the Dutch was nearing its end. But here we are interested in the act only because it gives evidence about the attitude of Virginia's leading men toward black slaves:

> Whereas the restriction of trade hath appeared to be the greatest impediment to the advance . . . of our present only commodity tobacco, Bee it enacted and confirmed that the Dutch and all strangers of what Christian nation soever in amity with the people of England shall have free liberty to trade with us, for all allowable commodities, . . . provided they give bond and pay the impost of ten shillings per hogshead laid upon all tobacco exported to any foreign dominions . . . always provided, that if the said Dutch or other foreigners shall import any negro slaves, they . . . shall . . . pay only the impost of two shillings per hogshead, the like being paid by our nation.[19]

Surely this law proves that Virginia, perfectly aware that the Dutch nation was the leading and virtually the only supplier of blacks in their part of the world, yearned both to sell more tobacco and import more black slaves. But it should not be concluded from this that Virginia wished to cease or even cut back on the importation of white labor. Indeed, Virginia continued to import white servants until the outbreak of the War for Independence. The same assembly that hoped to encourage the Dutch to bring them more blacks also passed a law removing discriminatory terms of service from the Irish, obviously hoping to increase the supply of Irish servants.[20] Edmund S. Morgan has argued in *American Slavery, American Freedom* that a sort of class conflict underlay Bacon's Rebellion, causing a self-conscious preference for black labor to white after 1676.[21] The view taken here is quite different: Virginians showed a marked interest in buying blacks well before Bacon's Rebellion and continued to buy white servants in significant numbers after it. Bacon's Rebellion was itself caused by some of the struggles that delayed the British development of a large-scale trade from Africa, especially the commercial and military warfare with the Netherlands. Virginians began buying more blacks than white servants when, at last, blacks were available in large numbers and at prices they could afford.

The last area we need to explore concerns sexual relations. W.F. Craven inclined to the view that the black population was slow to reproduce because a very few blacks were scattered throughout a much larger white population, and, at least among those registered for headrights, there were two men for every woman. Sexual relations with white people seem to have been regularly and severely punished. Finally, no Virginian seems to have observed for the record that blacks should be encouraged to reproduce. All of these points were well taken, but they do not tell the whole story.[22]

The courts of early Virginia did indeed punish couples of different races for fornication. But the same courts far more often punished white servants for fornication and bastardy. Blacks were not punished for sexual relations among themselves, which is surely significant. The county records, the oldest of which begin in the 1630s, make it quite clear that many blacks born in Virginia in that decade remained bound to service for life. One cannot escape the inference that planters regarded pregnancies and infants among their black women either with indifference or with approval, even though, as Craven says, no one ever positively asserted such a view. The same records indicate a fixed purpose to keep white women servants chaste throughout the term of their indentures and to punish them with whippings, fines, and additional years of service for unchastity.[23]

Two cases involving black women belonging to Lt. Robert Sheppard illustrate the point. They occurred in 1640 and 1641, and could possibly have referred to the same person. Parenthetically, these are two of several court cases and other evidences that appear in the records from 1640 onwards, convincing modern students that slavery existed by this time. Because nothing happened in 1639 or 1640 by way of legislation or social upheaval in Virginia, we have surely been reading this evidence too cautiously: the practice of 1640 was surely the practice long established. In any case, the court cited one Robert Sweat in October 1640 because he had "begotten with child a negro woman servant belonging unto Lieutenant Sheppard." The court ordered Sweat to do penance "at James City church in the time of devine service" and ordered the woman whipped.[24]

The case of John Graweere (or Geaweene) was remarkably different:

John Graweere being a negro servant unto William Evans was permitted by his said master to keep hogs and make the best benefit thereof to himself provided that the said Evans might have half the increase . . . . And whereas the said negro having a young child of a negro woman belonging to Lieut. Robert Sheppard which he desired should be made a christian and be . . . taught and exercised in the church of England, by reason whereof he the said negro did for his said child purchase its freedom of Lieut. Sheppard . . . with the good liking and consent of Tho: Gooman's overseer, as by the deposition of the said Sheppard and Evans appeareth, the court hath therefore ordered that the child shall be free from the said Evans or his assigns and to be and remain at the disposing and education of the said Graweere and the child's godfather, who undertaketh to see it brought up in the christian religion as aforesaid.[25]

Far from punishing Graweere and Lieutenant Sheppard's black woman, the court was here acting benevolently toward them, reflecting, no doubt, the good will of their respective masters and the somewhat mysterious overseer-godfather. If, as has been maintained here, Virginia planters in general were eager to keep the children of their blacks even at this early date, Lieutenant Sheppard was exceptional in his willingness to let the boy go free. But of course he was being paid to do so. The essential point is that Graweere had to pay for the freedom of his son; had he been an indentured servant, freedom would have come as a matter of course.

Finally, this case illustrates another of the puzzles hanging over early Virginia slavery. As his plea was stated by the court, Graweere was mainly concerned that his boy should be raised a Christian; the purchase of his freedom appears on the face of it to have been an essential condition of his becoming a member of the church. Yet it is difficult to see how Graweere could have taken the primary responsibility of raising his son a Christian if he were not a Christian himself. And he appears not to have been free. The following explanation may account for this apparent contradiction: just as *servant* might mean either slave or servant, depending on the context, so *Christian* still meant either "free denizen of a Christian nation," or "baptised member, formally enrolled in the church." Englishmen switched from one sense to the other quite unconsciously.[26]

The cases involving women belonging to Robert Sheppard indicate that chastity was a rule for white servants but not for black. A more striking proof of this is the estate inventory of William Stafford, late merchant of Cheeskiake, as listed in March 1644. Among the items were eight blacks, their values given in pounds of tobacco: Negro man, Anthonio, worth 2,700; Negro woman, Mitchaell, 2,700; Negro woman, Conchanello, 2,500; Negro woman, Palassa, 2,500; Negro girl, Mary, 4 years old, 700; Negro girl, Anne, 3 years old, 400; Negro boy, one year old, 400; and Negro boy, two weeks old, 200.[27] The list does not tell us who was related to whom in this group, but it has the merit, unusual in the seventeenth century, of giving the ages of the children. The adults, with their foreign names, were almost certainly born outside Virginia and may very likely have endured one or two violent kidnappings. Now they lived in the fields of tobacco-growing Virginia, rearing children with English names. We are not looking at indentured servants here; no Chesapeake planter ever had eight indentured servants of whom half were four years old or less. The children of indentured servants were considered a charge to the community; these black children were assets in Stafford's estate.

But at this stage in the historiography of slavery it should hardly be necessary to demonstrate that slavery existed in early Virginia, well before its legislature began defining the institution with a series of statutes. We know now—even those of us who more or less exclusively teach American history— that African slaves were in all the European colonies of America, virtually from their beginnings, and everywhere the practice of slavery preceded its legal definition. It would be amazing if slavery had *not* appeared in early Virginia. To speak of origins, however, is misleading, for slavery no more originated in Virginia than did the Church of England or the English language; like those it was imported, took root, and began to show distinctive characteristics of local adaptation. This proceeded slowly in Virginia, not because of any widespread prejudice against Africans, or even because of a preference for white labor, but because blacks were scarce and difficult to get until late in the seventeenth century. In conclusion we should also remember that there were also blacks bound for a limited period of service and free blacks in the years from 1619 to 1660; among the latter was the widely studied family of Anthony Johnson on the Eastern Shore. But the great majority of blacks were bound for life and that, surely, was the most important reason why many Virginians, including many of the wealthiest and shrewdest, sought them out and kept them.[28]

1. Charles E. Wynes, "Negroes," in *Encyclopedia of Southern History*, ed. D.C. Roller and R.W. Twyman (Baton Rouge, 1979), 886.

2. Evarts B. Greene and Virginia Harrington, *American Population Before the Federal Census of 1790* (New York, 1932), 134-36, 143-44.

3. *Shorter Oxford English Dictionary* (1933), 2: "servant," 1849; "slave," 1912.

4. *The Tempest*, Act 1, sc. 2, line 187, has Prospero call: "Come away, servant, come! Approach, my Ariel! Come!" Prospero to Caliban, act 1, sc. 2, lines 308-9, 319-20, 343-44.

5. Helen T. Catterall, ed., *Judicial Cases Concerning Slavery*, vol. 1 (Washington, D.C., 1926), 54; Susan M. Kingsbury, ed., *Records of the Virginia Company of London*, vol. 4 (Washington, D.C., 1935), 61; Edmund S. Morgan, *American Slavery, American Freedom* (New York, 1975), 128.

6. Charles Verlinden, *The Beginnings of Modern Colonization* trans. Yvonne Freccero (Ithaca, 1970), 35-36.

7. James B. Walvin, *Black and White: The Negro and English Society, 1555-1945* (London, 1973), 1; Towerson's first and second voyages are recounted in Richard Hakluyt, ed., *The Principal Navigations Voyages Traffiques & Discoveries of the English Nation*, vol. 6 London, 1589; (reprint, New York, 1965), 177-231, 200.

8. Walvin, *Black and White*, especially chapters 1 and 7.

9. H.R. McIlwaine, ed., *Minutes of the Council and General Court of Colonial Virginia, 1622-1632, 1670-1676* (Richmond, 1924), 33.

10. Ibid, McIlwaine, *Minutes*, 68, 71-73.

11. Kingsbury, *Records*, vol. 3 (Washington, D.C., 1933), 243.

12. W.F. Craven, *White, Red, and Black* (Charlottesville, Va., 1971; New York, 1977), 77-81; W.F. Craven, *Dissolution of the Virginia Company* (1932; reprint, Gloucester, Mass. 1964), 124-35.

13. Craven, *White, Red, and Black*, 82. Craven thinks "Virginia might have meant some other part of America," but most authorities, including Philip Alexander Bruce and Winthrop D. Jordan, believe the blacks landed in what is now Virginia.

14. On the role of the Dutch in the Atlantic slave trade and the development of European plantations in the Caribbean, see Cornelis Ch. Goslinga, *The Dutch in the Caribbean and on the Wild Coast, 1580-1680* (Gainesville, 1971) and C.R. Boxer, *The Dutch Seaborne Empire: 1600-1800* (New York, 1968); on the English adoption of Negro slavery in the Caribbean, see Arthur P. Newton, *The Colonizing Activities of the English Puritans* (New Haven, 1941) and Carl Bridenbaugh, *No Peace Beyond the Line: The English in the Caribbean* (New York, 1972).

15. K.G. Davies, *The Royal Africa Company* (London, 1957; reprint, New York, 1970) chap. 1.

16. Philip Curtin finds no overall increase in the Atlantic slave trade during the second quarter of the seventeenth century. The new flow of blacks to Barbados and the Lesser Antilles—with a slight but traceable overflow to the North American mainland— meant a greatly reduced supply for Spanish America; *The Atlantic Slave Trade: A Census* (Madison, 1969), 126. James A. Rawley, in *The Transatlantic Slave Trade* (New York, 1981), finds the Dutch struggling in the 1620s and 1630s, but succeeding in dominating the trade from the early 1640s to the mid-1670s. Like Curtin, he finds the trade to the mainland negligible before 1670 (see especially chap. 4).

17. Alden T. Vaughan, "Blacks in Virginia: A Note on the First Decade," *William and Mary Quarterly*, 3d ser., 29, no. 3 (July 1972):469-78, is so occupied with establishing "a deep and pervasive racial prejudice" (p. 478) that he has nothing to say about the possible motives of those who, according to the censuses that are his chief source, actually owned blacks. He notes the arrival of several blacks on ships from England, but does not explain their presence. But the article is valuable for locating every black or group of blacks present in Virginia before 1630. Craven mentions all these eminent Virginians except Wyatt; *White, Red, and Black*, 91, 92, 101n, 105n, 108n. He does not discuss the question why those who could most readily secure white labor were the main owners of blacks.

18. This valuable quotation may be found in Richard Lee Morton, *Colonial Virginia*, vol. 1 (Chapel Hill, 1960), 145.

19. W.W. Hening, *The Statutes at Large in Virginia* , vol. 1 (Richmond, 1810), 540.

20. Hening, *Statutes,* 539.

21. Edmund S. Morgan, *American Slavery, American Freedom: The Ordeal of Colonial Virginia* (New York, 1975).

22. Craven, *White, Red, and Black*, 100-102.

23. Philip Alexander Bruce, *The Economic History of Virginia in the Seventeenth Century*, vol. 2 (New York, 1896), 34-38, provides the best and virtually the only informed discussion on the subject of sexual rules and conduct among early Virginia servants.

24. Catterall, *Judicial Cases*, vol. 1, 77.

25. Ibid.

26. Winthrop D. Jordan, *White Over Black* (Chapel Hill, 1968), 92-98. Jordan and Catterall believe that "some of the first Negroes in Virginia had been baptized before arrival." The only evidence they adduce for this is that some of them had Spanish names.

27. *William and Mary Quarterly* 22, no. 4 (April 1914): 247.

28. For a recent and thorough review of the controversial literature on the so-called origins of slavery in seventeenth-century Virginia, see Joseph Boskin, *Into Slavery: Racial Decisions in the Virginia Colony* (Philadelphia, 1976).

2

Denmark Vesey's Peculiar Reality

WILLIAM W. FREEHLING

The title posed the puzzle. North American slaveholders entitled slavery the Peculiar Institution. They also denied that slaveholding was peculiar. Bondage, they boasted, was omnipresent throughout western history.

Then why was the Peculiar Institution peculiar?

An examination of moments of crisis helps answer that question. Insurrection scares were among the South's gravest traumas. Charleston, South Carolina's Denmark Vesey Conspiracy of 1822 was the severest antebellum scare. Both Charlestonians' explanations of why the Peculiar Institution momentarily shattered and their efforts to make the peculiar normal again illuminate how that mysterious title captured reality.

Denmark Vesey's Conspiracy, we have lately been told, was no window to reality. Richard C. Wade's influential 1964 essay reduced Vesey's threat to "loose talk" by a harmless handful of "aggravated and embittered men."[1] That thesis hinders understanding. Two minor documents misled Wade, apparently because he missed the pivotal document.

The full record is too revealing to tarry long on one scholar's partial reading. White Charlestonians differed on the conspiracy's cogency. But they agreed that evidence showed some threat. Contemporaries also agreed that the Peculiar Institution's peculiar tendencies toward softness gave Denmark Vesey his opportunity. Those agreements aside, an anguished governor and a tormented court fought over how the Peculiar Institution could be made as hard as less peculiar despotisms—and retain treasured peculiarities too.

Old South slavery was peculiar despotism for four related reasons. First of all, few absolutisms have been so private. Antebellum slaveholders normally coerced slaves with little state help or state interference. Public authorities only momentarily stepped between master and slave, and only in extreme cases of private power perverted or social control demolished. This possibility of public coerciveness constantly deterred private slaves from rising against solitary masters. But the institution remained unusual because The Man actually brandishing the gun was usually not a state official.

A second North American peculiarity was that this usually private despotism was enmeshed in an advanced public democracy. The slaveholder as democrat was a soul divided. His power as slaveholder violated his assumptions as democrat.

One way past schizophrenia was a third North American oddity: private despotism and public democracy allegedly cleaved at the color line. In the Old South, democratic public authority supposedly governed only whites, all supposedly equal to each other. Dictatorial private dominance supposedly applied only to blacks, all supposedly inferior to whites. Black and white. Inferior and superior. Dictator and democrat. Two colors, two abilities, two regimes, with nothing in between.

Alas, the in-between condition intruded. Mulattoes were sometimes born. Blacks were sometimes freed. Whites were sometimes stupid. Slaves were sometimes brilliant. Democratic and despotic suppositions were sometimes inseparable. Schizophrenic confusion often returned.

A measure of confusion was a fourth institutional peculiarity: public democracy moving past the color line to supply private dictatorship's model of legitimacy. The democrat as dictator craved one essential of democracy: subjects must consent before coercion becomes legitimate. These despots needed to believe that serviles accepted forcible deterrence voluntarily, just as a child, even while screaming, consents to father's spanking hand.

From that wish for childlike consent sprang the civilization's master metaphor, the institution's second title, and slaveholders' definition of their peculiarity. The Peculiar Institution was also called the Domestic Institution. Southern slavery was supposed to differ from other dictatorships in that master and slave were like father and son. Father power was expected to be deployed with benevolent firmness, so that the plantation family, including white and black dependents, consented to patriarchal direction.

The resulting charade of loving "Sambo" consenting to Massa's caring command was not that peculiar. Despots crave approval. Dictators adore being "elected." But what remained unusual about the dictator as democrat was how central the charade of domestic consent was to self-esteem and how continuously the familial put-on was demanded. In "Sambo's" command performance of loving gratitude, a private despotism enmeshed in a public democracy found comforts no wavering color line could supply.

The Massa/"Sambo," father/boy charade better conveyed slaveholder wish than institutional reality. On Massa's side of the script, the parental analogy was severely strained. Blacks considered to be degenerate performing service conceived to be degrading were different from father's white children. Nor were thirty-nine lashes, well laid on, the same as a spanking across the knee. Moreover, masters who scarcely pretended to partriarchy were legion, particularly in the nouveau Southwest.

Disconcerting gaps between the ideal and real explain why the proslavery argument was more a cry for slaveholders to achieve familial goals than an exaltation of domestic utopia achieved. Still, the paternalistic cry was at the foundation of many slaveholders' sense of self-worth. Wherever patriarchs took paternalism seriously, they struggled to take the strain out of the domestic analogy. Masters had to struggle because "Sambo's" performance also featured gaps between pretence and reality. The character of consenting "boy" was often played with a "childish" naughtiness driving posturing "fathers" to distraction. Blacks pretended not to understand orders, pretended to be sick, pretended not to understand why tools broke, all the while protesting adoration for the mighty patriarch. The "consenting" servile was partly a put-on, as "fathers" despairingly assumed.

Discrepancies between "Sambo's" script and performance were not usually so total as to destroy a crudely effective labor system or to demolish a crudely satisfying domestic illusion. Institutional strain, however, occasionally escalated. The domestic lackey sometimes plotted midnight murder while playing adoring child. Then the mask slipped off to reveal a killer.

Once the sword was drawn in domestic ambush, the Domestic Institution had to become undomestic despotism. Since "loving boys" had plotted patricide, serviles had to be tried and killed as men. Since patriarchal power had failed to provide public order, the private dictator had to abdicate. Public government designed for consenting whites had to coerce unconsenting blacks. But the democratic state required to take over despotic deterrence often felt compelled to remain democratically legitimate. The state sought to try "criminals" with some semblance of democratic justice, while also chilling the "boys."

With that newly strained mixture of democracy and despotism, the Peculiar Institution turned peculiarly distressing. Masters no longer mastered their people. Democratic government for whites no longer kept despotic hands off blacks. Black was white; grayness pervaded. Oh for the days when "Sambo" consented to papa's wishes.

Denmark Vesey lived at a time and in a place where an especially permissive brand of an especially deep-rooted paternalism had made the Domestic Institution especially vulnerable. The cult of domestic patriarchy flourished particularly in the ancient South, where "nigger-drivers" were scarcest and ancestral estates plentiful. Domestic pretenses also flourished particularly where slaves served intimate domestic circles instead of working far-off fields. Paternalistic slave management tended to be especially permissive when child-raising itself became most permissive.

Charleston in the early 1820s possessed all these preconditions for permissive domesticity. The city's hinterlands, sickly tidewater swamps, were the most productive and the most dangerous Old South area. Charleston, the relatively healthy center of this miasmatic area, was wealthy planters' favorite spot in sickly months. These planters brought large retinues of household slaves to town mansions; larger armies of field hands remained behind to work remote estates. Nowhere else were so many personal domestic servants so separated from impersonal agricultural gangs.

Charleston slaves who were not trusted house servants tended to be trusted skilled laborers. Individual craftsmen provided preindustrial Charleston's mechanical services. The Carolina low country was too demographically black to attract enough whites. Supposedly stupid slaves had special opportunities to become skilled artisans.

Charleston's unusually high percentage of house servants and skilled slaves came accompanied with a high percentage, for the lower South, of free blacks. Nearly one of every eight Charleston blacks was free. Black slaves and freedmen, taken together, comprised 57 percent of Charleston's population.

In the period immediately preceding Denmark Vesey's Conspiracy, Charleston patriarchs tended to treat their especially dense, especially talented, and especially domestic black population with special leniency. Although paternalism does not need to be permissive and fathers often rule remorselessly, grim deterrence was a parental style moving out of favor in the 1820s. The cult of romanticism was softening attitudes towards inferiors throughout the western world. Lenient childraising struck an especially responsive chord in Americans, with their increasingly egalitarian attitudes towards white males and their increasingly sentimental attitudes about white ladies' moral superiority and white children's innate virtues. English visitors to Jacksonian America saw little strict childraising, English-style. American youths were often begged and bribed to be papa's angel.[2]

In the 1818-22 period, Charlestonians, albeit with misgivings, sought to prove that the same lenient domesticity could control domestic slaves. "By far the greater number of our citizens," Charlestonians reported, "were rearing up" a "mild and generous" system, exulting "in what they termed the progress of liberal ideas." Slaves were permitted to hire out their labor. Slave domestics were permitted to learn to read and write. Black worshippers were permitted to form religious congregations. Gentlemen entertained "hope that as [slaves] were more indulged, they would become more satisfied with their condition and more attached to the whites." Instead of being brutalized into servility, slaves would obey out "of affection and gratitude."[3]

Permissive slave government, by relying heavily on "affection and gratitude" was doubly dangerous. Too little coercion left slaves too often unafraid of enslavers. Too many privileges left the semiprivileged too often desiring full privilege. Charleston slaves in the pre-Vesey years easily became proverbial men with the half loaf who desire the other half; and "father" had not always scared "boys" into thinking adulthood was unattainable.

Leaders of the Vesey Conspiracy exemplified expectations aroused, then thwarted. Denmark Vesey himself, a mulatto, was in-between in other ways North Americans were supposed to prevent. He was free where blacks were supposed to be enslaved. He was a brilliant skilled laborer where blacks were supposed to be stupidly unskillful. He had many enslaved wives and children; his bigamous family was no Christian Domestic Institution. Enraged that his children would remain slaves, he gambled everything he had achieved to destroy a system blunting his posterity's achievement.[4]

Monday Gell, a hired-out slave who had also achieved much, matched Vesey's rage at limited achievement. Gell ran his own harness shop, but he gave his owner a cut of what he made. He would cut The Man's throat for taking a thing. He became a principal in Denmark Vesey's plot.

Thwarted slaves in a free atmosphere were at liberty to use the white libertarian world view against antilibertarian whites. Vesey employed the Bible and the Missouri Controversy debates to provoke dissent. Pampered slaves, raged Vesey, had less than pampered masters. Men, he urged, must not consent to be petted "boys."

Denmark Vesey was a charismatic persuader. But he also saw that persuasion was not enough. For the moment, a leader of the underclass understood better than the master class that coercion must augment consent. The low level of slaveowners' physical deterrence handed Vesey opportunity to petrify those he could not persuade.[5] No black who heard of Vesey's conspiracy could simply walk away from a dangerous idea. A recruit was given the choice to kill or be killed. The slave Bacchus Hammett, for example, found the conspirators' arguments unconvincing. "Denmark then said," Bacchus shuddered, that " '*any person who don't join us must be treated as an enemy and put to death*'; and I said, '*if that is the case, well I will join you.*' "[6]

Vesey wished to extend Bacchus Hammett's "conversion" experience by creating a moment when the enslaved masses would have to choose between killing whites or being killed by blacks. Vesey envisioned a two-stage rebellion. Initially, a few dozen blacks would ambush Charleston's arsenals. Then thousands of slaves would aim captured guns at outnumbered whites. The few blacks siding with slaveholders would be assassinated.

Vesey believed that a handful of crudely armed conspirators could capture Charleston's lightly guarded or unguarded arsenals and gun stores. Most governmental arms were located in the state arsenal, a building usually unguarded on an exposed mid-city block. Over seven hundred muskets and bayonets were packed into two locations on Charleston's outskirts. Bacchus Hammett had a key to the larger storehouse, and no white watched the smaller structure at night.

If the surprise attack by a few on these vulnerable buildings succeeded, rebels armed initially with clubs, hoes, and pikes would command sophisticated firepower. Then all Charleston blacks would have to face Bacchus Hammett's choice. The masses, predicted the chiefs, would prefer fighting for freedom to being slaughtered as "Sambos."

The black masses would only face their moment of truth if Vesey's few ambushers remained confident and loyal. Again, the chief would bolster persuasion by reversing slavery's customary balance of terror. To make black revolutionaries seem more awesome, Vesey warned potential betrayers of horrid reprisals. Anonymous blacks, Vesey bragged, had pledged to murder his murderer. To make white terror seem less menacing, Vesey's prime lieutenant, Gullah Jack, promised protection from African gods. Jack, a conjurer back in Africa and a wizened little man with huge whiskers and violent gestures, claimed that his charmed crab claws would keep bearers safe.

Despite Vesey's rhetoric, black recruits remained nervous because they saw few rebels and little arms. Only several dozen attended Vesey's consciousness-raising harangues. Would that be enough? To waylay the question, Vesey bragged of thousands recruited. Plantation slaves, Vesey reminded city slaves, carried master's produce to city market on Saturday night. The marketeers, said Vesey, had agreed to take up guns from ambushers. Vesey also boasted of long lists of black converts. Peter Poyas claimed to have thousands on his list. Monday Gell boasted of another list. As for arms, Vesey claimed to have enough crude weapons to conduct a surprise attack on vulnerable arsenals.

Vesey knew that his opportunity carried within it its own obstacle, that a revolution based on thwarted expectations was a two-edged sword. The semiprivileged might guard the privileges already received rather than seek privileges currently denied. Some petted and pampered servile might truly love his master. Worse, the semiprivileged might reach for the greatest privilege by turning in freedom-fighters, hoping that grateful whites might emancipate turncoats.

Recruiters thus tried to avoid "waiting men who receive *presents of old coats, etc. from their masters.*"[7] But avoiding privileged "Sambos" meant not approaching the best potential recruits. Rolla and Ned Bennett, for example, were South Carolina governor Thomas Bennett's most treasured "family friends." These "Sambos," when approached by Vesey recruiters, declared thwarted expectations and became revolutionary leaders.

In late May 1822, a month before Armageddon, a recruiter approached the wrong "family friend." A trusted house servant proved trustworthy. He betrayed the rebels. At first authorities did not believe the informer. Ned Bennett, upon hearing his fidelity questioned, went voluntarily to the intendant (mayor) of Charleston. Ned laughed off patricidal charges and swore that he loved Massa Thomas. White "fathers," aching to believe black "boys," relaxed.

Vesey, tensing, moved the revolt up two weeks. Several days before the rescheduled ambush, however, another "Sambo" informed on black liberators. Hysteria ensued among establishment and rebels. Governor Bennett called out hundreds of white troops. Thousands of whites experienced a terrifying, sleepless night. Vesey, not sleeping either, desperately dispatched a fellow ignorant of the countryside to tell country recruits to march. The messenger never had a chance to get lost in the jungle. Vesey apparently never bothered to ask if he had left. Patrols were out. Ambush was impossible. White despots had become more frightening to Denmark Vesey's little band than the fearsome liberator.

As the story spilled out to the community, the Domestic Institution seemed shattered. Not only psychological comforts of the "Sambo" charade but also prevailing conceptions of permissive control lay in ruins. Uncoerced "Sambos," supposedly consenting to patriarchal direction because of "affection and gratitude," were unmasked as anti-"Sambos" ready to coerce their families. Time after horrifying time, those accused had been trusted serviles. Among the ambushers were those who had been trusted to sleep in the family yard or in the master's bedroom. How could the masters guard against the servants when the same servants had been charged to guard the masters?

John Potter, a prominent Charleston merchant, revealed in his correspondence the common dismay when Sambo was unmasked. Potter co-owned one accused rebel. The fellow had been loyal for "10 years. . . . When I left the City, I always directed him to sleep in the yard, which I thought safe under his charge." Potter cringed that if that protector "had made his way into my bedroom, in the dead of night. . . . " Well, the patriarch would not "own" up to such "unpleasant feelings . . . before my family, who have been more alarmed than I have ever seen."[8]

Families shivered throughout Charleston. John Drayton's cook, wrote Potter, "who had hitherto behaved well," had plotted murder. A chef could easily poison the pot. Another plotter had been Elias Horry's "favorite servant. . . . I believe his coachman!!" A driver could easily turn over the coach. "Good god," squirmed John Potter, "most of the coachmen and favorite servants in the City knew of it." Potter believed that if the beginning had been "but anyway successful, even for a moment, all or nearly all" his and everyone's favorite servants "would have joined!" Potter was trembling over precisely Vesey's strategy: only a few pretend "Sambos" need strike unguarded arsenals to test all "Sambos' " credibility.[9]

Elias Horry, unlike John Potter, believed "his people's" loyalty would survive all tests. When constables came to arrest Horry's coachman, the master "assured them they were mistaken. He could answer for [the man's] innocence. He would as soon subject himself." After hearing the evidence, Horry turned to his coachman. "Are you guilty?" he asked incredulously. "Yes." "What were your intentions?" The coachman, rage on a face where Horry had seen only smiles, whirled on his patriarch. He said that he sought "to kill you, rip open your belly, & throw your guts in your face."[10]

With words like these, the Domestic Institution lost its domestic illusion. The charade of consent was poisonous camouflage. Democrats' version of slavery had failed as social control because private coercion had insufficiently terrified the slaves. But how could a public democracy based on content legitimately coerce unconsenting private domestics?

Answers to that question differed according to different perceptions of how far slave dissent went. A handful of Charlestonians, led by Governor Bennett, believed that evidence indicated that only a few serviles had faked consent.[11] They wished only a little despotism. Most Charlestonians, led by the court trying Vesey conspirators, believed that conspiratorial facts cast doubt on all consent. They wished a little despotism at trials too.

Bennett emerged from his uncomfortable experience with his slaves' shams with his patriarchal assumptions intact. The embarrassed governor was the first patriarch whose household charade was exposed as phony. Three of the first five rebels captured were his "family friends." Two of the six most important rebel leaders, Ned and Rolla Bennett, were his trusted "boys." The most humiliating sham involved not Ned, even though that deceiver had thrown the government off stride by swearing adoration for the governor after the first betrayal. Bennett's greater chagrin concerned Rolla, who blew the "Sambo" role into a monstrous smokescreen after the second betrayal.

Before the conspiracy, Rolla Bennett, like John Potter's yardman, was trusted to guard white women and children when the patriarch left. The governor had no qualms about the household's lieutenant-governor. Yet black witnesses accused Rolla of lusting after virginal whites. *"When we have done with the fellows,"* Rolla winked at a black, *"we know what to do with the wenches."*[12]

Wenches! Rolla raped with words. The black "boy" defiled a white "angel" with the degrading language white chauvinists reserved for black "wenches." Still more debasing to Thomas Bennett, the "wench" Rolla had talked of deflowering was the governor's daughter!

Rolla, when hearing his words, displayed uncomprehending shock. His demeanor gave evidence of "utter ignorance of the intended insurrection."[13] His words shone with adoration for his white family. Would he kill, rape, wreck his own household? He begged his patriarch for protection against "outsiders."

The protector did what he could for his slave. Bennett hired a crack Charleston lawyer, Jacob Axson. Axson hammered at Joe LaRoche, one of Rolla's prime accusers. The lawyer proved that Rolla's wife used to be Joe's. Axson insinuated that Rolla, not Thomas Bennett, was the victim of domestic plotting.

The shrewd defense could not save the clever domestic. Joe, other witnesses reported, was glad to be free of a hated former wife. Furthermore, Joe and Rolla were described as being closer to each other than either was to the "wench." Accusers kept coming in with no reason to "get" Rolla. They told of the protector who would savage the protected.[14] Rolla, expert at feeling for the appropriate pose, now saw that the wide-eyed innocent stance was used up. He astounded his lawyer and his patriarch by confessing to threatening patricide.

Rolla's confessions to being anti-"Sambo" portrayed a refined "Sambo." Rolla conceded that Vesey "got me to join." But the slave claimed to have "said to myself, I cannot kill my master and mistress, for they use me, more like a son than a slave—I then concluded, in my mind, that I would go into the country" before the conspirators "were to commence."[15]

Here was the "Sambo" puzzle at an exasperating level of difficulty and an excruciating level of danger. An actor expert at fooling everyone here showed that no one, black or white, could know what slaves were thinking. Nor can posterity know which, if either, Rolla was real. In his dangerous situation, Rolla might have bet his safety on deceiving blacks. His rape talk may have been designed to prove allegiance to revolution. What a clever way to keep Denmark Vesey's hands off a turncoat's throat!

Another possibility is that Rolla bet his revenge on deceiving whites. Rolla may have personified, on a particularly vicious level, that break between the "Sambo" pose before whites and the truer self before blacks which was a widespread Afro-American slave personality. Rolla's rape fantasy seems a thoroughly human way for the man forced to play "boy" to bring his manhood to the household's attention.

Rolla also might have been sheerly an accommodator. This genius at "getting along" may have thought, each step of the way, only of the most plausible pose. "Sambo" always ran the danger of being empty inside, like freer citizens who mindlessly conform. In Rolla Bennett we come to the distilled essence of the academic debate over North American slave personality.

The mystery was not academic inside Rolla's domicile. In Thomas Bennett's family few illusions survived about Rolla's docility. "We, poor devils," shuddered Bennett's young niece, "were to have been reserved to fill their Harams—horrible." My "very beautiful cousin," Bennett's daughter, "was set apart for . . . one of their Chiefs."[16]

We do not know if the governor concurred that his daughter was reserved for his "boy's" harem. But we do know that whatever Thomas Bennett's disillusionment with Rolla, his illusions about Samboism survived. His statecraft in the post-Vesey period was based on conviction that the Domestic Institution had survived because the slaves had proved largely true. As Governor Bennett saw the situation, black tyrants such as Vesey had scared the Bennett family's "childish" blacks into a child's-play of revolution. The black race had proved its "indolence," its "cowardice," its "total absence of . . . intelligence" by planning an abortive uprising. The abortive had not transpired because servants full of "Fidelity" for white patriarchs had betrayed black authority figures. Slaves' domestic "attachments," then, should not be "destroyed by unnecessary rigor."[17]

The court trying conspirators, like the huge majority in the community, scoffed at Bennett's faith in "Fidelity." Had the master learned nothing from his slave panting after his daughter? Blacks, so most Charlestonians thought, had proved themselves not consenting "boys" but vicious men. The two or three full of fidelity who had betrayed the blacks full of murder had barely betrayed soon enough. Displaying little cowardice, less indolence, and no fidelity, a few dozen slaves had almost staged the ultimate test of a few thousand blacks' fidelity. White Charlestonians did not wish that examination rescheduled. Private slaves must learn that no matter how many masters such as the governor could be hoodwinked, the public government would crack down.[18]

Since Bennett conceded that some plotting against despots had occurred, the issue between governor and court was whether the plot was dangerously creditable. Bennett easily won part of the debate. He successfully urged that no threat was creditable *after* Charleston whites had wheeled out troops. The court claimed that even after the second betrayal, even after white troops had been deployed, an uprising almost transpired.[19]

Vesey's panic after the surprise attack lost the capacity to surprise undermined that viewpoint. As Bennett pointed out, a plot is hardly "within a few hours of consumation" when a leader must send a city lad ignorant of the countryside twenty-two miles into a jungle to find the right plantation blacks and tell them to begin. Nor was the plot still viable when the leader never bothered to find out if the messenger on the impossible mission had succeeded. The governor was trying to comfort the terrified; and troops did keep chances of a razor across the jugular a couple of days rather than a couple of hours away—if throats could enjoy such comforts.[20]

A second issue between the governor and the judges concerned whether ambush was creditable *before* whites heard of the plot. To Bennett, the court's *verbal* evidence, while proving a conspiracy, did not demonstrate a physically viable conspiracy. A plot able to deploy sufficient physical power, Bennett urged, would have left behind *physical* evidence to complement the verbal. But no list of thousands of recruits was found. Nor was so much as a pistol ever uncovered. Bennett concluded from the lack of physical remains that "less than a hundred" were involved, most only to the extent of "acquiescing" and all "unprovided with arms."[21]

The court answered that evidence unfound hardly proves that evidence never existed. Since several days had transpired between deployment of troops and arrest of ringleaders, Monday Gell, Peter Poyas, and Denmark Vesey had plenty of time to burn incriminating lists. Where no list discovered indicated to the governor that no lists ever existed, undiscovered lists implied to the court that additional conspirators were escaping detection.[22]

The court's estimate of the number of slaves involved, however, was compatible with Bennett's. "Any opinion formed as to the numbers actually engaged," cautioned the judges, "must be altogether conjectural." Their conjecture, like Bennett's, was that Vesey "greatly exaggerated" his numbers, "and perhaps designedly so," in order to give ambushers nerve to strike. Bennett, who could have written that sentence, might also have accepted the court's hazy conclusion: "considerable numbers were concerned."[23] Bennett's "less than a hundred" conspirators, after all, were a "considerable number" to mass against unguarded arsenals.

Nor were court and governor far apart on whether "considerable numbers," whatever that means, were armed. Where no arms physically uncovered spoke to Bennett of a "crude" plot "unprovided with arms," verbal testimony about crude arms indicated to judges an adequately armed ambush. Judges pointed to testimony about homemade pikes, one dagger, two pistols, seven swords, and the crude clubs, hoes, axes, and hatchets of agricultural workers. To these normal possessions of a servile people, concluded judges, must be added access to some of their masters' guns and a cogent plan to club, axe, and hatchet their way into unguarded arsenals containing a majority of Charleston's guns. Unarmed? Not altogether, and not at all after the strike.[24]

Since governor and judges agreed that the ambush plan involved far less than thousands of far from well-armed plotters, their disagreement centered on whether thousands would have joined if dozens had seized Charleston's guns. The racist governor still believed in the slave's consenting fidelity and scoffed at the possibility of many killers camouflaged behind smiles. Some urge, wrote Rolla's master, that "had the attempt been made by the small number who confederated, thousands would have joined." But that was "problematical." Conspirators shuddered to share their plans with the masses who would allegedly have joined them. Where rebels themselves "saw in thousands a Fidelity which they dared not tamper with," they could have "no confidence in such a contingency" as loyal servants switching into disloyal killers.[25]

The court replied that leaders distrusted the masses only *before* the ambush, only *before* blacks rather than whites possessed guns, only *before* the question was whether to kill for freedom or be killed by black brothers.[26] The court conceded that speculations about what would have happened *after* an ambush were "problematical." But then again, judges conceived, every plot of the few against the mighty is problematical. To avoid betrayal, conspiracies must be small. A few must create a confrontation situation which forces the many to take sides and gives them nerve to be free.

This logic of conspiratorial politics suggests that whites or blacks who believed Denmark Vesey's bragging about recruiting thousands probably exaggerated the participants and misunderstood the strategy. Both court and governor were probably right that Vesey was guarding his flanks by controlling his numbers and exaggerating his numbers so that ambushers would take heart. Vesey's was the nervy gamble that a surprise attack by dozens would give thousands faking fidelity nerve to fake no more.

Bennett found that view problematical because he did not believe fidelity was faked. Judges found Vesey's strategy viable because they no longer believed in consenting fidelity. The issue was unresolvable because neither undeniable verbal evidence nor missing physical evidence said a syllable about what thousands were thinking. The terror of Denmark Vesey was that a regime woke one night to find that safety rested on the invisible and unknowable.

The historian Richard C. Wade, in his effort to discredit the Vesey Conspiracy, went well beyond the amount of discrediting Governor Bennett conceived feasible. Bennett thought the verbal evidence of conspiracy too internally consistent to deny a plot. Wade charged the court with so falsifying slave confessions, when publishing trial records, as to leave no consistent and creditable verbal evidence. The governor knew better.

Wade attacked what he called "deliberate" discrepancies between slave confessions as printed by the court and the same slaves' confessions as found in manuscript. Wade found handwritten confessions of two Vesey conspirators, Bacchus Hammett and John Enslow, in Benjamin Hammett's (Bacchus' master) private papers at Duke University. The two unpublished depositions differ from the court's published versions. "Little confidence," concluded Wade, "can be placed in the authenticity of the official account."[27]

An unfortunate mix-up helped undermine Wade's confidence in the court. When comparing Bacchus Hammett's unpublished deposition at Duke University with Hammett's published confession, Wade unwittingly substituted John Enslow's for Hammett's. The historian found, not surprisingly, that the Enslow unpublished account differed from the Hammett published one. When one compares the Hammett unpublished account with the Hammett published one, facts are substantially the same and the language is only a little different.[28]

Comparing Hammett to Hammett does not negate Wade's argument that the Enslow published deposition adds information to the Enslow unpublished version. But Wade failed to discuss the alternative explanation of the Enslow discrepancies. Wade's uncharitable explanation is that the court falsified Enslow's confession. The more charitable possibility is that Enslow confessed to his master before confessing to the court, with judges then publishing the later confession they received.

A comparison of the two Enslow confessions makes the most charitable possibility the more plausible. Enslow's manuscript confession contains the words "master having read this over to me I do swear it is true and some facts left out." Enslow's published court confession contains no such words. Instead, Enslow's "owner, who was present, stated to the court that John . . . would reveal all." Wade could not understand why the published court confession should add information to a manuscript confession. The explanation on the face of the documents is that the manuscript confession was a preliminary statement to the master, while the published confession reported "all the information" about "facts left out" to the master.[29]

Governor Bennett's failure to pounce on alleged falsification of the printed court record makes the more-than-one confession explanation still more plausible. The court published its transcript in early November 1822, several weeks before Governor Bennett's special message to the legislature attacking the judges.[30] In that message, Bennett announced he was submitting the court's *manuscript* transcript.[31] If the court's publication falsified its transcript, surely its deadly opponent, with access to both manuscript and printed records, would have exposed the lies. Publishing the truth was in fact the only plausible course for judges knowing that their foe possessed true transcripts.

Wade evidently never saw the critical evidence proving that the courts had not falsified the published document. The *entire* manuscript court transcript is in the South Carolina Archives, filed with Governor Bennett's special message. Either this manuscript was out of place when Wade read the Bennett file or the theorist missed the disproof of his theory.[32]

A word-by-word comparison of the two slave confessions in question, as jotted down in the manuscript court record and then as published in the court proceedings, proves that no falsification occurred. The court printed precisely the John Enslow and Bacchus Hammett confessions contained in its transcript.[33] A word-by-word comparison of the *entire* manuscript court transcript with the entire published court record acquits judges of *ever* falsifying a quote. Judges justifiably claimed that they published language "as it was originally taken, without even changing the phraseology."[34]

Still, specialists will value the slightly fuller handwritten transcript. Judges made no pretense of publishing defense cross-examinations. The court instead printed accusations in full and then summarized defenses in part. Defenses such as Jacob Axson's cross-examination of Rolla Bennett's accusers can only be followed in manuscript.

Again, judges who presided over the main June-July trials made no pretense of publishing a transcript of later trials, occurring in August 1822 under different judges. The June-July court printed its accusations in full and then summarized August accusations; the August accusations can be followed only in manuscript.

Finally, in several instances in late July, when a witness knew nothing about a defendant's guilt or innocence the published court record omitted the testimony. These occasional I-know-nothing snippets were unpublished because they contained neither accusations nor defenses. But words useless to persecution and defense alike are useful, as we will see, in judging witnesses' integrity. The snippets can be recaptured only in manuscript.[35]

The sole way the published record gives a misleading impression of court proceedings concerns rearrangement of testimony. The printed proceedings read as if all trials followed the form of defendant put to trial and witnesses called to accuse. The manuscript transcript, however, shows that the June-July trials were divided into two phases. In mid-July, after Monday Gell turned state's witness, trials did assume the form of defendant indicted and accusers called.[36]

The manuscript record reveals that, in earlier trials, a different sort of witness sometimes led to more convoluted court proceedings. In late June and early July all accusers were unimportant followers. These underlings, remembering Denmark Vesey's threats that the black community would kill any betrayer, sometimes agreed to testify only anonymously, before those accused were in the courtroom. As a result, before trying anyone, the court took pretrial depositions from several witnesses. In the subsequent trial of each defendant, judges first pieced together this previously-given evidence. Then the accused and his lawyer were allowed to cross-examine other accusers not demanding anonymity.

When printing previously rendered accusations, judges cut out and rearranged pretrial testimony against each defendant. This rearranging for publication was neither indefensible nor dishonest. By printing rearranged accusations, judges reflected their rearrangements when deliberating. Furthermore, only rearranged accusations could fulfill judges' promises to print "the whole evidence, in each particular case, *in the order of its trial*" (emphasis mine).[37]

Order aside, the question is whether the rearrangement conveyed all pretrial depositions accurately and in context. A laborious tracing of judges' rearrangements acquits the court of falsification, deliberate or otherwise. Judges were at such pains to live up to promises "*not to suppress any part*" of the evidence (emphasis theirs) that at the one spot at which they suppressed a quote, they indicated the censorship with stars.[38]

We will come back to that revealing censorship. For now, the point about the published transcript of the early trials is that after the rearrangement was completed, almost all of the evidence was published, almost word-for-word as it was recorded in manuscript, with nothing out of context. Then in mid-July, after Monday Gell's confession opened up a wave of confessions from witnesses not demanding secrecy, the published court record follows word-for-word the manuscript transcript, in the order evidence was rendered. After reading this court record, no contemporary leader, least of all the Doubting Thomas in the governor's chair, could call the domestic threat "loose talk." Richard Wade's own protagonist conceded that some conspiracy had occurred and that some public deterrent was necessary.[39]

The unpublished document that Wade apparently missed is important not only for verifying the published document he dismissed but also for explaining the threat he discounted. Judges strewed astericks across one printed page rather than publicize one horror. Here are the forbidden words: the convicted conspirator Harry Haig told the court that Gullah Jack "was going to give me *a bottle with poison to put into my master's pump and into as many pumps as he could about town and he said he could give other bottles to those he could trust to"* (words censored for publication are italicized).[40]

There it was, in thirty-four unpublishable words, the peculiar nightmare of these peculiar masters. The court censored nothing about ambushes on arsenals. But a single domestic sneaking poison into a domesticity's water was too petrifying to broadcast. Stealthful domestic poison was the unmentionable sin because it suggested a second way Denmark Vesey meant to test "Sambo's" creditability. Vesey's main conception, ambushing arsenals and then seeing how deep fidelity ran, could easily be combated. A town could guard against surprise attack on arsenals. A modern army guarding modern firepower could crush several dozen slaves armed with pikes. The lesson of Denmark Vesey, not least to slaves, was that whites could overwhelm an uprising so long as officials bothered to guard the rifles.

But the individual household assassin hiding behind an accommodationist's mask was invulnerable to Denmark Vesey's collective vulnerabilities. The solitary servile slipping something into the water need not worry about whether pikes could conquer guns. He need have no concern about wide-awake troops outside the slumbering house. And when "his" white family started dying like flies, he would be all weepy solicitude, full of wonder about what strange sickness ailed the master's house.

The sleeping household, unable to guard against its solitary "family friends," was even more vulnerable to individual resistance crudely collectivized. Patriarchs could not protect their homes if their "gullible boy" was given ideas by "Sambos" beyond the house. Harry Haig's master was helpless before Mr. Pritchard's slave's vial of vile stuff. The judges' stern households were vulnerable to Governor Bennett's pampered serviles.

All Charlestonians thus realized that while dispatching troops could destroy Vesey's primary strategy of a test of servile loyalty after a collective ambush, no army could deter the secondary test of individual fidelity within the house. A regime peculiar because based on domestic "consent" at least momentarily required some public force to reach inside overly permissive masters' houses and scare conspirators seeking to poison other masters' families. But, again, how could the public state, the source of collective deterrence, repress dictatorially and remain democratic—or sustain a dictatorship supposedly private and domestic?

The South Carolina government had legal capacity to coerce blacks. South Carolina law guaranteed republican justice only to whites. When a slave was accused of a capital crime, any justice of the peace would select another justice of the peace and from three to five freemen to join with him in forming a court. The JPs and freemen were judge, jury, and court of last resort. As judge, they could use any procedure. As jury, they could convict by a simple majority. Nothing required them to give accused blacks any rights.[41]

Nothing except the conscience of a democracy. Before public procedures began, Gov. Thomas Bennett privately demanded that trials be democratic. But the governor remained incensed that other dictators' slaves had corrupted his "boys." He hoped dictatorial pretrial fact gathering would trace corruption to its course. He privately urged Charleston authorities to form a "Court of Investigation," whose deliberations would "precede the state courts" trying the accused. The preliminary despotic court, "untrammeled by the usual forms could pursue fearlessly the mazes of the labyrinth." Then regular courts could give the accused a democratic trial.[42]

Judges brushed aside the governor's suggestion. Some blacks whose testimony in closed court could lead to convictions were wary of open courtrooms because they were terrified of Vesey's threatened reprisals. Bennett's plan might despotically yield incriminating evidence and then democratically allow scared incriminators not to testify at trials. No convictions would ensue. A liberator could remain the most creditable terrorizer.[43]

The court was determined to seize the balance of terror. Judges meant to inject fear of whites inside all houses. Blacks must learn, wrote Charleston's intendant (mayor) James Hamilton, Jr., that "there is nothing they are bad enough to do, that we are not powerful enough to punish."[44]

Judges considered Bennett the epitome of the community's problem. The man seemed two times too permissive. First of all, as a private despot he seemed to be a weak patriarch whose soft regime had almost ended with his gentle daughter in his dissimulating slave's embrace. Secondly, as a public ruler, he appeared to be a paralyzed republican whose scruples could not keep poison out of his neighbors' water wells. It was time to force some hard despotism on such soft democrats. Thus the court went ahead trying three Bennett slaves and several other conspirators, limiting confrontations between accused and accuser and permitting no testing of justice in the open air.[45]

Fearing conflict-of-interst charges, Bennett waited until his slaves were tried before pressing his protest. Then he wrote Robert Y. Hayne, attorney general of the state, asking whether a republican court could try a man for his life "with closed doors" and without allowing the defendant to question all accusers. Hayne answered, rightly, that under South Carolina law accused slaves had no legal rights. Trials proceeded, while Bennett silently suffered.[46]

In his special message to the legislature at the end of the year, Bennett went public with his protest. Bennett "deeply lamented" that a criminal court should "close its doors upon the community," thereby shutting "out those accidental rays which occasionally illuminate . . . innocence and guilt." He deplored testimony "received under the pledge of inviolable secrecy," leaving the accused "convicted, and sentenced to death, without seeing the persons, or hearing the voices, of those who testified to their guilt." Bennett attacked the court's rationale that several witnesses were scared of open courtrooms. "The state," claimed the state's executive, "was competent to protect." Months after witnesses testified, reported the governor, turncoats whose identities were "distinctly and generally known . . . pass unmolested."

True, continued Bennett, accusers faced the accused in later phases of the trials, after Monday Gell turned state's evidence. But at that point, in Bennett's opinion, witnesses' collaborations poisoned justice. Monday Gell and others who later confessed, Bennett pointed out, differed from earlier turncoats. Later witnesses had already been convicted. They thought survival depended, charged Bennett, on "the number of convictions" they "could make."

Monday Gell's and Charles Drayton's chance to make convictions, continued Bennett, increased because they were once "closeted together" for hours. They could have perfected a collaboration to kill others indiscriminantly, under court auspices. Then a grateful court might not kill them. Nothing could exceed their "chilling depravity."[47]

Bennett summed up his principle when writing another South Carolina governor four years later. "I never could and cannot at this hour," declared Bennett, "separate myself from the conviction, that all the forms, proceedings, and solemnities of a trial affecting the life of a fellow being, should be the same whether *White* or *Black*."[48]

Considering those words, Thomas Bennett deserves an honored place in the southern liberal tradition. But his liberalism must be kept in perspective. His was the noblesse-oblige of the patriarch convinced that the superior race must be fair to the lesser. He saw no need for coercive court procedures because he considered blacks an innately childlike race, incapable of effective conspiracy and inclined toward consenting fidelity. The coercive court, while more offensive to later-day jurists, was closer to the later-day assumption that a race capable of resistance had to be coerced into enslavement.

Nor was Thomas Bennett a modern advocate of liberal justice. He was for giving pretrial investigators despotic power. He trusted that truth would out in later trial procedures. He failed to comprehend the way pretrial tyranny corrodes democratic trials. Even this outraged republican was democrat and despot too.

The judges too struggled to live within their democratic conscience. Their mix of democracy and dictatorship was closer than Bennett's to sheer despotism. But, like the governor, they revealed the mixed assumptions of this peculiar regime by striving to increase dictatorial coercion while still remaining "honorable" democrats.

The court totally rejected only Bennett's demand for public trials. The court was "certain that no colored witness would have ventured to incur the resentment of his comrades, by voluntarily disclosing his testimony in a public court."[49] Judges dismissed Bennett's ex post facto counterargument that the state proved it could protect accusers *after* trials. Accusers had to accuse *before* the public state could establish its credibility as a coercive force.

In every other way, the court sought a degree of democratic procedure. Defendants were guaranteed the right to have a lawyer and their master at the trial, to present their defense, and to cross-examine anyone except the minority of witnesses demanding anonymity (a big exception). Judges, with another big exception noted below, followed the common law on conspiracy: for capital offenses, two witnesses must be creditable.[50] Although they were judge and jury and had legal power to convict by majority vote, all convictions except two (two more big exceptions) followed the jury requirement of unanimity.

The court's handling of its despotic exceptions showed its democratic qualms. The two nonunanimous convictions afflicted free blacks. In both cases, the divided court sought to expel rather than kill. Judges granted Prince Graham his request for transportation to Africa. The court sentenced Saby Gaillard to death but recommended that Governor Bennett commute the sentence to banishment from the United States.[51] Bennett, jumping not on the lack of unanimity but on the only time the court failed to require a second collaborating witness, commuted Gaillard's sentence to banishment from the state.[52] The court, maybe secretly relieved about this outcome of a verdict repellent by its own standards, protested not at all.

Judges protested most against Bennett's charge that they allowed Monday Gell and Charles Drayton to form a league to kill other blacks. A democratic court's obligation to ascertain witnesses' creditability is key to conspiracy convictions; and here judges sought to be as scrupulous as if they had been trying whites.[53] Their results undermine Bennett's accusations. The manuscript trial record, by providing August cases as well as times in late July cases when witnesses testified to knowing nothing, allow a fuller estimate of the court's gullibility and witnesses' creditability than does the published record. The transcript shows that Charles Drayton was called against forty defendants. He testified that twenty-eight were guilty. Monday Gell was called against forty-five defendants. He testified that thirty-two were guilty. These 70 percent rates of accusation hardly show indiscriminate determination to slaughter.[54]

Nor would a republican court have thrown out the Gell-Drayton testimony, as Bennett implied, because the two spent some time together and might have united on their stories. The key criterion of collaboration is whether stories in court were the same. Drayton and Gell testified in the same trial thirty-one times. They agreed with each other seventeen times, disagreed fourteen times.[55] This "united" collaboration was disunited almost half the time.

In the end, uneasily despotic judges, in a time of extreme hysteria, acquitted almost half their defendants. Sixty-seven blacks were convicted, sixty-four set free. Of those convicted, thirty-five were hung, thirty-two banished from the state or United States.[56]

A governor and court with different degrees of uneasiness about a democratic state's excursion into tyranny were both anxious that the process should be quickly ended. The court wished to convict ringleaders and show slaves of "soft" masters that the white state could be more terrifying than the most tyrannical liberator. Then judges wanted out of the despotism business. In late July, "conceiving that enough had been done to serve as an example," the original court decided "to pursue the investigation no further." Bennett, relieved, ordered no more hangings of those previously convicted. "I conceived that I consulted the best feelings of my fellow citizens," he wrote, "in arresting these dreaded punishments, which were becoming but too familiar, ceased to produce a salutory terror, no longer served for example, and at which humanity wept."[57] Both a despotic court struggling to provide somewhat democratic trials and a democratic governor who desired pretrial despotism were delighted to return to halcyon days when the Peculiar Institution divided public democracy and private despotism at the color line.

Governor Bennett's special message at the end of the year was an appeal to slaveholders in the legislative body assembled to judge the judges. Bennett asked the legislature to condemn the court and to pass laws protecting black defendants. But 1822 was not Governor Bennett's year. The governor who had lost control over his household and lost control over the court system had no control over the legislature. South Carolina solons voted 80-35 to table Bennett's message without printing it. The court stood vindicated.[58]

The victory was not a lasting one. Eleven years later, immediately after that Nullification Crisis which Denmark Vesey indirectly helped provoke, South Carolina's governor urged reform of the slave codes. The reforming governor was none other than Robert Y. Hayne, the attorney general back in 1822 who had instructed Governor Bennett that black defendants had no legal rights. "While rigid discipline should be enforced," wrote Governor Hayne, "the law ought . . . to afford complete protection" against injustice.[59]

The legislature responded by allowing appeal in capital cases from a Court of Magistrates and Freeholders to the state's regular circuit court. The circuit court could return the case to another freeholders court for retrial. Trial judges would never be regular judges. A jury would never be involved. But at least the circuit court responsible for white justice could negate injustice to blacks.[60]

With this movement towards, while hardly all the way to, color-blind justice, Governor Bennett's not altogether color-blind tradition won an important victory. It would be tempting to close with the irony of the white loser ultimately winning. But in the wake of Denmark Vesey's domestic threat, all white patricians were losers. Governor Bennett could win vindication concerning the unusual circumstances when public government had to coerce private slaves. The democratic despot was partly democratic in attitudes towards state authority, as even Vesey's judges strived to show. But what was left of domestic domains such as Governor Bennett's in the more normal times after Vesey struck and the court withdrew?

The inescapable answer is that the Domestic Institution must have been far tenser than before Vesey's domestic assault. Illusions about "family friends" consenting without coercion were hard to come by when patriarchs recalled those plans for domestic rapes and well poisonings and slitting-your-guts-out-and-throwing-them-in-your-face. Dreams of a paternalism for blacks as softly permissive as paternalism over white children were shattered. Paternalism over blacks would have to be tougher, more coercive, with fewer illusions about loving willingness to obey.

The result, probably in the Bennett household as in many others, was a wary household relationship with the slaves. Slave religion, blossoming on blacks' terms before Vesey, was far more controlled by whites. A public whipping station opened. Permissions to live out, hire out, and marry out were curtailed.[61]

Despite some stricter controls, the charade of domestic consent remained. The democrat as despot needed the "Sambo" scenario to live easily with himself and defend his peculiarities. But the Peculiar Institution had been more comfortable for whites when the charade better matched reality, when paternalism had been more permissive and loving, when one did not distrust "Sambo's" smile.

The whites of Charleston killed Denmark Vesey. He had killed not a man but a myth. In the peculiar world of the democratic dictator, the losing democrat might win later victories. But the greatest loser who could never altogether lose was the liberating tyrant who proved such a domestic menace to the Peculiar Institution.

1. Richard C. Wade, "The Vesey Plot: A Reconsideration," *Journal of Southern History* 30 (May 1964): 144-61.

2. See, for example, C.B. Marryat, *Second Series of A Diary in America* (Philadelphia, 1840), 255.

3. Petition of Charleston citizens to the state legislature, 1822, printed in Robert S. Starobin, ed., *Denmark Vesey: The Slave Conspiracy of 1822* (Englewood Cliffs, N.J., 1970). This book combines well-chosen documents with astute editorial comments. Bob and I were researching the Vesey problem at the same time and derived mutual satisfaction from our concurrence on many, although not all, points. Using his book now, I am the more saddened that he, as one of Kenneth Stampp's finest students, did not live to enrich the present volume.

4. Unless otherwise noted, my narrative of the Vesey plot is taken from Lionel H. Kennedy and Thomas Parker, *An Official Report of the Trials of Sundry Negroes, Charged with an Attempt to Raise an Insurrection . . .* (Charleston, 1822). For a book-length accurate narrative, see John Lofton, *Insurrection in South Carolina: The Turbulent World of Denmark Vesey* (Yellow Springs, Ohio, 1964).

5. Eugene Genovese, *From Rebellion to Revolution: Afro-American Slaves in the*

Making of the New World (Baton Rouge, 1979), 8-10, is extremely insightful on Vesey's use of terror.

6. Confession of Bacchus, the slave of Mr. [Benjamin] Hammett, in William and Benjamin Hammett Papers, Duke University Library, printed in Starobin, *Denmark Vesey*, 61-65, especially p. 62. Emphasis in the original.

7. Kennedy and Parker, *Trials of Sundry Negroes*, 75.

8. John Potter to Langdon Cheves, June 29, 1822, Cheves Papers, South Carolina Historical Society, printed in Starobin, *Denmark Vesey*, 76.

9. Potter to Cheves, July 10, 16, 20, 1822, Cheves Papers, printed in Starobin, *Denmark Vesey*, 77-79.

10. As reported in Martha Proctor Richardson to My Dear James, Aug. 7, 1822, Arnold-Screven Papers, Southern Historical Collection, University of North Carolina at Chapel Hill, printed in Starobin, *Denmark Vesey*, 83.

11. Justice William Johnson, of the United States Supreme Court, Bennett's brother-in-law, was the only prominent leader who publically supported the governor. For an excellent account of Johnson's position and actions, see Donald G. Morgan, *Justice William Johnson, the First Dissenter* (Columbia, 1954), 126-40.

12. Kennedy and Parker, *Trials of Sundry Negroes*, 63.

13. Ibid., 66n.

14. Axson's cross-examination, briefly summarized in the published court record, can be followed more fully in the manuscript trial transcript. See Document B, copy 2, accompanying Gov. Thomas Bennett's MS. message no. 2 to the Senate and House of Representatives, Legislative Papers, South Carolina Archives, June-July trials, pp. 10-11.

15. Kennedy and Parker, *Trials of Sundry Negroes*, 68.

16. Anna Hayes Johnson to Elizabeth E. W. Haywood, June 23, 1822, Ernest Haywood Papers, Southern Historical Collection, printed in Starobin, *Denmark Vesey*, 72.

17. Bennett's MS message no. 2, esp. pp. 14, 17.

18. The best summaries of the majority position are in Kennedy and Parker, *Trials of Sundry Negroes*, 17-60, and in James Hamilton, Jr., *An Account of the Late Intended Insurrection* (Charleston, 1822).

19. Kennedy and Parker, *Trials of Sundry Negroes*, 36, 55.

20. Bennett's MS. message no. 2, pp. 15-16.

21. Ibid., 14.

22. Kennedy and Parker, *Trials of Sundry Negroes*, 24-26.

23. Ibid., 25, 27.

24. Ibid., 31-34.

25. Bennett's MS. message no. 2, p. 14.

26. Kennedy and Parker, *Trials of Sundry Negroes*, 37-38.

27. Wade, "The Vesey Plot," 156. Six years after Wade published this article, Starobin, *Denmark Vesey*, 61-66, accurately printed Enslow's and Hammett's previously unpublished depositions.

28. Compare Wade, "The Vesey Plot," 155-56, with Hammett's and Enslow's manuscript confessions (Starobin, *Denmark Vesey*, 61-66) and Hammett's and Enslow's published court confessions (Kennedy and Parker, *Trials of Sundry Negroes*, 141-47).

29. Compare the first sentence of the last paragraph of the manuscript Enslow confession (Starobin, *Denmark Vesey*, 66) with the court's preface to its version (Kennedy and Parker, *Trials of Sundry Negroes*, 146).

30. The Charleston *Southern Patriot*, Nov. 9, 1822, announced the court publication was ready for distribution. Bennett's message to the legislature was dated Nov. 28.

31. Bennett's MS. message no. 2, p. 1.

32. Bennett actually submitted two copies of the court transcript. They are identical, except that the transcript which the South Carolina Archives Department has labelled Document B, copy 1, stops entirely after the trials on July 26, while the transcript labelled Document B, copy 2, omits the last several pages for July 26 but contains the August deliberations. The two transcripts are thus nicely complementary.

33. For the Hammett confession, compare Document B, copy 2, June-July trials, pp. 15-19, with Kennedy and Parker, *Trials of Sundry Negroes*, 141-45. For the Enslow confession, compare Document B, copy 2, June-July trials, p. 34, with Kennedy and Parker, *Trials of Sundry Negroes*, 146-47.

The manuscript court transcript reveals that Bacchus Hammett's statement in the court's hands actually consisted of two confessions, dated July 12 and July 17, respectively, strung together without so explaining in the published proceedings. The July 12 confession ends at p. 144, line 28, in Kennedy and Parker *Trials of Sundry Negroes*; the July 17 confession commences at line 29. The Bacchus confession in the Benjamin Hammett papers is obviously yet a third deposition which the court either never saw or never entered in its trial transcript.

34. Kennedy and Parker, *Trials of Sundry Negroes*, iii.

35. Such snippets can be found in Document B, copy 2, June-July trials, pp. 37-39, 42, 44.

36. The shift is evident at Document B, copy 2, June-July trials, p. 14.

37. Kennedy and Parker, *Trials of Sundry Negroes*, iii.

38. Ibid., iv, 107.

39. Wade had an unfortunate mode of phrasing which erroneously implied that his favorite contemporaries *might* have concurred in his "loose talk" thesis. "The Governor *probably* believed in a plot of some kind," wrote Wade ("The Vesey Plot," 153; emphasis mine). But Bennett *did* believe in a plot of "some kind"; he was so convinced of certain conspirators' guilt that he refused to grant them executive clemency (see MS. message no. 2, pp. 8-10). Again, when summing up Bennett's niece's final opinion, Wade wrote that *if she believed a conspiracy existed at all*," she thought it exaggerated ("The Vesey Plot," 152; emphasis mine.) But the lady *did* believe those hung "were guilty most certainly" (Anna Hayes Johnson to Elizabeth E.W. Haywood, July 24, 1822, printed in Starobin, *Denmark Vesey*, 74). Any balanced account of the Vesey controversy must concede that differences over its extent occurred within a unanimous concurrence that more than "loose talk" happened.

40. Document B, copy 2, June-July trials, p. 21.

41. Kennedy and Parker, *Trials of Sundry Negroes*, vii-xv, reprints the relevant laws.

42. Bennett's MS. message no. 2, p. 4.

43. Kennedy and Parker, *Trials of Sundry Negroes*, vii.

44. Hamilton, *Account of the Insurrection*, 4.

45. Kennedy and Parker, *Trials of Sundry Negroes*, 61-87.

46. Robert Y. Hayne to Bennett, July 1, 1822, filed with Bennett's MS. message no. 2, South Carolina Archives; Bennett's MS. message no. 2, pp. 4-7.

47. Bennett's MS. message no. 2, pp. 5-8.

48. Bennett to Richard I. Manning, April 11, 1826, Williams-Chestnut-Manning Papers, on loan to the South Carolina Library, University of South Carolina.

49. Kennedy and Parker, *Trials of Sundry Negroes*, vii.

50. Ibid., vi.

51. According to Kennedy and Parker, *Trials of Sundry Negroes*, all convictions,

whether for capital offenses or not, were rendered *"unanimously"* (emphasis theirs) except Saby Gaillard's (p. 125) and Prince Graham's (p. 163).

52. Bennett's MS. message no. 2, pp. 9-10. Both Saby Gaillard and Prince Graham were probably sent to freedom rather than slavery elsewhere, although the record is not clear on this point.

53. Kennedy and Parker, *Trials of Sundry Negroes*, 56, 110, 174-75.

54. Document B, copy 1, pp. 42-43; Document B, copy 2, June-July trials, pp. 23-46, August trials, pp. 1-8.

55. See note 54 above.

56. Kennedy and Parker, *Trials of Sundry Negroes*, 183-88.

57. Ibid., 59; Bennett's MS. message no. 2, p. 11.

58. *Charleston City Gazette,* Dec. 4, 1822; *Charleston Mercury,* Dec. 11, 1822. The anti-Bennett feeling was more lopsided than even the 2:1 numbers indicate, because many of the 35 voting against tabling wished an investigation to clear the court of Bennett's charges (*Charleston City Gazette*, Dec. 14, 1822).

59. Quoted in Howell M. Henry, *Police Control of the Slave in South Carolina* (Emory, Va., 1914), 59.

60. Ibid., 63-64.

61. William W. Freehling, *Prelude to Civil War: The Nullification Controversy in South Carolina, 1816-1836* (New York, 1965), 67, 72-76.

PART II

Race and Slavery in Antebellum Northern Politics

3

The Republican Party
and the Slave Power

WILLIAM E. GIENAPP

In *Home as Found*, James Fenimore Cooper presents a biting commentary on American society and values before the Civil War. At one point in the book, Aristabulus Bragg, the archetypal democratic politician always out to curry popular favor while looking out for his own interests, has the unpleasant duty of inducing some apprentices to stop playing ball on his client's property. Afraid to oppose the majority on any question, this self-proclaimed champion of the sovereignty of the multitude is rudely rebuffed when he tries to convince them to play in the street. Frustrated, he hits upon the clever strategy of pointing out that playing ball among roses is aristocratic. The change in the players' attitude is instantly apparent. Several announce that they never liked playing there, and the group quickly adjourns to the street. Boasting of their republican principles, mid-nineteenth century Americans, as Cooper recognized, nurtured a deep-seated hatred of anything that smacked of aristocracy.

The rediscovery of Cooper as a social critic of pre-Civil War America has paralleled the development among historians of a more sophisticated comprehension of the ideological basis of early American politics. An increasing number of works, spanning the nation's history from the Revolution to the end of Reconstruction, depict ideology as a central and persistent feature of political conflict. Reflecting this emphasis, recent work on the sectional conflict points to the critical role of belief systems in the coming of the Civil War. More than simply a means to win office, differences between parties in the antebellum period represented a fundamental cleavage over the nature of American society and its future development. Despite this general recognition, however, no agreement prevails concerning the causes of party realignment in the 1850s, the central feature of which was the birth of the Republican party and its astonishingly rapid rise to national power. The nature of the party's persuasion, why voters responded to it, and its relationship to the deepening sectional crisis, remain subjects of sharp historical debate.[1]

In seeking to distill the essence of the early Republican party's appeal, historians have stressed a number of different ideas—the promotion of industrial capitalism, nativism and anti-Catholicism, moral opposition to slavery, racial hatred of blacks, and stopping the extension of slavery, among others— and Eric Foner has demonstrated how, once matured, the party's ideology could simultaneously exhibit a number of these not entirely compatible sentiments. In general, however, discussions of the Republican persuasion have not sufficiently recognized that the party's ideology did not spring forth fully developed. Just as it took time to construct a viable organization, so it also took time for leaders to meld various ideas and concerns into a coherent and effective party creed. In the first years of the party's existence antagonism to certain groups or policies motivated many voters more than a positive identification with the Republican party. Only over time did voters develop an affirmative loyalty to the party and its program, and consequently much of the Republican appeal before the Civil War focused on what the party opposed.

Eric Foner has written the most extensive and what is probably the most influential interpretation of Republican ideology. His book provides a wide-ranging treatment of the subject, and no one has more sensitively analyzed the ambiguities and contradictions in Republican thought. Foner argues that a belief in free labor and the need to protect its concomitant social values of mobility, economic opportunity, and individual liberty constituted the framework of the party's ideology. Cognizant of the different impulses that contributed to the Republicans' hostility to slavery, he nevertheless emphasizes the party's opposition to the institution's expansion, which he views as arising out of a commitment to preserve and extend the North's free labor society.

Foner's interpretation has many virtues, one of which is the number of diverse themes that he integrates into a coherent Republican world view. Still, his argument that the idea of free labor provided the ideological foundation of the party's creed and accounted for its mass support contains difficulties. The ideology of free labor may have distinguished northerners from slaveowners, but that it divided Republicans from northern Democrats is questionable. All northerners, and not just Republicans, shared a belief in the values associated with free labor. Indeed, some have argued that these values were not exclusively northern, and that southerners including slaveowners embraced them.[2]

Michael F. Holt has recently advanced a different interpretation of Republican ideology. Holt stresses fear for the survival of republican government, rather than opposition to the extension of slavery, which he regards a distinct and subordinate concern among party members, as constituting the core of the party's appeal, and he argues that Republicans considered the Slave Power the major threat to republicanism. His book skillfully explains how fears in both the North and the South for the safety of the Republic ultimately came to dominate the sectional conflict.

Holt's forceful interpretation enhances our understanding of the ideology of the early Republican party. His emphasis on republicanism is well taken and builds on a growing body of literature, but at the same time his analysis ignores some important aspects of Republican thought. Despite the critical importance he attributes to the concept of the Slave Power, he gives little attention to how Republicans defined this symbol. Furthermore, though he recognizes that specific events inflamed Republican fears during the 1850s, he considers these fears to be essentially static and consequently does not analyze how they evolved in response to political developments. Finally, an alternative interpretation is possible that draws a more direct link between fears for republicanism and opposition to the extension of slavery.

While no summary can do justice to the nuances, qualifications, and many insights of these works, sufficient questions remain to justify a new examination of the party's appeal. The idea of a Slave Power and its role in Republican thought, in particular, needs more analysis. Close attention to what Republicans said indicates that they were concerned less about slavery than the Slave Power, that it was white planters—not black slaves—whom they hated, and that it was the growing threat to white liberties, not black, that they most feared. Because it united a number of diverse themes into a coherent intellectual construct, the concept of the Slave Power provides the essential key to dissect and comprehend the central thrust of Republican ideology.[3]

When Republicans raised the issue of slavery, they spoke much more frequently about the evils of its expansion than of its existence. Yet as Holt points out, if Republicans used the slavery extension issue to publicize their cause, curbing slavery's spread was not their primary motivation. Kansas simply offered the most convenient point on which to conduct a larger, more basic struggle. Even such an intense antislavery man as Charles Sumner acknowledged that the Kansas crisis was incidental to a more fundamental conflict. "For a long time my desire has been to make an issue with the Slave Oligarchy; & provided this can be had, I am indifferent to the special point selected," he told Henry J. Raymond in 1856, although he agreed that "at this moment Kansas is the inevitable point." In much the same fashion, the *Cincinnati Commercial* emphasized that the territorial issue "is merely a temporary form—a single manifestation of one that is infinitely more important." At the heart of the crisis, it continued, was the survival of republican government, against which the slaveocracy posed the foremost threat.[4]

As the master symbol of the Republican party, the Slave Power was the primary means by which party spokesmen defined the precise nature of the political crisis of the 1850s. In Republican propaganda, the Slave Power was simultaneously both a symbol of many undesirable features of American life and a description of the basic controlling force of the nation's political system. The concept furnished an uncomplicated explanation of the origins and progress of the conflict between the North and the South, while at the same time it indicated the program of action required to resolve this crisis.

Republicans portrayed the sectional crisis as a contest for national political supremacy between the Slave Power and the Republican party. In a speech delivered in 1856, William H. Seward told his listeners that "the question now to be decided is, whether a slaveholding class exclusively shall govern America." Four years later, the *New York Times* claimed that "possession of the Federal Government is what both the North and South are striving for," an interpretation endorsed by James Russell Lowell, who contended in the same year that the Slave Power aimed at permanent political ascendancy. The political overthrow of the Slave Power, Sumner announced, was "the practical purpose of the Republican party."[5]

When party members spoke of the Slave Power, or its equivalent the slaveocracy, they most frequently meant the slaveowners of the southern states—"the privileged class," as Seward denoted it, of 350,000 individuals who ruled their section without challenge and who sought to maintain by any means necessary their national power. Yet there were ambiguities even in this deceptively simple definition. Some Republicans, such as Horace Greeley, limited membership to slaveowners with a significant investment in slaves (normally 10 or more). Gamaliel Bailey of the *National Era,* on the other hand, included the families of slaveowners and estimated the Slave Power's strength at about two million people. Other Republicans excluded not only small slaveowners but also women, minors, and owners who did not live in the South. By this line of reasoning, Edmund Quincy, in a widely read article in the *Atlantic Monthly,* calculated the true strength of the Slave Power as "not much more than FIFTY THOUSAND voting men."[6]

As Quincy's reference to voters implies, central to the concept of the Slave Power was the notion of political power. The author of a three volume history of the sectional conflict, Henry Wilson designated the Slave Power as "the *political influence* . . . that results from the holding of four million men as property." Similarly, John Gorham Palfrey, who did much to popularize the idea of a Slave Power in a series of newspaper articles in the 1840s and 1850s, defined the slaveocracy as "that control in and over the government of the United States which is exercized by a comparatively small number of persons, distinguished from the other twenty millions of free citizens, and bound together in a common interest, by being owners of slaves."[7]

Although party spokesmen frequently noted that the Slave Power's influence also derived from the enormous capital sum (upwards of $2 billion) represented by the institution of slavery, they did not specify whether northern businessmen who serviced this investment were part of the Slave Power. A few Republicans, most notably Palfrey, advocated expanding the definition of the Slave Power to include northerners with extensive commercial ties to the plantation South, but most party propagandists were content to leave the precise relationship unspecified. The accusation of an alliance between southern planters and northern business interests—the lords of the lash and the lords of the loom—held much greater attraction for abolitionists, who had often been victims of businessmen-led mobs in the 1830s, than it did for Republicans, who despite disagreement over specific policies generally favored the promotion of economic growth. Most party members considered northern businessmen who sympathized with southern demands as simply tools of the slaveocracy rather than legitimate members.[8]

Also left ambiguous was whether the Slave Power encompassed northern politicians who defended southern rights. Republicans typically viewed such men as dupes or agents of the Slave Power rather than full-fledged members, although even this identification was sufficient to damn them. Yet on occasion party leaders suggested that these men played a more insidious role. In his 1858 senatorial campaign Abraham Lincoln, for example, characterized Franklin Pierce, James Buchanan, and Stephen A. Douglas, all prominent northern Democrats, as active leaders of a conspiracy hatched in the interest of the Slave Power. More common, however, was the viewpoint of the *Kennebec Journal,* which was edited by James G. Blaine, that the Slave Power easily bent northern Democrats to its will through its control of the party. When these doughfaces were no longer useful, their southern masters contemptuously cast them aside.[9] As a prime illustration, Republicans pointed to Stephen A. Douglas's fate after he opposed the proslavery Lecompton constitution.

Republicans also differed over the degree of unity manifested by the Slave Power. Some painted it as a tightly-knit, well disciplined, efficiently organized force. Thus one New England paper said of the Slave Power: "It is directed by one will, and moved by a common purpose. It has a fixed system of diplomacy, and a well organized and thoroughly trained corps of agents. The Czar of Russia has not more skilled and unwearied diplomatists."[10] Other Republicans, while not endorsing such a sweeping vision, agreed that the slaveholders' power derived from their unity as a distinct social class with a common interest. "Held together like the feudal barons of the middle ages by a community of interest and of sentiment," the *New York Times* commented, slaveowners acted "together always for the promotion of their common ends." Political divisions among southerners were of no significance, the *New York Evening Post* argued, because when it came to the extension of slavery, all southern politicians "act in concert . . . they amuse the North, it is true, with a show of belonging to different parties, but they belong in reality to but one—the party of slavery."[11]

As the vehicle of social, political, and economic privilege, the Slave Power represented the forces of aristocracy in American life. Convinced that the slave masters ruled their section without challenge, Republicans depicted society south of the Mason-Dixon line as completely in the grip of a political oligarchy that monopolized power and prestige, used this power solely for its own advantage, and oppressed nonslaveholding whites. Slaveowners were less than 5 percent of the southern white population, the *New York Times* noted, "yet in every one of these States the Slaveholders wield the whole political power,— make just such laws as their own interests require or their own projects dictate, and hold the great body of the white population in a condition of political subserviency quite as absolute as that of their Slaves." Slaveholders dominated public offices, dictated legislation, kept the southern masses in ignorance and poverty, and allowed no one to hold office who was not a spokesman for slavery. Although Republicans recognized the planters' extraordinary prominence in southern life, they revealed only a limited understanding of the sources of this power, and in particular greatly exaggerated the role of intimidation and coercion while unduly minimizing that of deference and perceived common interests.[12]

Also integral to the concept of the Slave Power was a belief in conspiracy. Republicans claimed that southern politicians were merely the most visible agents of a conspiracy to protect and enlarge the power and position of slaveowners, yet party leaders advanced no consistent theory of when this plot had first taken shape. Salmon P. Chase, who did much to develop the idea of a Slave Power, traced its organization back to the adoption of the Constitution. Some Republicans pointed to the Missouri crisis of 1819-1820, others emphasized the struggles during the 1830s over abolitionist petitions and use of the mails, while a number believed that the administration of John Tyler, which had accomplished the annexation of Texas, marked the ascendancy of the Slave Power in national councils. Whenever they dated its emergence, party supporters agreed that by the time of the Mexican War it had become an aggressive force in American politics.

Republicans ascribed the aggressive nature of the Slave Power to several factors. Blaming malevolent individuals such as John C. Calhoun or David Rice Atchison was one easy answer.[13] Carl Schurz, however, linked southern aggression to the institution of slavery itself. Like many Republicans, he accepted the idea endorsed by some southerners as well, that slavery had to expand to survive. Without fresh lands and new outlets for the surplus slave population, slavery would wither economically and eventually collapse. All the Slave Power's "demands and acts are in strict harmony with its interests and attributes," the German leader contended, "they are the natural growth of its existence."[14] Other Republicans attributed this aggressiveness to the influence of slavery on the southern character. Slavery inevitably developed "the most intense spirit of personal pride, a love of class distinctions, and the lust of dominion," Henry Wilson explained. "Hence arose a commanding power, ever sensitive, jealous, proscriptive, dominating and aggressive."[15]

These questions concerned only party elites. To ordinary Republicans, what mattered was that the Slave Power existed and (by their standards) was acting aggressively. By the mid-1850s, the idea of a Slave Power functioned, in part at least, as a partisan slogan. Joshua Leavitt, a veteran antislavery agitator, had prophesied this development during the 1840s. Noting that the term *Slave Power* was "now indissolubly incorporated in the political nonmenclature of the country," he told Chase: "We must make the most of that word. It is not necessary that they who use it should ever know who taught it to them—the name and the thing—but the incessant use of the term will do much to open the eyes and arouse the energies of the people."[16]

Actually the concept's ambiguity offered certain advantages, for it allowed Republican orators to shift its meaning somewhat to support most effectively their argument. As always intellectual rigor was not necessary for political success. Two ideas, however, were invariably present: first, that the slaveowners constituted the heart and soul of the Slave Power and supplied its driving force; and second, that the Slave Power posed a serious threat, not only to northern interests, but to the nation's republican tradition as well. This threat to America's republican heritage, rather than the precise definition of the Slave Power, formed the core of the Republican appeal to northern voters. In the 1830s a small group of abolitionists developed the Slave Power concept to attack and end slavery.[17] Republicans transformed this idea by shifting the emphasis from ending slavery to destroying the South's political power as a requisite step to preserve republicanism.

The major impetus behind the party's free soil program was that by stopping the advance of slavery and refusing to admit any new slave states, the growth of the Slave Power would be halted, thereby enabling the North to take control of the federal government. This theme had emerged during the controversy over the Wilmot Proviso in the 1840s, but then its thrust had been to break southern control of the Democratic party. By the 1850s the South was more unified politically, and the challenge to its national power now came from the Republican party, whose supporters as a group were more concerned about the power wielded by slaveholders than slavery per se. As one wrote Sumner, "In this country, Slavery is really fostered as a *source of political power,* & not as an economical or social disideratum." Prominent Republicans repeatedly denied that the party had any intention or desire to interfere with slavery in the southern states. In a speech which defined the purpose and policy of the Republican party, Seward repudiated any intention of attacking slavery itself. Instead, he advocated that the power of the slaveocracy be broken by stopping the extension of the institution, and "that is enough."[18]

At stake was nothing less than control of the country's destiny. The *Cincinnati Commercial* asserted that the South desired new territory "with a view, by the multiplication of slave States, to increase the political power of the slave interest in the government. In short, to contrive ways and means to keep the government of the country in the hands of a Southern minority has been, from first to last, the end and aim of all parties at the South, ever since the introduction

of cotton culture." The *New York Times* made the same point four years later in
the Lincoln campaign. Slavery was "merely an incident of the real controversy,"
it commented, "the real contest is for political power."[19] One reason southerners
reacted so strongly to Lincoln's election was their perception that they had lost
control of the government after years of exercising authority.

The notion of a Slave Power expressed northern resentment over the
political power of the South and especially slaveholders. At its core was the
belief that the South had long dominated the national government and dictated
federal policy at will. "The powers of the government are in their keeping,"
George W. Julian said of the slaveowners. "They are the reigning lords and
masters of the people, white and black. Look at the facts." Republican sources
documented southern preponderance since 1789 in federal offices, headed by
the presidency, which the South held for all but twenty-two years before the Civil
War. The president, Seward complained, was little more than "a deputy of the
privileged class." In like manner, Schurz called the federal government "the
very citadel of the slave aristocracy."[20]

According to Republicans, government policy systematically favored the
South's and especially slavery's interests. The address of the Pittsburgh convention in 1856 maintained that despite the North's superiority in population,
wealth, and enterprise, "slavery . . . controls all departments of their [Amer-
icans'] common government, and wields their power on its own behalf." Under
the direction of the Slave Power, the national government had been perverted
into an engine for slavery expansion. Flushed by its earlier territorial gains, the
South now aimed for Kansas. Success there, party spokesmen cried, would
make the Slave Power impregnable.[21] Yet this insatiable slave oligarchy did not
confine its schemes merely to the national domain. The purpose of filibustering
expeditions against Latin American countries and of demands for the reopening
of the African slave trade, Republicans proclaimed, was "to convert this Republic into the grandest and most powerful Slaveholding Empire the world has ever
known."[22]

Led by Salmon P. Chase, who argued that the Founding Fathers opposed
slavery and had expected it to die soon after the Constitution was adopted,
Republicans accused the Slave Power of subverting the Republic's original
purposes. Party spokesmen contended that southerners overturned this goal by
demanding that slavery be allowed to expand, and in response the institution had
become a powerful, aggressive force that threatened to engulf the entire nation.
The only remedy was to return to the original policy, divorce the federal
government from any support of slavery, and treat it strictly as a local institution.[23] To be sure, Chase greatly exaggerated the Revolutionary generation's
commitment to antislavery, especially in terms of policy, but in so doing he
created more than just a usable past; he also formulated a concise explanation of
why the nation developed in the direction it had. Republicans of all persuasions

uncritically embraced Chase's constitutional theory, which allowed them to identify with the revered Founders of the American Republic, while it placed the Slave Power in stark opposition to the country's heritage.

It was not southern obstruction of economic legislation or the federal government's intimate ties to slavery—disturbing though these were—that made control of the national government seem so pressing. Instead, what made southern political power ominous to Republicans was the South's attempt to restrict the basic rights of northern white men. To party members, nothing less than the preservation of republican government and society was at stake in the sectional struggle.

In advancing this argument, Republican spokesmen drew upon the ideology of republicanism, which the Amerian Revolution had enshrined in the nation's political creed. Republicanism did not lose its importance after the adoption of the Constitution, yet this body of thought was not a fixed set of principles immune to social and political developments. Historians have traditionally emphasized the continuities in republican thought, but more attention needs to be paid to its discontinuities, especially for the years after 1815. The growth of the Republic after 1789 and the broadening experiences of subsequent generations altered the meaning of republicanism, so that it was no longer the same in the 1850s as in the 1780s or even the 1830s. Recognition of the changing nature of republicanism is essential for understanding how the Republicans used this tradition for partisan purposes.

By the last decade before the Civil War, certain ideas that were once central to the ideology of republicanism no longer commanded widespread assent. These included the concept of virtue, the fear of government power, and opposition to political parties. Certainly the Republicans no longer endorsed the traditional Country Whig hostility to an active, centralized government or to policies designed to promote economic and social modernization. At the same time, other basic beliefs had undergone change. For example, representative government remained a central ideal, but in the wake of the rise of democracy it was not accompanied by a much stronger insistence on the principle of majority rule; furthermore, the older concept that property formed the basis for political citizenship had been superseded by a belief in universal (white manhood) suffrage and the desirability of officeholding by ordinary citizens. Much greater importance was also attached to basic civil liberties, such as freedom of speech, of the press, and of political action than had been true in the eighteenth century. At the same time, other components of this creed retained much of their earlier content. Socially, for example, republicanism continued to extoll the value of individual liberty and equality, and thus it promoted a strong animus against, even a hatred of, aristocracy and elite rule. But the most striking continuity in republican thought between the Revolution and the Civil War was the popular fear of a conspiracy to subvert liberty. Drawing on the experience of earlier generations, Republican spokesmen identified this internal threat as emanating from aristocractic tendencies in American life. By this period, republican theory stipulated that government was bound by law and was responsive to and controlled by the people, and that its purpose was to promote liberty and equality by vigilantly protecting society from aristocratic privilege.

Although they shared several common values, the ideology of republicanism was not the same as that of free labor. Despite some attention to social and political questions, the thrust of the free labor argument, whose roots lay in traditional liberalism, was economic; its central tenet was a belief in the moral benefits of economic development, and it extolled the superiority of the northern social order in terms of access to opportunity and social mobility. The doctrine of republicanism, in contrast, placed greater emphasis on political than economic considerations. It laid heavier stress on protecting basic civil liberties and on the necessity of maintaining a government that represented the interests of the people rather than a privileged aristocracy. The lack of a free and open democratic political system, the aggrandizement of political power in the hands of the planter class, and the curtailment of the fundamental rights of southern whites, rather than the economic disadvantages slavery entailed on non-slaveowning southerners, caused Republicans to view the South as an unrepublican society.

After an initial period of ideological uncertainty, the Republican party's fundamental appeal finally took shape during the 1856 campaign in response to the caning of Charles Sumner and the continuing turmoil in Kansas which culminated in May with the "Sack of Lawrence." Because the extension of slavery was only part of this larger crisis perceived by Republicans, the caning of Sumner was as critical to the party's appeal as the situation in Kansas.

"The issues now before the people, are those of Despotism or Freedom," a letter to the *New York Independent* affirmed after the Sumner and Lawrence incidents. "The question has passed on from that of slavery for negro servants, to that of tyranny over free white men." Schuyler Colfax used virtually identical language in a letter to a local Republican convention in 1856, while a New York Republican insisted that nothing less than "the right to speak, to think, to write" was at stake in the contest.[24] Charles A. Dana of the *New York Tribune* was convinced that southern aggression against northern rights provided the Republicans with a winning issue. Neither the Pope nor immigrants could govern the country or endanger its liberties, he insisted, "but the slave breeders and slave traders *do* govern it, and threaten to put an end to all other government than theirs. Here is something tangible to go upon," he continued, "an issue on which we will . . . surely succeed in the long run."[25]

The Sumner caning effectively symbolized several Republican themes: the arrogance and insolence of southern leaders, the barbarism of southern culture, and the Slave Power's determination to silence all critics and eradicate free speech if necessary to maintain its ascendancy. Not only had Preston S. Brooks insulted northern manhood and attacked northern equality, his fray with Sumner in the Senate Chamber in retaliation for the Massachusetts senator's recent speech seemed a direct attack on freedom of speech.[26] Events in Kansas raised precisely the same issue, for Republicans claimed that freedom of speech and of the press, as well as purity of the ballot box, were all being violated in that far-off territory. Both in Kansas and in the nation's capital, men seemed to be attacked for what they said and thought. Slavery propagandists, the *Cincinnati Gazette* asserted, "cannot tolerate free speech anywhere, and would stifle it in Washington with the bludgeon and the bowie-knife, as they are now trying to stifle it in Kansas by massacre, rapine and murder." The war on the free state settlers in Kansas, the *Ashtabula Sentinel* declared, vividly demonstrated the Slave Power's determination to "wield the General Government against freedom—not only in Kansas, but every where else." The notorious Kansas legal code enacted by the proslavery territorial legislature, which severely circumscribed traditional civil liberties, intensified Republican fears. The *Atlantic Monthly* designated these laws a direct attack on republican government, for they "aimed a fatal blow at the four cornerstones of a free commonwealth,—freedom of speech, of the press, of the jury, and of suffrage." Here seemed irrefutable proof of the ultimate design of the Slave Power. All of these developments, summarized Henry Ward Beecher, were part of a "long-formed, deeply-laid plan, of destroying free speech in the Republic, and making SILENCE NATIONAL!"[27]

Republican emphasis on northern liberties did not end with John C. Frémont's defeat. Developments during the next four years, especially the Dred Scott decision and the ill-fated attempt to admit Kansas under the proslavery Lecompton constitution, reinforced Republican anxiety. Alarmed by these events, as well as by the attempt to prevent Republican orator George William Curtis from speaking in the city, and by Democratic leaders' open advocacy of lynching abolitionists after John Brown's raid, the Philadelphia conservative Sidney G. Fisher reflected: "[Southern] politicians are . . . connecting the cause of abolition with the cause of liberty, order & civil rights. These have been destroyed in the southern states for the sake of slavery. . . . Events are showing that . . . [our rights], the Union & slavery, are incompatible. . . . Which then shall we sacrifice? . . . Every right-thinking, conservative man will answer, preserve all three if possible; if that be not possible, sacrifice slavery first."[28] In 1860 a northern congressman told his southern colleagues: "Your aggressions forced the North into this contest—to defend the liberty of speech and of the press; to maintain the right of petition; to secure their citizens['] rights, plainly and in terms guaranteed by the Constitution, and assailed by your unjust and unconstitutional laws." The black abolitionist Frederick Douglass discerned a fundamental truth when he observed, "The cry of Free Men was raised, not for the extension of liberty to the black man, but for the protection of the liberty of the white."[29]

Having allegedly eradicated the basic rights of southern whites, the Slave

Power, according to Republicans, now aimed to do the same with the liberties of northern white men. By such rhetoric, Republicans made the threat posed by the Slave Power seem much more real and personal, and they used the slave-master relationship, the essence of everything northerners feared and hated, to define this threat. Thus the *New York Evening Post* asked after the Sumner caning: "Has it come to this, that we must speak with bated breath in the presence of our Southern masters? . . Are we too, slaves, slaves for life, a target for their brutal blows, when we do not comport ourselves to please them?" Even earlier a Republican paper in Maine raised the same cry. After a discussion of a long list of instances of southern interference with northern civil liberties, it warned: "These things are not accidental. They are the true exponents of an overshadow-ing, relentless oligarchy, that is as ready to fasten its manacles upon *our* limbs, as it ever has been upon those of the meanest slave."[30]

As Michael Holt has emphasized, slavery had a meaning for antebellum Americans independent from the institution of black slavery.[31] It connoted a person's loss of independence, his inability to control his own life and destiny, his subjection to the wishes of another. As such, slavery symbolized the antithesis of republicanism, and thus when Republicans denounced slavery, they often meant the threatened loss of *white men's* liberties. "It is high time that the people of the whole country should know and understand, that the degraded negro is not the only class of *slaves* among us; but that the arrogance of the *'slave power'* tramples ruthlessly upon *all* who presume to fix limits to its dominion," an Ohio man wrote to Benjamin F. Wade.[32] Adding force to this point were the heedless editorials in prominent southern newspapers that urged the enslavement of lower class whites. Wide circulation of these editorials in the Republican press made this idea seem much more in accord with southern attitudes than was really the case.

Republicans consciously identified their crusade with the forefathers' struggle for liberty during the American Revolution. Then the British were conspiring to enslave the colonists; now the Slave Power manifested a similar intention. "Now is the beginning of the second 'American Revolution,'" one Republican wrote during the 1856 contest. "The North is the band struggling for freedom. The south is the despotic power which wishes to enslave the north." In making the same comparison, a New Hampshire Republican paper contended that "the Liberties of our country are in tenfold the danger that they were at the commencement of the American Revolution." The crucial difference between the crisis of the 1850s and that of the 1770s was that "we then had a distant foe to contend with. Now the enemy is within our borders."[33] The symbolic impor-tance of this identification with the Republic's birth should not be minimized. Not only did it reaffirm the belief that the party's program paralleled that of the founding generation, it also gave a sense of legitimacy to the Republican fear of a conspiracy against liberty.

Republicans' perception of southern society further fanned their fears. When Republicans looked south, they saw a society that seemed to repudiate some of the most fundamental American values. Party members were acutely aware that freedom of speech, at least on the topic of slavery, had largely disappeared in the South and that political rights were circumscribed as well, a situation that led to considerable exaggerations in the Republican press about conditions in the South. In a speech on "The Dominant Class in the Republic" delivered during the 1856 campaign, Seward emphasized the absence of freedom of speech, of the press, of the ballot box, of education, of literature, and of popular assembly in the South, all of which he traced to the power of the slaveholding class. Republicans readily projected similar intentions toward northern society. Reckless demands by southern newspapers after the Sumner caning that other Republican leaders be thrashed, accompanied by assertions that no discussion of slavery be tolerated, certainly did not alleviate Republican anxieties. Scoffed one Republican congressman in response to these threats, "Verily, this is a *model . . .* Republic."[34]

As the proponent of slavery, of aristocracy, of tyranny, and of minority rule, the Slave Power was, in Republican thought, the absolute negation of the country's founding principles. A Republican congressman asked in June, 1856: "Are we to have a government of the people, a real representative Republican Government? or are the owners of slave property, small in number but with the power now in their hands, and strongly intrenched in every department, to rule us with arbitrary and undisputed sway?"[35] Republicans repeatedly raised the cry that the nation was in danger of being transformed into a slaveholding oligarchy. "Slavery is essentially an anti-republican institution," one Republican paper declared, "and if it ever arrives at undisputed predominance in this country, will in reality, if not in name, subvert our republican form of government. . . . The most important object of political action, at the present day, is unquestionably to check this anti-republican influence, and to assert the predominance of freedom in the Republic." Recent events, the address of the Pittsburgh convention asserted, allowed no doubt that the Slave Power "is resolved upon the dethronement of the principles of republicanism, and the establishment in their stead, of an OLIGARCHY bound together by a common interest in the ownership of slaves."[36]

Here was the Republicans' reply to the accusation that they were fomenting trouble by meddling in southern affairs. They reversed the argument: it was the Slave Power that interfered with northern society, seeking to circumscribe civil liberties and subvert the Constitution. It was slavery that would not leave northern free men alone. Charles Francis Adams answered the question, "What makes slavery a question of national concern?," by recounting southern attacks on northern civil liberties since the 1830s. Northerners had to meet this issue if they were to preserve republican government. The truth was, Greeley recalled, that "Slavery never let the North alone, nor thought of so doing."[37] Republicans insisted that they sought only to return to the policy of the Founding Fathers and that they contemplated no aggression on southern rights. It was the South, not the Republican party, that was acting aggressively.

Denunciation of the Slave Power enabled the Republicans to avoid the aristocratic stigma that had so burdened the Whigs. William Henry Seward took the lead in defining the basic conflict between the two sections as one of aristocracy versus democracy. In a speech that Richard Henry Dana, Jr. termed "the key note of the New Party," the New York leader warned when speaking of the slaveholding class that "an aristocracy has . . . arisen here . . . [which] is already undermining the republic." And he pointedly asked if republicanism was to be sacrificed for the convenience of 350,000 slaveowners:

The republican party is sounding throughout all our borders a deep-toned alarum for the safety of the constitution, of union, and of liberty. Do you hear it? The Republican party declares, that by means of recent treacherous measures adopted by congress and the president . . . the constitutional safeguards of citizens, identical with the rights of human nature itself, are undermined, impaired, and in danger of being overthrown. It declares that if those safeguards be not immediately renewed and restored, the government itself, hitherto a fortress of republicanism, will pass into the hands of an insidious aristocracy, and its batteries be turned against the cause which it was reared to defend.[38]

The image of the Slave Power as a vehicle of aristocracy exerted a powerful influence on northern voters, long nurtured on egalitarian rhetoric. Horace Greeley's *New York Tribune* noted that the word *aristocracy* politically repelled the common men of the North, while the *Springfield Republican* caustically observed that "one of the peculiar effects of southern slavery is to develop . . . among the proprietors, the aristocratic feeling, and to destroy the American sentiment of social equality." The climax of the struggle against aristocracy in America occurred, not in the Jeffersonian challenge to the Federalists in the 1790s, or in the Jacksonian-Whig battles in the 1830s, but in the Republican assault on the Slave Power in the 1850s. In accounting for the Republican party's strength in the 1856 election, a thoughtful Bostonian told a southern friend that other arguments were insignificant compared to "the aristocratic nature of . . . slavery" and the accompanying issue of whether a small class of slaveholders should continue to control the government. "If there is anything in this country fixed," he succinctly remarked, "it is the prejudice against aught which has the appearance even of aristocracy."[39]

Closely connected to this conception of the crisis was the issue of majority rule, the cardinal principle of republican government. Socially the agent of aristocracy, the Slave Power politically was the proponent of minority rule. In both its social pretensions and political principles, Republicans identified the Slave Power with values utterly repugnant to northern voters' republican ideals.

The radical *Cincinnati Commercial* claimed: "If our Government, for the sake of Slavery, is to be perpetually the representative of a minority, it may continue republican in form, but the substance of its republicanism has departed." The *Ohio State Journal,* a much more conservative Republican paper, dismissed slaveowners as "an arrogant little Aristocracy" and went on to maintain that "majorities rule, or should rule, in this Republican land." Control of the nation by "a mere handful of Southerners," contended a newspaper published in southern Illinois, represented the "paradox of a republican government, in which a minority rules the majority."[40]

For Republicans, Lincoln's victory in 1860 starkly raised this issue. At last the northern majority possessed the power to which it was entitled. Yet southerners refused to accept the popular verdict and eventually eleven states seceded. So long as they had power, an angry James Russell Lowell wrote, southerners were satisfied with the political system, but now in defeat they "question the right of the majority to govern, except on their terms. . . . Their quarrel is not with the Republican party, but with the theory of Democracy." The prominent conservative Republican Edward Bates insisted that to submit to threats of disunion "would be a clear surrender of the one [and] only principle of representative government—the right of the majority to govern the country; according to the forms of the constitution."[41]

While these themes were not new in 1856, their powerful hold on northern public opinion was. The events of the past twelve months had converted thousands of northerners to the Republican viewpoint. What made the Republican argument compelling was that these latest "outrages" formed part of a long series of alleged assaults on northern civil liberties. Their cumulative effect, coupled with the particularly dramatic nature of the caning of Sumner and the raid on Lawrence, persuaded many northerners that these charges were more than political propaganda. The assault on Sumner was "not merely an *incident,* but a *demonstration,*" Hannibal Hamlin's father-in-law asserted. Citing the repeal of the Missouri Compromise, the invasions of Kansas, the behavior of southern congressmen, the policy of the Administration, and the acts of violence of the period, he concluded: "bring all the proofs together, & do they not furnish a clear demonstration of a settled purpose to annihilate freedom? . . . It seems to me the demonstration is as certain as any demonstration in mathematics. Incidents are no longer incidents—they are links in the chain of demonstration, infallible, plain, conclusive." Practical illustrations, not abstract moral philosophy, Schurz observed, finally caused the northern masses to recognize the threat to democratic institutions.[42]

Republican strategists realized that concern for the welfare of blacks, free or slave, had never been strong in the free states and that appeals based on the immorality of slavery were doomed to political failure. One advantage the symbols of Bleeding Sumner and Bleeding Kansas offered was that they enabled Republicans to attack the South without directly attacking slavery. By appropriating the abolitionist symbol of the Slave Power and linking it to the threat to northern rights, Republicans made a much more powerful appeal to northern sensibilities than they could have otherwise. As John Van Buren warned James Buchanan during the 1856 campaign, this issue was especially effective among old Jacksonian Democrats. The acrimonious struggle between the Van Buren Democrats and southern political leaders in the 1840s had made them very sensitive to charges of southern arrogance and dictation. One rank-and-file Democrat, who joined the Republican party in 1856 because of what he considered the Slave Power's insolent aggression in Congress, in Kansas, and in the country generally, informed a longtime political associate: "Reserve no place for me. *I shall not come back.*"[43]

The concept of the Slave Power offered the additional advantage of allowing Republicans to attack southern policy while sustaining the fiction that they did not hate the South. Party adherents insisted that they opposed the Slave Power and not the mass of white southerners. "When we speak of the South as distinguished from the North by elements of inherent hostility," the *Atlantic Monthly* explained, "we speak only of the governing faction, and not of the millions of nominally free [southern] men who are scarcely less its thralls than the black slaves themselves."[44] However soothing this theoretical distinction was to troubled party members, it was not an easy one to draw in practice. The 1856 election dramatically revealed the intensity of antisouthern feeling in the Republican ranks, and the subsequent four years did not ameliorate this hostility. Some Republicans, sensitive to the accusation that their party was a sectional organization that threatened the Union, denied that it was impelled by antipathy to the South.[45] But nothing party leaders did or said altered its image or reassured southerners.

The Republicans' emphasis on the Slave Power and its threat to republican values had such obvious strategic advantages, it seems puzzling in retrospect that they did not adopt this appeal immediately. The inevitable confusion that accompanies the collapse of any party system and the formation of a new party accounts for some of this delay. A more serious impediment to adopting this approach was the taint of abolitionism that the Slave Power concept bore. Because abolitionists had initially developed this idea, and because they had harped on it for over two decades, it was decidedly disreputable in most northern circles. Although the war with Mexico, the Compromise of 1850, and the repeal of the Missouri Compromise gave the notion of a Slave Power more plausibility, most northerners remained suspicious of any idea spawned by abolitionists. Additional and more direct assaults on northern liberties were necessary to overcome their scepticism.

It was not mere coincidence that the party's ideology formalized in 1856. The impact of the caning of Sumner and the continuing chaos in Kansas account for both the focus of the Republican appeal and its persuasiveness. By raising more directly than anything since the mail and petition controversies of the 1830s the issues of civil liberties, of northern rights, and of republicanism, these events directed public attention to issues other than the existence of slavery, and Republican leaders understood the strategic advantages of downplaying the question of slavery in favor of an attack on the Slave Power.

After 1856, the Republican appeal continued to center on the threat to republicanism and to northern rights posed by the Slave Power, and the party's main goal remained wresting control of the government from the slave oligarchy. The momentous events of 1857-60, however, dramatically magnified the threat confronting the North and added new dimensions to the party's creed. Beginning in 1857, Republicans increasingly emphasized the growing belief that slavery would be forced not just on Kansas and other territories, but on the free states as well. Unless the North acted, slavery would soon become a national institution.

The fear that slavery would ultimately expand north had been voiced, albeit sporadically, during the struggle over the Nebraska bill in 1854. The violence and frauds in Kansas strengthened the plausibility of this idea, and during the 1856 campaign papers such as the *Cincinnati Commercial* and the *Phildelphia North American* earnestly raised this concern.[46] Statements such as Robert Toombs's oft-quoted and subsequently denied boast that he would call the roll of his slaves on Bunker Hill and the southern argument that slavery had the same rights as any other property under the Constitution fueled Republican anxiety. Critics North and South ridiculed these fears, yet without question many sincerely believed that the threat was real. One of Buchanan's correspondents noted with astonishment that "many honest men believe that if Fremont shall fail in his election, slavery will be established in all the free states."[47]

In 1856 this idea was inchoate and not accepted by all or even most Republicans, but developments during Buchanan's administration reshaped the thinking of many party members, so that by 1860 the threatened nationalization of the institution had become a major Republican theme. The one event that, more than any other, convinced thousands of northerners that such fears were not hysterical was the Supreme Court's Dred Scott decision, which invalidated any congressional ban on slavery in the territories as a violation of the constitutional guarantee of due process. "There is such a thing as THE SLAVE POWER," shrieked the *Cincinnati Commercial* when the decision was announced. "It has marched over and annihilated the boundaries of the states. We are now one great homogeneous slaveholding community." The real meaning of the court's ruling, the *Illinois State Journal* claimed, was that a person could bring slaves into Illinois "with impunity, hold them here as long as they please and then take them back again, thus virtually making our soil a *slave State*."[48]

Lincoln and other Republican leaders noted that all that was needed was one more Dred Scott decision that a state could not bar slavery and the objective of the Slave Power to nationalize slavery would be accomplished. There seemed no way to prevent such a decision, for the court had a proslavery majority that had already demonstrated its willingness to ignore past precedents to propound a decision favorable to slavery.[49] Ominously, the California Supreme Court upheld a slaveowner's right to retain his property contrary to the state's constitution.[50] Other Republicans expressed apprehension that the United States Supreme Court would nationalize slavery by simply affirming the right of indefinite transit for slave property in a free state. In Philadelphia Judge John K. Kane had already issued such a ruling in the trial of Passmore Williamson, and an appeal to the Supreme Court of the Lemmon case, which raised the same issue, seemed likely. Fearful of the outcome of such an appeal, the *New York Tribune* insisted that if the right of transit were endorsed, "We shall see men buying slaves for the New-York market. There will be no legal power to prevent it." These forebodings intensified with the commencement of what appeared to be a concerted campaign to prepare northern public opinion for this outcome. Near the close of 1857, the *Washington Union,* the Democratic party's national organ, announced that the clear implication of the Dred Scott decision was that all state laws prohibiting a citizen of another state from bringing his slave property into the state, either permanently or temporarily, were unconstitutional.[51]

Apprehension that slavery would become national was not an infrequent theme voiced by a few excited politicians; it permeated Republican thought after 1856, and its advocates included the party's most thoughtful spokesmen. In his famous speech "The Irrepressible Conflict," Seward charged that the slaveholders had a "plan of operation" to extend slavery "throughout the whole Union." The contest meant that "the United States must and will, sooner or later, become either entirely a slaveholding nation, or entirely a free-labor nation."[52]

Already embarked on the path that would take him to the White House, Abraham Lincoln formulated the most forceful and carefully argued analysis of this threat in the years 1858-60. "The House Divided Speech," delivered when he accepted the Republican nomination for senator, contained his best known statement on the subject. Taking as his text the biblical verse that "a house divided against itself cannot stand," the Illinois leader began by prophesying that the nation would eventually cease to be divided between freedom and slavery. "It will become *all* one thing, or *all* the other." Either slavery would be placed "in course of ultimate extinction; or its *advocates* will push it forward, till it shall become alike lawful in *all* the States, *old* as well as *new—North* as well as *South.*" Then in a sentence most historians consider anticlimatic but which in fact was the critical transition between these opening general remarks and the main theme of the speech, Lincoln asked his audience: "Have we no *tendency* to the latter condition?" The existence of a concerted program to make slavery a national institution, in which he implicated his opponent Stephen A. Douglas, served as the keynote for Lincoln's senatorial campaign. All the pieces were now falling into place. "We shall *lie down* pleasantly dreaming that the people of *Missouri* are on the verge of making their State *free*," he warned, "and we shall *awake* to the *reality*, instead that the *Supreme* Court has made *Illinois* a *slave* State."[53]

For the most part, historians have dismissed the fears of Seward and other Republicans as excessive if not patently ridiculous, and Lincoln's biographers, writing in the shadow of his wartime statesmanship, have been constantly embarrassed by his use of this argument.[54] Southerners at the time also responded with a chorus of denunciation. Except for the most extreme elements, they denied any intention or even desire to nationalize the institution. Robert Toombs of Georgia ridiculed the claim, and Jefferson Davis waved it aside as "absurd."[55] Without close scrutiny, historians have taken men such as Toombs and Davis at their word. In so doing, they have ignored the fact that men frequently do not perceive the full implications of their arguments, indeed often resist accepting them even when they are made clear. Too little attention has been given to the compromise plan Davis introduced following Lincoln's election. The Mississippi senator proposed a constitutional amendment to put slave property on the same footing as any other property and to exempt such property from impairment by Congress or any state or territory. His amendment would have essentially legalized slavery in *every* state in the Union. Here, and not some crack-brained class theory of slavery, was the logical outcome of the slaveholders' philosophy.

As the burgeoning Republican alarm over the nationalization of slavery illustrates, the party's ideology was not static but continued to evolve after Frémont's defeat. Historians have not appreciated, however, the extent to which these changes took place within the basic outline formalized during the 1856 presidential campaign. It is true, as Holt argues, that fear of black slavery was not the same as fear of white slavery. Nevertheless, the anxiety that slavery would spread northward, like the party's continuing commitment to block the institution's expansion into the territories, was integrally connected to the party's overriding commitment to preserve republicanism.[56] The primary reason Republicans opposed the extension of slavery was not because of racial or economic concerns, as some historians have asserted. Racism occupied only a minor place in Republican thought, and although the belief that free labor could not compete with slavery was of greater importance, it too was distinctly subordinate to other concerns. In fact, while little doubt exists that slavery could have taken hold in the free states, as the long struggle to exclude it from Indiana and Illinois earlier in the century demonstrated, its economic significance would have been limited. Instead, what made the possible expansion of slavery north so alarming to party supporters was the belief that the institution's presence would annihilate republicanism. Slavery would foster a hierarchical society, one ruled by an oligarchy hostile to fundamental republican values and committed to eradicating basic republican institutions. The existence of slavery, in short, would create a privileged slaveholding aristocracy that would control the state and strip whites of their liberties, just as had happened already (at least according to Republican propaganda) in the South. The result would be, Republicans were certain, that America's republican heritage would become only a memory.

Identical assumptions explain why southerners gravitated towards what appears to be a desperate policy to nationalize slavery. In essence, what the South objected to was any discussion of slavery. Southerners (as well as Republicans) were convinced that if slavery existed in a state, the interest of the institution would predominate. Republicans were keenly aware that slavery lacked overweening economic strength in the border states yet was politically invincible, with Delaware and its infinitesimal slave population being the most glaring example. The outcome would be the same in the free states if slavery were legalized. Climate would be no bar. Remove the legal barriers to slavery and the *Chicago Tribune* predicted that the North's "codfish and cotton aristocracy" would immediately introduce slavery.[57] Every state would then contain a ruling slaveholding aristocracy with a vested interest, both economic and psychological, in maintaining bondage. The no longer peculiar institution finally would be safe in an increasingly hostile nineteenth century world.

In accounting for the growing popular belief in the North in the Slave Power, some historians have delved beneath the deteriorating relations between the two sections and sought an explanation in the social and psychological realm. David Brion Davis provides the most extensive analysis of the acceptance of this idea in his book *The Slave Power Conspiracy and the Paranoid Style*. Davis concedes that events "gave increasing substance to the northern view of a Slave Power conspiracy," but he finds the significance of this idea, and the explanation for its hold on the northern popular mind, elsewhere. He borrows from Richard Hofstadter's argument that Americans have been peculiarly susceptible to a view of history as the unfolding of some gigantic conspiracy and emphasizes instead underlying social and psychological tensions in American society. Noting that "the imagery of counter-subversion may give symbolic expression to the deepest fears and needs of a people," he traces the roots of the idea of a Slave Power conspiracy to the rapid and often bewildering changes that beset American society in the decades before the Civil War. Economic, social, and intellectual flux produced popular anxiety and a confusion over social roles, and because it was an important symbol by which many antebellum Americans defined their values and roles, the Slave Power conspiracy was a primary means of relieving stress in their daily lives.[58]

Davis's argument has much to commend it. It places the idea of the Slave

Power conspiracy in a larger context by relating its themes to other countersubversive movements of the antebellum period. By linking these ideas to the inner needs and anxieties of Americans, it firmly establishes the social milieu in which these ideas took hold. Aware of the internal contradictions and ambiguities of this cluster of ideas, Davis skillfully incorporates them into a thoughtful interpretation of their significance. In so doing, he has greatly expanded our knowledge of countersubversive movements in pre-Civil War America.

For all its strengths, however, Davis's argument ultimately is not convincing. One problem is his assertion that the diffusion of anxiety among the general population produced by rapid social and economic change accounts for the attraction held by the idea of a Slave Power conspiracy. Rapid social and economic change has by now become a catch-all to explain a myriad of political movements. Jacksonians, anti-Masons, abolitionists, proslavery ideologues, and Know Nothings—as diverse a collection as one could imagine—have all been interpreted as a product of this phenomenon. Moreover, even if relevant, popular anxiety alone cannot explain why some of these movements gained a much greater popular following than others. Of the various countersubversive movements, none took such deep root in the northern popular mind as the Slave Power conspiracy. Nor does Davis's interpretation explain why this idea exhibited great popularity only in the 1850s and not earlier. The concept had been formulated in the 1830s and persistently agitated since then, yet not until the final decade before the war did it have central significance in American politics. There is no evidence that the 1850s was a time of more rapid change, or of greater social unease and popular anxiety, than the 1830s. Whatever role these factors played in the genesis of the concept, they cannot account for its sudden attractiveness in the 1850s after two decades of neglect.

Analysis of the relationship between Republican ideology and the brewing political crisis of the 1850s offers a more fruitful approach. While a few historians have seen some validity in Republican claims, most have dismissed the idea of a Slave Power as fantastic. They note that slaveholders did not have the same interests or perceptions, that the South was never united politically before the Civil War, and that it was impossible for the minority South to rule the country without northern aid. At no time did southern representatives vote as a bloc in Congress, and the 1860 presidential election revealed how deeply southerners were divided over how to deal with the sectional crisis.[59] Such arguments suggest that Republicans' acceptance of the idea of a Slave Power was at best foolish and unreasonable, at worst pathological and paranoid.

In attacking the idea of a Slave Power, historians have concentrated on the most extreme Republican rhetoric. Certainly it is not difficult to discover the elements of the so-called paranoid style in Republican thinking. Party loyalists, both leaders and among the rank and file, frequently invoked the concept of conspiracy to explain the American past. Without question a number of Republicans interpreted the nation's politics since some critical date as the unfolding of this conspiracy, existence of which was revealed through the pattern of events. Republican speeches and editorials frequently enumerated a list of occurrences and attributed each to the malevolent workings of the Slave Power, and sometimes even predicted future developments which it would bring to fruition as soon as possible. In such rhetoric, the slave oligarchy, united and aggressive, stood at the center of American history, "always the secret spring which sets events in motion."[60] With no cognizance of the role of accident, personal ineptness, coincidence, or unforeseen consequences, this simplistic view of history as the product of a vast conspiracy that secretly controlled men and events fully exemplified the mind-set Hofstadter described.

Historians have had an easy task demonstrating that such statements were greatly exaggerated. Even some Republicans ridiculed the party's "political Cassandras," as Representative Eli Thayer denoted them, "who are continually saying that slavery has always had its own way, and always will have it."[61] Though examples exist throughout the party's ranks of men who endorsed such extreme claims, they were particularly numerous among pronounced antislavery men, who formed the radical wing of the party, and among former Democrats. The radicals' frustration stemming from years of unsuccessful agitation against slavery, their tendency to concentrate narrowly on a single issue, and their uncharitable assessment of their opponents' motives, help account for the zeal with which they embraced the concept of an all-powerful Slave Power conspiracy. Another explanation, as Foner suggests, is that the idea of a Slave Power emerged in the 1830s, at a time when abolitionists' basic civil rights came under direct attack. The Democratic-Republicans' penchant for conspiratorial theories stemmed from the struggle during the 1830s and 1840s for control of the Democratic party. Displaced from their accustomed ascendancy in the party, they attributed their eclipse to a conspiracy led by John C. Calhoun and first hatched during the nullification crisis to seize control of the Democratic machine. Their belief as Republicans in the Slave Power conspiracy was a direct outgrowth of these earlier struggles.

Although some party leaders employed this exaggerated rhetoric, it did not represent the mainstream of Republican thinking. More reasonable and thoughtful party spokesmen, most notably Seward and Lincoln, who were by the end of the decade the party's two most prominent leaders, presented a much more restrained point of view. While both men cautiously suggested the existence of a conspiracy to extend slavery, they generally avoided the word; instead, they spoke loosely of a plan, design, or preconcert, or used the metaphor of coordinated efforts (Lincoln's reference to the building of a platform in which various Democratic leaders each contribute a precut piece, all of which fit perfectly together, is well known).[62] As leaders of the moderates, always the largest group in the party, what Seward and Lincoln emphasized, and what historians have unduly slighted, was the *tendency* of events. What direction, they asked in great earnestness, was the nation headed? What would a reasonable man conclude was the probable outcome of the crisis?

Sound reasons existed for their concern. Granted, in some ways politics naturally partakes of the conspiratorial: strategies are devised in secret, and commitments are made and agreements reached beyond the gaze of the public. None of these acts need be sinister. Southern behavior, however, went well beyond these normal activities. The successful movement to annex Texas was the work of a small group of talented southern politicos. Many of these same men led a concerted drive to oust Martin Van Buren from control of the Democratic party in 1844 which culminated in James K. Polk's nomination. Four powerful southern senators who were disciples of Calhoun—the F Street mess—bore primary responsibility for the repeal of the Missouri Compromise ten years later. The election-day invasions of Kansas were the products of an organized movement along Missouri's western border in which Senator David Rice Atchison took the leading role. The subsequent attempt to make Kansas a slave state by the Lecompton constitution while ignoring Buchanan's pledges concerning a fair vote on the issue of slavery deepened the Republican belief in a conspiracy. In the face of this sequence of developments, use of the term *paranoia* to describe Republican fears is neither appropriate nor accurate.[63]

In their analyses, Lincoln and Seward were closer to the truth than historians who have cavalierly dismissed the idea of a Slave Power. Southern demands in the 1850s *were* extreme, and they grew *more* extreme as the decade progressed.[64] Actions of southern men such as the attack on Lawrence, the electoral invasions of Kansas, the attempt to fasten the Lecompton constitution on that territory, and the caning of Sumner, were startling enough. Even more frightening, however, was that southern public opinion generally seemed to endorse these acts. Not only extremists but also respected southern leaders and newspapers spoke out in support, often vying with one another to make their endorsements as ardent as possible. As party members recognized, the few southerners who denounced Brooks's attack on Sumner or the election frauds in Kansas had no influence outside the border states. Those who wielded power over southern public opinion overwhelmingly refused to condemn such actions. Moreover, the tendency throughout the 1850s had been towards greater, not less, political unity among southerners. Southern political divisions increasingly disappeared in response to the growing sectional crisis. Only nine southern congressmen voted against the Kansas-Nebraska Act in 1854, and even fewer (only two, both border state men) dared to vote for Brooks's expulsion.

As southern political unity grew, southern demands became more and more extreme. By 1860 the majority of southern Democrats had adopted the radicals' position in favor of a congressional slave code, something that would have been unthinkable a decade earlier. At the same time, the southern press rang with arguments that startled virtually every northerner (Democrats included): that areas suitable to slavery be seized and annexed to the United States, that northern books and magazines be barred from the South, and—most shocking of all—that the African slave trade be reopened to diffuse the ownership of slaves more widely throughout southern society. The reply that only a minority of southerners supported these proposals was not reassuring. Not only were they voiced by some of the most prominent journals in the South, such as the *Richmond Enquirer* and *DeBow's Review,* both of which were well known in the North, but even more unsettling was the progress of southern public opinion. Arguments considered absurd in 1850 were taken seriously in 1860. George Templeton Strong, a level-headed conservative Republican and a man not easily alarmed, privately recorded his conviction that the Democratic party would soon call for a resumption of the African slave trade. "Opinions develop fast in this age," he wrote in his diary. "Four years ago, no Northerner would have dreamed such a thing possible."[65]

As the decade progressed, Republicans understood more clearly than their opponents, and more clearly than even southern leaders, that the South's program led ultimately to the position that only the nationalization of slavery would make the institution secure. In the sense of a tightly knit conspiratorial group, fully united in purpose and strictly drilled, the Slave Power never existed. But this was never the image of the Slave Power that most Republicans invoked. In the more common version as a vested interest based on the ownership of slave property, which had a unique set of economic, social, and political concerns, and which wielded disproportionate power in state and national affairs, the Slave Power was not a figment of the Republican imagination. In stipulating the existence of a Slave Power bent on maintaining its power by overriding northern liberties and making slavery national, Republicans grasped the central meaning of the political crisis of the 1850s. Secession and civil war would bring Republicans to the final realization, which grew out of their interpretation of the sectional crisis, that in order to save republicanism they had to destroy slavery.

Research for this essay was partially funded by a grant from the Mabelle McLeod Lewis Memorial Fund, Stanford, California. I would especially like to thank Eric Foner, George B. Forgie, George Fredrickson, Michael F. Holt, and Richard H. Sewell, who read an earlier draft of this essay, for many helpful comments and suggestions.

1. See Eric Foner, *Free Soil, Free Labor, Free Men: The Ideology of the Republican Party before the Civil War* (New York, 1970); Michael F. Holt, *The Political Crisis of the 1850s* (New York, 1978); and Joel H. Silbey, "The Surge of Republican Power: Partisan Antipathy, American Social Conflict, and the Coming of the Civil War," in *Essays on American Antebellum Politics, 1840-1860,* ed. Stephen E. Maizlish and John J. Kushma (College Station, Texas, 1982), 199-229.

Like other historians, I am employing the term *ideology* to refer to a cluster of relatively coherent ideas, rather than a rigid theory, that "made it possible for members of the party to perceive a pattern in the happenings around them, to define a group identity in terms related to that pattern, and to sketch a course of action that could make the pattern change" (Lance Banning, *The Jeffersonian Persuasion: Evolution of a Party Ideology* [Ithaca, 1978], p. 15). I have used ideology interchangably with appeal and persuasion.

2. Bruce Collins, "The Ideology of the Ante-bellum Northern Democrats," *Journal of American Studies* 11 (April 1977): 103-21, especially 103-5; James Oakes, *The Ruling Race: A History of American Slaveholders* (New York, 1982), 226-27.

3. Rather than present a full discussion of Republican ideology, this essay seeks to define its central core or primary focus, to which other themes, though important, were subordinate. Nativism is the most important element of the party's creed that is not touched on here. For an analysis of the literature on the party's appeal, see William E. Gienapp, "The Origins of the Republican Party, 1852-1856" (Ph.D. diss., University of California, Berkeley, 1980), 1055-75.

4. Charles Sumner to Henry J. Raymond, March 2, 1856, Henry J. Raymond Papers, New York Public Library; *Cincinnati Commercial,* April 11, 1856.

5. *The Works of William H. Seward,* ed. George E. Baker, 5 vols. (Boston, 1853-84), 4: 274-75; *New York Times,* July 4, 1860; James Russell Lowell, "The Election in November," *Political Essays* (Cambridge, 1904), 21; Charles Sumner, *The Slave Oligarchy and Its Usurpations* (Washington, 1855), 14.

6. Seward, *Works,* 4: 225-40; *New York Tribune,* June 25, July 1, 1856; Gamaliel Bailey, *The Record of Sectionalism* (Washington, 1856), 4; [Edmund Quincy], "Where Will It End?" *Atlantic Monthly* 1 (Dec. 1857): 243.

7. Henry Wilson quoted in Russel B. Nye, *Fettered Freedom: Civil Liberties and the Slavery Controversy, 1830-1860,* rev. ed. (East Lansing, 1963), 293; John Gorham Palfrey, *Five Years' Progress of the Slave Power* (Boston, 1852), 2.

8. Palfrey, *Progress of the Slave Power,* 25-26; Edward L. Pierce, *Memoir and Letters of Charles Sumner,* 4 vols. (Boston, 1877-93), 3: 187.

9. Roy P. Basler et al., eds., *The Collected Works of Abraham Lincoln,* 9 vols. (New Brunswick, 1953-55), 2: 465-66; [Augusta] *Kennebec Journal,* Oct. 5, 1855; James Shepherd Pike, *First Blows of the Civil War* (New York, 1879), 333, 335.

10. *Kennebec Journal,* Oct. 5, 1855; David Brion Davis, *The Slave Power Conspiracy and the Paranoid Style* (Baton Rouge, 1969), 56.

11. *New York Times,* June 10, 1856; *New York Evening Post* quoted in the *Portland Advertiser,* July 27, 1855.

12. *New York Times,* June 10, 1856; Lowell, "The Election in November," *Political Essays,* 32; "The Reign of King Cotton," *Atlantic Monthly* 7 (April 1861): 455; Carl Schurz, *Speeches of Carl Schurz* (Philadelphia, 1865), 11-12.

13. Davis, *Slave Power Conspiracy,* 70; Samuel Fessenden to William Pitt Fessenden, Jan. 16, 1857, Fessenden Family Papers, Bowdoin College; Joshua R. Giddings, *History of the Rebellion: Its Authors and Causes* (New York, 1864), 373.

14. *Speeches, Correspondence and Political Papers of Carl Schurz,* ed. Frederic Bancroft, 6 vols. (New York, 1913), 1: 131; letter from W.M.W., *Toledo Blade,* May 18, 1855; Henry Ward Beecher quoted in Milton A. Rugoff, *The Beechers* (New York, 1981), 383.

15. Henry Wilson, *History of the Rise and Fall of the Slave Power in America,* 3 vols. (Boston, 1875-77), 1: 2, 2:187-89; (Concord, New Hampshire) *Independent Democrat,* May 29, 1856; Timothy C. Day to Friedrich Hassaurek, May 30, 1856, Friedrich Hassaurek Papers, Ohio Historical Society.

16. Joshua Leavitt to Salmon P. Chase, July 7, 1848, quoted in Foner, *Free Soil, Free Labor, Free Men*, 93.

17. For the origins and development of the concept of the Slave Power, see Nye, *Fettered Freedom*, 282-96; Davis, *Slave Power Conspiracy*, 18, 62-64; and Foner, *Free Soil, Free Labor, Free Men*, 90-98.

18. Stephen Higginson to Charles Sumner, Feb. 22, 1858, Charles Sumner Papers, Harvard University; Seward, *Works*, 4: 237; *Cincinnati Commercial*, Nov. 13, 1856.

19. *Cincinnati Commercial*, Nov. 3, 1856; *New York Times*, May 30, 1860.

20. George W. Julian, *Speeches on Political Questions*, ed. Lydia Maria Child (New York, 1872), 70; Seward, *Works*, 4: 235, 274-75, 295; Schurz, *Speeches*, 27.

21. *Toledo Blade*, Jan. 11, July 17, 1855; *Portland Advertiser*, Oct. 13, 1856; "The Kansas Usurpation," *Atlantic Monthly* 1 (Feb. 1858): 500.

22. *New York Times*, Oct. 10, 1854; *Toledo Blade*, Oct. 23, 1856; David Wilmot to Towanda meeting, Feb. 4, 1854, quoted in Charles B. Going, *David Wilmot, Free-Soiler* (New York, 1924; reprint, Gloucester, Mass., 1966), 451.

23. Foner, *Free Soil, Free Labor, Free Men*, 73-87.

24. Letter signed C., *New York Independent*, June 5, 1856; George Rathbun to Eli Slifer, Aug. 23, 1856, Slifer-Dill Papers, Dickinson College; Ovando J. Hollister, *Life of Schuyler Colfax* (New York, 1886), 101.

25. Charles A. Dana to Henry C. Carey, Nov. 27, [1856], Henry C. Carey Papers, Historical Society of Pennsylvania.

26. William E. Gienapp, "The Crime Against Sumner: The Caning of Charles Sumner and the Rise of the Republican Party," *Civil War History* 25 (Sept. 1979): 229-32.

27. *Cincinnati Gazette*, May 24, 1856; *Ashtabula Sentinel*, July 17, 1856; "The Kansas Usurpation," *Atlantic Monthly* 1 (Feb. 1858): 496; Henry Ward Beecher correspondence, *New York Independent*, June 12, 1856.

28. Nicholas B. Wainwright, ed., *A Philadelphia Perspective: The Diary of Sidney George Fisher Covering the Years 1834-1871* (Philadelphia, 1967), 340-41, 374.

29. *Congressional Globe*, 36th Cong., 1st sess., Appendix, 180; Frederick Douglass quoted in Eric Foner, "Politics, Ideology, and the Origins of the American Civil War," in *A Nation Divided: Problems and Issues of the Civil War and Reconstruction*, ed. George Fredrickson (Minneapolis, 1975), 30.

30. *New York Evening Post*, May 23, 1856; *Kennebec Journal*, Oct. 12, 1855.

31. Holt, *Political Crisis of the 1850s*, 134-35.

32. W.B. Theak to Benjamin F. Wade, Aug. 5, 1856, Benjamin F. Wade Papers, Library of Congress.

33. Thomas H. Hicks to Wade [late May-early June 1856], Wade Papers; *Independent Democrat*, June 5, 1856; Moses Davis to John Fox Potter, Oct. 25, 1857, quoted in Holt, *Political Crisis of the 1850s*, 190-91.

34. Seward, *Works*, 4: 258; *National Era*, May 21, 1857; O.B. Matteson to John A. King, June 14, 1856, John A. King Papers, New-York Historical Society.

35. Henry Bennett quoted in Richard H. Sewell, *Ballots for Freedom: Antislavery Politics in the United States, 1837-1860* (New York, 1976), 305; Lyman Trumbull to Jonathan B. Turner, Oct. 19, 1857, quoted in Horace White, *The Life of Lyman Trumbull* (Boston, 1913), 71.

36. *Bangor Whig and Courier* quoted in the *Kennebec Journal*, Feb. 23, 1855.

37. Charles Francis Adams, *What Makes Slavery a Question of National Concern?* (Boston, 1855), 11-17, 22, 24, 44-45; Horace Greeley, *The American Conflict*, 2 vols. (Hartford, 1865-66), 1:354-55.

38. Seward, *Works,* 4:226-27, 241, 279-80, 302, 372; Robert F. Lucid, ed., *The Journal of Richard Henry Dana, Jr.,* 3 vols. (Cambridge, 1968), 2: 681.

39. *New York Tribune,* April 29, 1856; *Springfield Republican,* Jan. 9, 1857; John Murray Forbes to J. Hamilton Cowper, Dec. 4, 1856, quoted in Sarah Forbes Hughes, ed., *Letters and Recollections of John Murray Forbes,* 2 vols. (Boston, 1899), 1: 156-57.

40. *Cincinnati Commercial,* April 11, Nov. 3, 1856; *Ohio State Journal,* June 13, 1856; *Southern Illinoisian,* Sept. 26, 1856, quoted in the *Ashtabula Sentinel,* Oct. 16, 1856.

41. Lowell, "E Pluribus Unum," *Political Essays,* 57-58; Edward Bates to Wyndham Robertson, Nov. 3, 1860, quoted in Marvin R. Cain, *Lincoln's Attorney General: Edward Bates of Missouri* (Columbia, Mo., 1965), 118-19.

42. Stephen Emery to Hannibal Hamlin, May 27, 1856, Hannibal Hamlin Papers, University of Maine; Schurz, *Speeches,* vi.

43. John Van Buren to James Buchanan, June 10, 1856, James Buchanan Papers, Historical Society of Pennsylvania; James F. Chamberlain to Ansel J. McCall, June 21, July 11, 29, Oct. 28, 1856, McCall Family Papers, Cornell University. See the excellent discussion of former Democrats in Foner, *Free Soil, Free Labor, Free Men,* 149-85.

44. "Where Will It End?" *Atlantic Monthly* 1 (Feb. 1858): 247.

45. For example, Greeley to Charles A. Dana, April 2, 1856, in *Greeley on Lincoln, with Mr. Greeley's Letters to Charles A. Dana and a Lady Friend,* ed. Joel Benton (New York, 1893), 141; Lowell, "The Election in November," *Political Essays,* 43; Oliver Wendell Holmes to Sumner, Dec. 28, 1855, Sumner Papers.

46. *Cincinnati Commercial,* May 22, Aug. 30, Nov. 3, 1856; *Philadelphia North American,* Oct. 14, 30, 1856.

47. Ranson H. Gillet to Buchanan, Oct. 2, 1856, Buchanan Papers; George Hoadly, Jr. to Timothy C. Day, April 5, 1856, in Sarah J. Day, *Man on a Hill Top* (Philadelphia, 1931), 168; [Concord] *New Hampshire Patriot,* Nov. 26, 1856.

48. *Cincinnati Commercial,* March 12, 1857; *Illinois State Journal,* March 9, 1857.

49. Lincoln, *Collected Works,* 2: 466-67; *New York Tribune,* March 11, 1857; Samuel Fessenden to William Pitt Fessenden, Jan. 16, 1857, Fessenden Family Papers; *Jamestown Journal,* March 13, 1857.

50. William E. Franklin, "The Archy Case: The California Supreme Court Refuses to Free a Slave," *Pacific Historical Review* 32 (May 1963): 137-54; Paul Finkelman, "The Law of Slavery and Freedom in California 1848-1860," *California Western Law Review* 17 (1981): 437-64.

51. *New York Tribune,* March 11, 1857; *Washington Union,* Nov. 17, 1857. For the Lemmon case, see Paul Finkelman, *An Imperfect Union; Slavery, Federalism, and Comity* (Chapel Hill, 1981), 296-310.

52. Seward, *Works,* 4: 292, 294.

53. Lincoln, *Collected Works,* 2: 461-69, 3: 29-30, 233, 369, 404-5.

54. Two exceptions are Sewell and Finkelman, who point to the threat posed by the southern-controlled Supreme Court. Finkelman demonstrates that southern legal opinion was steadily moving in the direction of making slavery national, and he presents a carefully reasoned argument that the legal basis had already been laid for the Taney Court eventually to propound such a ruling; *An Imperfect Union,* 287-93, 313-38.

55. Ibid., 322; Foner, *Free Soil, Free Labor, Free Men,* 100.

56. Contrary to the analysis presented here, Holt argues that concern for white freedom remained the party's principal motivation throughout the decade and that Republicans agitated unfounded fears that slavery would go north merely to reinforce

popular hostility to the Slave Power. While I agree that concern for the safety of republicanism was central to the party's appeal, I think he errs in insisting that this consideration was separate and distinct from the fear that slavery would become national, especially after the Dred Scott decision was announced; *Political Crisis of the 1850s,* 202-3, 209-11.

57. *Chicago Tribune,* March 19, 1856; Sewell, *Ballots for Freedom,* 297-98.

58. Davis, *Slave Power Conspiracy,* 4, 6, 18-19, 26-27, 29-31, 59, 82-84; Richard Hofstadter, "The Paranoid Style in American Politics," *The Paranoid Style in American Politics and Other Essays* (New York, 1965), 3-40.

59. The classic statement is Chauncey S. Boucher, *"In Re* That Aggressive Slavocracy," *Mississippi Valley Historical Review* 8 (June-Sept. 1921): 13-79. Sympathetic to the idea of a Slave Power are Nye, *Fettered Freedom,* 282-315, and especially Lee Benson, "Explanations of American Civil War Causation," *Toward the Scientific Study of History* (Philadelphia, 1972), 307-26. For more cautious assessments, see Foner, *Free Soil, Free Labor, Free Men,* 99; Sewell, *Ballots for Freedom,* 302; and Holt, *Political Crisis of the 1850s,* 180-81.

60. "Where Will It End?" *Atlantic Monthly* 1 (Feb. 1858): 245. Other examples include Wilson, *Rise and Fall of the Slave Power,* 1: 30, 50-56, 120-23, 148-52, 339-43; James Ashley, *Reminiscences of the Great Rebellion* (np, [1890]), 9-21; Benjamin F. Hall, *The Republican Party and Its Presidential Candidates* (New York, 1856), 435-36; Sumner, *Slave Oligarchy and Its Usurpations.*

61. Quoted in Foner, *Free Soil, Free Labor, Free Men,* 101.

62. For other careful endorsements, see Trumbull's speech in Chicago, *National Era,* Sept. 2, 1858; Fessenden's remarks in the Senate, *Congressional Globe,* 35th Cong., 1st sess., 609-18.

63. James H. Hutson argues that only after 1830 did the fear in American politics of persecuting power become "paranoid," since he contends—astonishingly—that the Slave Power could not be fairly accused of interfering with the rights of white Americans. Likewise, C. Vann Woodward, in discussing the sectional responses of the 1850s, speaks of "paranoia" inducing "counterparanoia." Such terminology hinders an understanding of the sectional crisis by suggesting that the fears of the North and the South were pathological. I do not think that any explanation that posits mass psychosis on such an unprecedented scale will ever take us very far toward an understanding of the causes of the Civil War. Hutson, "The Origins of 'The Paranoid Style in American Politics': Public Jealousy from the Age of Walpole to the Age of Jackson," in *Saints & Revolutionaries: Essays on Early American History,* ed. David D. Hall et al. (New York, 1984), 371-72; Woodward, *The Burden of Southern History* (Baton Rouge, 1960), 68.

64. John V. Mering, "The Slave-State Constitutional Unionists and the Politics of Consensus," *Journal of Southern History* 43 (Aug. 1977): 395-410, shows that even the most conservative southerners escalated their political demands in this period.

65. *The Diary of George Templeton Strong,* ed. Allan Nevins and Milton Halsey Thomas, 4 vols. (New York, 1952), 2: 307.

4

Race and Politics in the Northern Democracy: 1854-1860

STEPHEN E. MAIZLISH

In the fall of 1862, less than one month after Abraham Lincoln announced his intention to issue the Emancipation Proclamation, Cincinnati's Democratic newspaper, the *Enquirer,* urged its readers to vote in the coming election for "the White Man's Ticket—the ticket of the Union, and the Constitution as it is, and the negroes where they are."[1] Across the North, other Democratic papers issued similar appeals. In Harrisburg, Pennsylvania, for example, the *Patriot and Union* declared the electon to be "a contest between the white and black races for supremacy. President Lincoln and the Abolitionists have made it so." "The only question asked," the paper concluded, should "be 'are you White?' or 'are you Black?' "[2]

Clearly Lincoln's plan to free the slaves had given the northern Democracy an opportunity to make race a key issue in the 1862 campaign. Emancipation, the party press warned, would only lead to greater bloodshed. "The proclamation of the President is an outrage upon the humanity and good sense of the country," declared the *Patriot and Union.* "Now . . . the negroes have a chance. . . . They may rise, if they will, and massacre white men, women and children till their hands are smeared and their appetites glutted with blood."[3] Put simply, the proclamation was "an invitation to the enslaved population to rise against their masters."[4] The result, predicted the *Illinois State Register,* Springfield's Democratic state organ, would be to "let savages loose, and reenact the drama of St. Domingo."[5] In Cincinnati, the *Enquirer* was no less certain about the consequences of emancipation. It would lead, the paper argued, "to the massacre of mothers, wives, and children."[6] Even the usually mild New York press warned of a "vengeful bloodbath" and of "the subjugation and extermination of Southern whites."[7] But, according to the northern Democracy, southern whites would not be the only ones to suffer from Lincoln's plan. The *Cincinnati Enquirer* insisted that "Seven or eight hundred thousand negroes, with their hands reeking in the blood of murdered women and children, would present themselves at our southern border, demanding to cross over into our State, as Ohio's share of the free slaves," ready to compete with northern white labor.

"Every white laboring man in the North, who does not want to be swapped off for a free nigger should vote the Democratic ticket," urged the paper.[8]

Faced with the political demands of the election in 1862, Democrats had intensified their agitation of the race issue and by the time Lincoln's proclamation took effect the following January, race had come to form an essential part of the Democracy's political appeal. The Republican commitment to black freedom, explained Democrats throughout the North, threatened white security, white labor, and, by leading to the prolongation of the war, would also threaten the Union itself.[9] Race had clearly become the centerpiece of the Democratic argument. It offered a context within which other issues of concern could be viewed and understood. Yet how new was this Democratic emphasis on race? Had not race always served the northern Democracy as a key mobilizing issue? Particularly in the 1850s, when sectional questions came to dominate electoral contests, was not race just as central to the northern Democracy then as it would be in the late 1860s, following emancipation?

In the wake of the civil rights movement of the 1960s, a number of historians looking closely at the antebellum years for signs of the racism they were beginning to confront in their own environment concluded that the racism displayed so prominently in 1862 and 1863 was significant politically in the 1850s as well. James Rawley, Eugene Berwanger, C. Vann Woodward, Leon Litwack, and Chaplin Morrison all made impressive cases for the pervasive nature of mid-nineteenth century northern anti-black prejudice.[10] Writing in his 1969 study of the Kansas dispute and the coming of the Civil War, Rawley explained that he hoped "to lift from the shadows and to place in the light . . . the almost universal racial bias of a proud people who boasted to the world of their doctrines of liberty and equality." Racial inequality, Rawley argued, was "a folk belief which most white Americans held."[11] Many other American historians also writing in the 1960s agreed. Concentrating especially upon those usually thought of as the standard bearers of American freedom, these historians tried to demonstrate that the Republicans' "triumph over slavery" was, as Woodward put it, accomplished "in the name of white supremacy." "The present," concluded Woodward of racial prejudice, "seems depressingly continuous with the past."[12]

Since the 1960s, a number of scholars have attempted to modify this view. Eric Foner, Richard H. Sewell, and most recently Kenneth M. Stampp, have tried to resurrect the image of the early Republican party.[13] In his *Free Soil, Free Labor, Free Men,* Foner explained that "Racist expressions" by Republicans were "to a large extent . . . political replies to Democratic accusations rather than gratuitous insults to the black race." Furthermore, insisted Foner, "Republicans did develop a policy which recognized the essential humanity of the Negro, and demanded protection for certain basic rights which the Democrats denied him."[14] Republicans, Foner concluded, were simply not as deeply motivated by racial prejudice as previous historians had suggested. Yet, while at least partially discounting the role of racism in the Republican party, Foner and others did not dismiss the significance of race in the politics of the 1850s altogether. Rather, they argued that racist appeals were "concentrated" in the Democratic party. "Racial attitudes," argued Stampp, "played an important role in the political realignments" of the pre-Civil War years. For the Republicans, Stampp explained, "race was an issue on which [they] . . . were always on the defensive," but for the Democrats, the issue was their "stock-in-trade from the 1850s to the end of Reconstruction."[15] As Sewell concluded: "Republican racist pronouncements palled beside the brutish negrophobia of Northern Democrats."[16]

Examining the legislative record in the years before the Civil War, there is little doubt that the Democratic party was indeed strongly committed to racist policies. Throughout the North, Democrats were consistently the leading advocates of state laws limiting Negro liberties. In Wisconsin, for example, Democrats in the legislature opposed a referendum on black suffrage, and when, in 1857, the Republicans were finally able to have the measure placed before the public, Democrats voted overwhelmingly against it. In New York, at least 90 percent of the Democrats in the legislature opposed giving Negroes the vote, and when that state held a referendum on the issue in 1860, Democratic areas were strongly opposed. In Illinois Democrats defended their state's Black Laws from Republican attack, and in Ohio Democrats tried three times to pass legislation excluding blacks from entering the state. In Iowa they did the same, and in Indiana they made sure that such legislation already on the books was not repealed.[17]

These stands against political and social equality were based upon a strong belief in Negro inferiority which the Democratic press clearly and repeatedly articulated throughout the 1850s. In 1854, for example, the *New York Herald* explained that "nature has placed on this continent three distinct and separate races of human beings, endowed with different moral, mental and physical qualities, to each of which a peculiar and well defined sphere and duty have been allotted." And for the *Herald* there was little question as to which sphere the blacks belonged. "God made them," the paper assured its readers, "to be servants of the white man."[18] "They are," declared the *Albany Atlas and Argus,* "a separate race, which can never amalgamate with the white race and must always continue a distinct and peculiar people." "The only safe and true course," the paper concluded, "is to regard this as a government of the white race."[19]

Few northern Democrats seemed ready to disagree with these sentiments or challenge their party when it enacted restrictive, antiblack legislation. Yet the question remains: How important were racial issues to most Democrats? Granted Democrats freely expressed racist views and, when offered the opportunity, did not hesitate to advocate laws limiting racial equality, but was race a central Democratic concern in the 1850s? Did it play a significant role in Democratic politics? Did it provide the rank and file with a perspective for viewing the sectional strife and political conflict of the time?

These questions are critical, for they take us beyond the mere identification of positions Democrats held to the far more difficult and crucial task of ranking Democratic political concerns. Such an assessment of the relative importance of racial issues to one of the country's major political parties might reveal much about the significance of racial beliefs to northern society as a whole.

Yet finding the appropriate method for exploring these critical questions is not easy. Some historians searching for answers have looked at the public pronouncements of leading Democrats or at the legislative record of the northern Democracy. But though a record of racist legislation can confirm Democratic support for antiblack policies, it cannot indicate the relative importance of these policies in Democratic thinking; and though speeches by Democrats which made use of racial arguments may reveal an underlying prejudice, they do not provide a context for judging either the depth or the breadth of racial views.

While it does not offer a perfect solution, an analysis of a number of Democratic newspapers can be a useful way to acquire a perspective on the significance of a variety of issues to the Democratic party. The Democratic press in the mid-nineteenth century generally attempted to reflect the views of the party as a whole. Party editors were always ready to agitate whatever issue they believed would bring political advantage. A reading of a representative sample of newspapers over a period of time can give us a picture of the consistency with which the party held to its positions as well as a sense of its priorities.

Looking at a selection of northern Democratic newspapers over a period extending from the introduction of the Kansas-Nebraska Bill in 1854 to the election campaign of 1860, race does not appear to have been as critical a political issue as we might have concluded from an examination of the Democracy's legislative record or from an analysis of its leaders' racial beliefs. Race simply did not play as large a part in defining Democratic perceptions of the political environment in the late 1850s as it would after emancipation. The Democratic press often ignored race completely both when reacting to the leading sectional issues of the day and in conducting political campaigns. At times Democratic papers did employ racial arguments, but this occurred so erratically that it is difficult to conclude that the race issue was central to Democratic politics. A certain amount of racial imagery was, it is true, also present in almost every northern Democratic newspaper at one point or another, but again, not with enough consistency or to a large enough extent to play a dominating role in the party's political appeal.

In one of the nation's most widely read Democratic newspapers, the *Herald* of New York, racial arguments appeared only occasionally in discussions of political controversies between 1854 and 1860. If the *Herald* used race at all, it was usually just to label the opposition, and the paper did even this with little regularity. In the campaign of 1855, for example, the *Herald* referred to the Republicans as "our Northern nigger worshippers." In mid-1856 the paper's racial imagery broadened to include the "nigger drivers" of the South, but, as in the previous year, there was no substantive agitation of racial fears in connection with the basic political issues of the day. In the fall of 1856, the paper actually dropped its racist labels, giving no attention whatsoever to race in its political columns during the entire presidential election campaign. How central an issue could race have been if such a mild use of it could be so easily discontinued? In the 1857 campaign the *Herald* resumed the practice of name calling with occasional references to the "nigger loving" opposition, but in 1860 the paper again withdrew this form of racism.[20] Though the paper's antiblack prejudice was clear, it never treated race as a fundamental political concern.

Other Democratic papers of more limited circulation followed the *Herald*'s lead. In upstate New York, the *Albany Argus* at times actually seemed less concerned than the *Herald* with the racial aspects of the key issues of the decade. The paper hardly ever talked of race the few times it dealt with sectional questions before 1856, and in that year the paper's only expression of political racism was a reference to the Republicans as a "mongrel party."[21] In the remainder of the decade the paper rarely made greater use of racial issues in forming its electoral appeal.

There were Democratic papers in the North that invoked racial arguments with more frequency than the *Argus,* but few that adopted race as a central part of their political stand.[22] The *Key Stone,* for example, ignored race in its discussion of political issues from 1854 until 1859. Then, before John Brown's raid, the paper suddenly began publishing articles about "The Negro Equality Doctrine of the Republicans."[23] Here at last was evidence that an important Democratic paper was presenting the Republican threat in racial terms. But the paper dropped this racist theme as quickly as it had picked it up. Aside from one or two articles on "The Negro Race" in the 1860 campaign, race was not a dominant issue for the Harrisburg paper in that critical election year.[24] Given this uneven record, race could hardly be said to be a basic political concern of the paper.

This erratic use of the race issue also characterized many of the Democratic newspapers of the Old Northwest. The Democracy's sporadic racism in this area, often thought of as the most deeply racist in all the North, must raise further doubts about the issue's significance to Democratic politics.[25]

The *Cincinnati Enquirer,* located near the border with slavery, in a city plagued by controversy over the admission of fugitive slaves and the status of its significant black population, used race often in its political rhetoric, but not with enough regularity to place the question at the core of the paper's political beliefs. In 1854, the newspaper, wishing to avoid the year's divisive sectional issues, refrained from any discussion of either race or slavery expansion, but the following year, with Salmon Chase as the opposition's gubernatorial candidate, the *Enquirer* spoke repeatedly of the threat of "nigger suffrage, *niggers* in the public schools, and . . . nigger Emancipation."[26] For the remainder of the decade, the paper repeated this on again off again pattern of racism. In the presidential campaign of 1856, the Union was the issue and the *Enquirer* barely mentioned race. The following year, though antislavery leader Chase was once again the Republicans' choice, the Democrats, hoping to demonstrate the irrelevance of their opponents' sectional argument, decided to downplay the race issue just as it had in 1854.[27] By 1858, the *Enquirer* had dropped political discussions of race almost entirely, yet in 1859 race appeared once again, as a key issue. The Republicans, charged the *Enquirer,* were possessed by an "almighty regard for the negro" which was leading them to "advocate a policy to flood Ohio with fugitive slaves." "The welfare of the whole white race," warned the *Enquirer,* "is put at stake by the success of such a movement."[28] But despite their intense agitation of racial anxieties, in the next year, with the Union endangered by southern secession, the *Enquirer* seemed to forget the threat to white purity. Almost never referring to the Republicans' racial policy, the paper emphasized instead its fears for the nation and for the American economy.[29]

A similarly erratic pattern of racism characterized the *Illinois State Register* during the 1850s. In the 1854 campaign, the paper, like the *Enquirer,* did not make race an issue. However, unlike the *Enquirer,* the *Register's* silence on race continued throughout 1855, and, while the *Enquirer* was relatively free of political discussions of race in the 1856 campaign, the *Register* was actively charging the opposition with seeking "to make the negro the white man's equal."[30] In 1857 the paper again reversed itself and published relatively little on race beyond some references to the "negro worshipping" Republicans. But in 1858, the year the *Enquirer* withdrew its racist charges, the *Register* made the race issue central, especially in its coverage of the Lincoln-Douglas debates. Still, race did not remain important to the Illinois paper for long. As if to consciously alternate its use of race with its sister Democratic paper in Cincinnati, the *Register* dropped the issue in the 1859 campaign, even though the Illinois state election followed John Brown's raid, and then picked up the issue again in 1860 declaring that year's contest to be one between "the men who love the Union and its laws, and . . . those who love the Negro better than the white man."[31] How central an issue could race have been if it could be so easily and quickly discarded by papers in areas generally thought of as severely racist?

Racism undoubtedly took different forms in some Democratic newspapers not examined here. But the point remains that there was no uniform pattern of racism in northern Democratic political appeals during the 1850s. Though Democrats were prejudiced and racism was present in many of their campaigns, the use of race as a political issue was determined more by local conditions than by the demands of a northern Democratic ideology. Even in the West, where race was obviously an important issue, Democrats did not agitate racial fears consistently as a central part of their political program.

Far more crucial to the northern Democracy was a concern for stability, order, and "the peace and quiet" of the nation. Worries over the possibility of racial disruption were of less importance to most Democrats in the North than were fears of anarchy and disunion. As early as 1854, the *New York Herald* expressed these fears in an editorial entitled: "Duty of the Friends of Order at the Coming Election." Under Republican rule, warned the *Herald*, "the laws will be violated, the peace broken, the South embittered, and the Union brought into contempt."[32] For most northern Democrats no opposition leader symbolized better this Republican threat to stability than New York's William Henry Seward. In 1858, after his famous speech proclaiming the existence of an "irrepressible conflict" between the sections, the *Herald* declared that Seward's sentiments were "dangerous in their tendencies to the peace of the Union, the supremacy of the law, and the safety of society." In describing the consequences of a Seward victory, the paper never mentioned the danger of racial unrest. Rather it predicted "sectional strife, disunion, revolution, anarchy, and the bayonet system of elections peculiar to Mexico and the fighting states and factions of South America."[33]

Democrats in the Old Northwest also placed prime importance upon the future security of the Republic. Our opponents, explained the *Enquirer* of Cincinnati, are "hostile to our National Government, traitors to the Union, and are more to be feared than a foreign enemy." If the Republicans won the election, the paper insisted in 1856, "the Union and the Constitution will be at an end." As in the East, Democrats in the West rarely spoke of race in summarizing the dangers posed by their political opponents. "Peace and prosperity," remained the party's main concerns.[34]

When Democrats did discuss the Republicans' racial program, they often viewed it as simply another challenge to the stability and order of the country. Racial equality was one among many of the consequences of a Republican victory that would turn the world as the Democrats had known it upside down. "Shall seven white men cut each other's throats because one black man is held in bondage?" asked the *Cincinnati Enquirer*. The triumph of "this Northern abolition party," would in any case only "rivet . . . [the Negroes'] chains . . . tighter" and "its success would be the signal for the dissolution of the Union." "Are you prepared to see this Confederacy shattered to fragments, and our glorious nationality destroyed? Shall we, the descendants of the men of 1776 and 1789, prove ourselves unable to maintain that Government which our fathers purchased for us after a terrible sacrifice of blood and treasure?" the paper demanded. The coming election, concluded the *Enquirer* in 1855, will decide "whether the rights of all shall be conserved and the harmony of this confederacy perpetuated, or that the blackness of night shall cover our hopes as a pall."[35] In Illinois, the *State Register* saw the conflict over black rights in much the same way. Equality would certainly bring a rapid deterioration of the superior race, the paper predicted. But, perhaps worst of all, it would make the United States like South America where "anarchy reigns in the land—there is no fixed and permanent government—all is confusion and disorder."[36]

The Democracy's enthusiasm for order thus gave meaning and importance to its racial concerns. Race was a significant issue for most northern Democrats, but it gained greater urgency and recognition when party leaders could demonstrate its relationship to the Democracy's deeper commitment to peace and harmony. While acknowledging the racial turmoil the "nigger worshippers" threatened to inflict upon the North, Democrats concluded that their opponents' greatest crime would be the disruption of "the public peace," and the introduction of "anarchy and its fruits . . . the curses of civil war."[37]

A close examination of three major sectional crises of the antebellum period reveals clearly the primacy of the themes of order and stability in Democratic thought. The Kansas-Nebraska Act, the organization of the Kansas territory, and the raid on Harpers Ferry by John Brown, all raised questions of black-white relations, but in none did race play a major role in the Democratic response. Rarely did the Democratic press even refer to the race issue in its discussion of these controversies, except perhaps to show that the Republican stance on race would bring anarchy and disunion.

Stephen Douglas's Kansas-Nebraska Act of 1854, allowing slavery into part of the Louisiana Purchase territory under the principle of popular sovereignty, jarred the nation and placed the slavery extension controversy at the center of American politics for the remainder of the decade. Yet, while the Kansas-Nebraska controversy directly involved the future status of the country's black population, the Democratic press rarely dealt with the racial aspects of the issue.

Some Democratic papers preferred to avoid the Kansas-Nebraska controversy altogether. Fearing they would only exacerbate internal Democratic divisions over an issue that had little popular appeal, both the *Albany Argus* and the *Harrisburg Key Stone* hardly mentioned Douglas's measure either during the early months of 1854, when Congress debated it, or in the course of the state elections the following fall. Democratic papers that did discuss the measure spoke exclusively of the threat to national unity posed by those who attacked Douglas's sectional compromise. The *Cincinnati Enquirer,* lashing out at these instigators of sectional discord, claimed that "There are no enemies to this Union half as formidable as those who are bending their energies to array one section of it against another in hostile division upon the question of slavery," destroying the "peace and quiet" that has "prevailed throughout the country."[38]

The *Illinois State Register* in its response spoke only of the "tranquility and safety of the republic," as did the *Herald*.[39] None of the papers examined here discussed in any way the issue of race relations raised by the question of slavery in the territories. Occasionally the *Herald* would employ some racial imagery to make a point, but other than that paper's few references to "hybrid mulatto compromises," northern Democrats simply did not seem to perceive this greatest of all antebellum sectional controversies in racial terms.[40]

For at least four years following the passage of the Kansas-Nebraska Act, the sectional dispute focused on Kansas and the fate of slavery there. The most serious controversy over Kansas stemmed from the proslavery Lecompton Constitution of 1857, passed by a minority of Kansas residents and yet endorsed by the Democratic administration of James Buchanan. Northern Democrats split over the constitution; some supported it and the stance taken by their administration, while others, including Stephen Douglas, opposed it. But whatever their position, the race issue did not appear to enter into their considerations. Much of the Democratic press never mentioned race at all in relation to the Kansas issue. The pro-Lecompton *Albany Atlas and Argus, Harrisburg Key Stone,* and *Cincinnati Enquirer* ignored race completely when they spoke out in favor of the administration's position.[41] Except for a certain amount of name calling, the anti-Lecompton *Illinois State Register* was almost as free of racial comment. Republican spokesmen at times became "leaders of niggerism" and Republicans generally were often "Black Republicans," but beyond these slurs, little racism appeared in the *Register*'s discussion of Lecompton.[42] The *New York Herald,* which held a middle position on the controversial Kansas constitution, also limited its use of racism to occasional name calling. Talk of "nigger worshippers" and "nigger agitation" was not uncommon, and at one point the paper bemoaned the preoccupation of the country with "a contemptible border squabble over a handful of niggers in Kansas," but never did race become a central feature of the paper's Kansas argument.[43] The use of racist labels by the Democracy was certainly a clear indication of the party's insensitivity and prejudice, but not necessarily a sign of the significance of race in Democratic thought. Throughout the Kansas dispute, the Democratic press confined its use of racism to simple imagery, while national stability and the preservation of the Union continued to dominate its coverage of the territorial issue.

Race did not even play an important part in the Democrats' treatment of the sectional issue most likely to provoke racial comment—John Brown's 1859 raid on the federal arsenal at Harpers Ferry, Virginia. Though Democrats vigorously condemned Brown's attempt at initiating a slave insurrection, they did not perceive it as a primarily racial threat. As in other crises, it was the order and stability of the Union that Democrats believed the raid endangered most.

Upon hearing the news of the raid, the *New York Herald* declared: "The first overt act in the great drama of national disruption which has been plotted by that demagogue, Wm. H. Seward, has just closed at Harper's Ferry." The raid, explained the *Herald,* was an attack on the basic tenent of the Constitution which allowed each state to establish its own domestic institutions. By challenging this constitutional doctrine, Brown and his Republican allies were assaulting the very "theory of political self-government" upon which the nation was founded. To endorse the raid, to apologize for its perpetrators, would only lend support to those who threatened the peace and prosperity of the Union. "Merchants, farmers, manufacturers, mechanics, laborers, your best and deepest interests are involved in this question," the paper warned. "The welfare of the South is necessary to the welfare of the North." The *Herald* never directly mentioned the obvious threat to racial harmony posed by the raid. Rather the paper's concern was for "the future peace of the Union."[44]

Other northern Democratic papers were not as free as the *Herald* of racial allusions in their treatment of Brown's action. In Albany, the *Atlas and Argus,* which had hardly dealt with the race issue at all since 1854, denounced the raid's "cowardly instigators at the North" for plotting "against the lives of women and children," and setting loose "wild Murder and Lust embodied in the half-savage negroes."[45] The *Patriot and Union* in Harrisburg also showed concern for the "shrieks of the white women and girls of the South," and the *Enquirer* of Cincinnati condemned those who "let loose hellish passions engendered by bondage." "Traitorous scoundrels, with white faces, but black hearts," the *Illinois State Register* called them, infamous agitators whose goal it was "to stir the southern slaves to bathe their hands in the blood of the whites of the South."[46]

Underlying fears for the safety of the white race clearly were present in these Democratic reactions to the raid, but as in previous sectional confrontations, they remained of secondary importance. A racial catastrophe would accompany the continued agitation and future triumph of the Republicans, but that would not be the worst consequence of the opposition party's actions. If the Republicans were not rebuked, the *Atlas and Argus* declared after Brown's assault, "there is an end of fraternal peace in this Nation, and the Union is already dissolved." "The Federal compact, which binds together States of different and independent institutions, was intended first of all to be a compact of peace," explained the paper. Now, in the aftermath of Brown's raid, which had challenged the basic assumptions of that compact, "There is an end to peace."[47]

John Brown's attempted incitement of the South's blacks to rebellion had not altered northern Democratic priorities. The protection of the white race from the assaults of "savage" Negroes was a concern of many Democrats, but the preservation of the Republic came first. It was the "blood of Civil War" that the Democrats feared most from a victory of the Republicans—the "party of anarchy and disunion."[48]

Emancipation, as we have seen, changed northern Democratic attitudes dramatically. After 1863, there could be no question that the Republican commitment to black freedom would be realized. This, Democrats were convinced, would make a quick and painless reunion impossible. Lincoln's program would strip southerners of their slave property and so leave them with nothing to lose if they chose to prolong the war by continuing their resistance. Now, Democrats argued, Republican policies toward black Americans were directly threatening the Union. In addition, by freeing the slaves, Republicans, Democrats insisted, were encouraging a black inundation of the North. Democrats had always feared that this would be the consequence of a Republican victory, but, with emancipation, what had been a relatively abstract concern became more immediate. Political appeals based upon these racial fears could now have a wider impact. Soon race would become a mainstay of the Democratic political arsenal.

In the decade before the Civil War, Democrats also demonstrated a commitment to white supremacy, but the issue of race rarely dominated their politics to the extent that it would in the postemancipation era. Those who hold racially prejudiced views do not have to be concerned only or even primarily with race, and Democrats in the 1850s were mainly motivated by other interests. As they faced a world soon to collapse around them, northern Democrats thought far more about peace, stability, and the future of the Union than they did about the future of the white race.

1. *Cincinnati Enquirer,* Oct. 14, 1862.
2. *Harrisburg Patriot and Union,* Sept. 25, 1862.
3. Ibid., Sept. 24, 1862.
4. Ibid., Jan. 1, 1863.
5. *Illinois State Register,* Oct. 2, 1862.
6. *Cincinnati Enquirer,* Jan. 3, 1863.
7. *New York Herald,* Jan. 2, 1863; *Albany Atlas and Argus,* Jan. 6, 1863.
8. *Cincinnati Enquirer,* Oct. 9, 1862.
9. Ibid., Oct. 14, 1862.
10. James Rawley, *Race and Politics, "Bleeding Kansas" and the Coming of the Civil War* (Philadelphia, 1969); Eugene Berwanger, *The Frontier against Slavery* (Urbana, 1967); C. Vann Woodward, "The Northern Crusade against Slavery," in Woodward, *American Counterpoint* (Boston, 1971); Leon Litwack, *North of Slavery* (Chicago, 1961); Chaplin Morrison, *Democratic Politics and Sectionalism* (Chapel Hill, 1967).
11. Rawley, *Race and Politics,* vii-ix.
12. Woodward, "The Northern Crusade against Slavery," 148, 162.
13. Eric Foner, *Free Soil, Free Labor, Free Men: The Ideology of the Republican Party before the Civil War* (New York, 1970); Richard H. Sewell, *Ballots for Freedom: Antislavery Politics in the United States, 1837-1860* (New York, 1976); Kenneth M. Stampp, "Race, Slavery, and the Republican Party of the 1850s," in *The Imperiled Union* (New York, 1980).
14. Foner, *Free Soil, Free Labor, Free Men,* 266, 261.

15. Stampp, "Race, Slavery, and the Republican Party of the 1850s," 116.

16. Sewell, *Ballots for Freedom*, 327. See also Jean Baker, *Affairs of Party* (Ithaca, 1983) for an important presentation of the view that race was central to the Democracy.

17. Sewell, *Ballots for Freedom*, 335; Foner, *Free Soil, Free Labor, Free Men*, 286-87; Phyllis Field, "Republicans and Black Suffrage in New York State: The Grass Roots Response," *Civil War History* 22, no. 2 (June 1975):140-41.

18. *New York Herald*, June 2, 1854.

19. *Albany Atlas and Argus*, Nov. 7, 1860. For just one other example of Democratic racial theories see the *Harrisburg Key Stone*, June 18, 1854. (The *Harrisburg Patriot and Union* was called the *Harrisburg Key Stone* until 1859. The same editor edited both papers.)

20. *New York Herald*, Aug. 15, 1855; June 3, 1856; Oct. 27, 1857.

21. *Albany Atlas and Argus*, Oct. 19, 1856. (The *Argus* became the *Atlas and Argus* in 1856. There was a continuity of editors between the papers.)

22. A definite exception to this generalization was the *New York Day Book*. Not only did its pages flow with racism throughout the 1850s, it also presented a vigorous defense of slavery. Its readership was very small and largely limited to Irish Catholics.

23. *Harrisburg Patriot and Union*, Oct. 8, 1859. See also issues of the same paper on Oct. 5, 1859 and Oct. 17, 1859.

24. Ibid., Oct. 29, 1860.

25. See Berwanger, *Frontier against Slavery*.

26. *Cincinnati Enquirer*, Oct. 4, 1855. See also issues of the same paper on Oct. 4, 1855 and Oct. 6, 1855.

27. See for example the *Cincinnati Enquirer*, Nov. 11, 1856. One example of racism in the 1857 campaign can be found in the *Enquirer*, Oct. 4, 1857, but it is unusual.

28. *Cincinnati Enquirer*, Oct. 11, 1859; Oct. 9, 1859; Oct. 18, 1859.

29. See especially the *Cincinnati Enquirer*, Oct. 9, 1860 and Oct. 12, 1860.

30. *Illinois State Register*, Oct. 27, 1856. For more examples of racism see also Oct. 28, 1856 and Oct. 30, 1856.

31. *Illinois State Register*, Nov. 14, 1857; Oct. 8, 1858; Nov. 2, 1860.

32. *New York Herald*, Nov. 1, 1854.

33. Ibid., Oct. 19, 1858; Nov. 4, 1858.

34. *Cincinnati Enquirer*, Sept. 28, 1855; Feb. 24, 1856; June 3, 1856.

35. Ibid., July 15, 1856; Sept. 30, 1855.

36. *Illinois State Register*, Oct. 9, 1858.

37. *New York Herald*, Aug. 19, 1855.

38. *Cincinnati Enquirer*, Feb. 1, 1854.

39. *Illinois State Register*, June 1, 1854.

40. *New York Herald*, Jan. 25, 1854.

41. For examples of the three papers' views on Lecompton see: *Albany Atlas and Argus*, March 24, 1858; *Harrisburg Key Stone*, Feb. 10, 1858; *Cincinnati Enquirer*, Feb. 4, 1858.

42. See for example, *Illinois State Register*, Nov. 13, 1857.

43. See for example, *New York Herald*, Nov. 10, 1857, Nov. 21, 1857, March 24, 1858, and Dec. 10, 1857.

44. *New York Herald*, Oct. 19, 1859; Nov. 10, 1859.

45. *Albany Atlas and Argus*, Oct. 21, 1859.

46. *Harrisburg Patriot and Union*, Oct. 22, 1859; *Cincinnati Enquirer*, Dec. 3, 1859; *Illinois State Register*, Oct. 20, 1859.

47. *Albany Atlas and Argus*, Oct. 24, 1859; Nov. 10, 1859.

48. *Illinois State Register*, Oct. 25, 1859.

PART III

Civil War and Reconstruction

5

The Creation of Confederate Loyalties

REID MITCHELL

In April 1863, Lt. Leonidas Lafayette Polk of the 43rd North Carolina Regiment (C.S.A.) took part in an expedition into the eastern part of his home state, an area that had been held intermittently by Union forces. Elected to the state legislature as a Unionist, Polk had nonetheless volunteered very early in the war and regarded himself as a man of southern sentiments; he was a slaveholder loyal to the state of North Carolina. By spring of 1863, however, Lieutenant Polk had considerable misgivings about the Confederate war effort. Speculation and corruption were creating a "rotten aristocracy" in the South; wealth kept the rich man from the army while the poor boy was forced into service. And while Polk recognized the need for military discipline, he resented the restrictions placed upon his freedom: "A man ceases to be himself when he enlists in the ranks."

The expedition of April 1863 came close to demoralizing Lieutenant Polk entirely. He wrote his wife that he could see no point in the campaign except conscripting men of eastern North Carolina. What particularly saddened him was that he himself was obliged to round up men and force them into the army.

While performing my duty as enrolling officer I witnessed scenes & compelled compliance with orders which God grant I may never do again. To ride up to a man's door, whose hospitable kindness makes you feel welcome & tell him, in the presence of his faithful & loving wife & sunny-faced children, that he must be ready in 10 minutes to go with you, and see the very looks of sadness and dispair seize the wife & a cloud of apprehension cover the smiling faces of his children—their imploring looks and glances—the tears of sorrow—the Solemn silence—the affectionate clasping of hands—the fervent kisses—the sad & bitter Goodbye—the longing glance at the place most dear to him on earth, as he slowly moves out of sight—this is indeed a sad & unplesant task. When we left doors on the road crowded with the faces of frightened & crying & helpless women with the question, "For God's sake are you going to leave us at the mercy of the Yankees" made me ask often what have we gained by this trip?

Three months later Lieutenant Polk was wounded at the battle of Gettysburg. Recuperating in a Petersburg hospital, he continued his frequent letters to his wife. He expressed his doubts about a growing peace movement in North Carolina; he feared that the North would offer no terms except a return to the Union and the abolition of slavery. Still, he admired "the good old Republican spirit evinced by the plain spoken Sons" of North Carolina, and he longed for peace. In the fall of 1864 he left the service and returned to the state legislature to which he had been elected as a soldiers' candidate. In the interval between his election to office and his resignation from the service, he was courtmartialed for cowardice, an accusation he believed to be politically motivated. He was found innocent.[1]

Polk was not the paradigmatic Confederate soldier, that statistical average and sum of impressions known as "Johnny Reb." Nonetheless, his wartime career displays elements common to the experience of most confederate soldiers. Thousands of southern white men in the Confederate army shared his dislike of discipline, his love of the South, and his hatred of speculation and class favoritism—as well as the physical facts of soldiering. This shared experience, too complex to be expressed by the rhetoric of Lost Cause orators, the fancies of filiopietistic neo-Confederates, or the condescension of historians who write of "deference" and "planter hegemony," created loyalties to that sectional fiction—the Confederate nation—at the same time that it revealed the class bias and racism at the heart of southern society. To understand the Confederate soldier, one must move beyond sentimentality or simplistic class analysis to a realization of the complexities of the wartime experience.[2]

Both secession and Confederate volunteerism require careful handling. Secession probably generated far less enthusiasm among the mass of southern whites than the war itself did. The prospect of Yankee invasion united the white South. The northern army was real and concrete, compared to the phantoms that the fire-eaters had raised. Furthermore, while a southern white man might deplore secession as a policy, he resented any attempt on the part of the North to tell the South—to tell him—what to do. The invasion was a threat to his community and he quickly rose to meet it.

It has been argued that the leaders of the secession movement managed to override the popular will by distorting the election returns. If this was the case, the cause of secession paid for it. If a substantial majority of the white South had not been converted to secession by democratic means, the enthusiasm of 1861 would not suffice. Men whose loyalty was drummed up by flagwaving rather than elicited by ideological persuasion might not always stay loyal. If the secessionists were aware that they did not lead a popular movement, then they required a short, successful war.[3]

If secession could not be characterized as a popular movement, it was nonetheless greeted with considerable display of enthusiasm by many southern whites, both the slaveowners and the slaveless. J. Mills Thornton interprets secession as the last crisis of the Jacksonian era—the heir of the war against the monster bank, a symbolic crusade fueled by a tension-ridden, expanding market economy. While this interpretation ignores the fact that secession was also an attempt on the part of the slaveholders to cement the loyalty of the nonslaveholding class to the South's "peculiar institution," it does help explain why many southern whites supported secession.

The existence of a "subsistence culture" with a premarket ethos in antebellum America is debatable. It is certain that during the first half of the nineteenth century the United States underwent an economic transformation that deserves to be called a revolution and that this transformation produced a wide variety of responses among citizens North and South, ranging from wholehearted acceptance to ambiguity to rejection. During the crisis of the 1850s, the slaveholding class tended to support modernization and the spread of the market, while what resistance existed came from the nonslaveholding class. But the Southern Rights movement of the same period succeeded in part with identifying the ills created by economic transformation with northern domination.[4]

Secessionists played on white racial fears as well. The nonslaveholder, who may have resented the planter, very rarely had love for the slave. He too could be stirred by tales of abolitionist incendiarism. And if the worm of upward mobility ate at him, if he had decided to seek the spoils of the market economy, the slave system offered him the way to wealth. The twin motives—fear of a black uprising and the desire for economic advancement—created a loyalty to the southern social order on the part of many white nonslaveholders.

The secessionists, however, did not succeed in creating universal support for their cause among southern whites. Large pockets of Unionism, located in the areas farthest removed from market activity, plagued the Confederacy throughout its brief life. And disaffiliation among individuals who could in various ways resist the war effort was another constant problem. And, indeed, historian Kenneth M. Stampp has gone so far as to suggest that a sort of latent Unionism within the souls of many Confederates prevented them from making the struggle for southern independence the all-out effort they so often proclaimed it to be.[5]

The initial enthusiasm for war, the 1861 counterpart to what Charles Royster calls the "rage militaire" of 1776, proved inadequate to prosecute a long and exhausting conflict. The secessionists did not get their short, successful war. Rather, they were plunged into a war that revealed the strains and cracks within southern society. The demands that the war placed upon the southern people were not shared equally; those whom Bell Wiley called "the plain people of the Confederacy" bore a disproportionate share. The Confederacy, which was born of the crisis of the Old South, died, in part, from its own contradictions.[6]

Secessionists claimed, for instance, that the Confederacy would be a bulwark against modern Yankee incursions of power on the autonomy of

individuals and small communities. Yet the new government actually encouraged the operation of the market, the growth of industry, and the encroachment
of a national government upon individuals and into communities. It tried to
control agricultural production and the labor force. Taxes and impressment of
food brought farmers into contact with the agents of the state much more
frequently than had been the case in the antebellum South. The Confederate
Conscription Act of 1862 was the first in American history. Individual autonomy was more threatened by the Confederacy than it had ever been under the
United States. Politicians such as Zeb Vance of North Carolina and Joe Brown of
Georgia were able to gain tremendous popularity among southern whites by
their attempts to place the doctrine of state's rights between the Confederate
citizen and Jefferson Davis's government at Richmond; at least one historian of
the Civil War has claimed that the Confederacy died of state's rights.[7]

Nor was the Confederacy a classless, white man's utopia; it proved class-
ridden and dominated by the interests of the well-to-do. Conscription, for
example, clearly favored the wealthy over the poor. The original conscription act
of 1862 was accompanied by a series of exemptions that placed the burden of
service primarily upon poorer men. The "twenty-nigger" law, the most notorious, provided exemptions for planters owning twenty or more slaves and for
overseers of large plantations. Such class legislation was justified by its supporters as necessary for the functioning of the southern economy, but it created
considerable resentment among small slaveholders and nonslaveholders alike.
James Skelton voiced a popular sentiment when he wrote his sister Emily, "I do
not think it is right for me to go through the hardships of camp life and the
danger of Battle and others living at home enjoying life because they have a few
negroes." And his brother A.H. Skelton, a conscript, wrote his sister from a
camp near Vicksburg in January 1863, "so here we all go to Hell together and I
dont care damn how soon the Big fis was made to eat the little ones any-
how dont this Lat [exemption] Law [beat] all the laws that you ever did see they
intend to kill all the poor men and the fools go in to it just like they ware a bliged
to do it now if they are a mind to do t all Right But if they ware Like me I would
see them in Hell before I would do it." There was nothing one man could do by
himself against such injustice, he told his sister, and he had only one final
resistance to the Confederate state: "I can think." And independent thought
provided the only possible basis for opposition to the planter class during or after
the war.[8]

The Confederate conscription act was reformed in 1864 to extend the
exemption to smaller planters and to eliminate many other exemptions, but the
impression the earlier act made persisted. As Charles A. Wills wrote on June 12,
1863, "it looks like the will never be peace anymore for poor people the rich is
getting out of the war on every hand," and the cliché "a rich man's war and a poor
man's fight" proved an enduring one.[9]

Widespread corruption marked the Confederate experience. In the chaos of the time, profiteering and speculation were rampant. Men made fortunes—bright, glittering, and insecure—by trading with the enemy, engrossing necessities, speculating in gold, in Confederate currency, and in Yankee greenbacks, and running the blockade. Rhett Butler was not purely a creature of Margaret Mitchell's imagination. These profiteers were the men Lieutenant Polk referred to as the emerging "rotten aristocracy."

Finally, the Confederate state was notoriously incompetent. One of the greatest charges that could be made against such procedures as conscription and impressment was that they failed. The armies in the field were almost always undermanned and underfed. Confederate authority failed the mass of southern white people. As the war kept on, and as evidence of Confederate incompetence, corruption, and class bias mounted, there was a gradual withdrawal of support on the part of many southern whites. This withdrawal, which Paul Escott has labelled "the quiet rebellion of the common people" defeated the attempt to establish a southern Confederacy.[10]

In view of this "quiet rebellion," the loyalty of the Confederate soldier, both during and after the war, becomes harder to explain. After all, most Confederate soldiers came from the common people; Confederate authority failed the Confederate soldier as surely as it did the civilian population. Even if the enthusiasm of 1861 had been simply the product of "planter hegemony" or mass hysteria, the fact that the soldiers remained loyal to the Confederate cause long after large numbers of their class had abandoned it suggests that the military experience was involved in the formation of Confederate loyalties.

In one important sense Confederate loyalties did not last until the end of the war. Desertion was a constant problem. When convinced that the cause was hopeless or that his family needed him more than the army did, the Confederate soldier voted with his feet. Desertion had reached epidemic levels by the time Lee, Johnston, and Kirby Smith actually gave up the fight. Indeed, one may speculate that had they waited much longer they might have had nobody other than their personal staffs to surrender when the time came.

Nonetheless, many soldiers served until the end of the war. The Confederate soldier became a folk hero because of his bravery and endurance, and this heroic myth had a basis in fact. The white men of the South made good soldiers. But if fine soldiering was defined as ready deference to superiors and familiarity with discipline, the Confederates of 1861 must have disappointed their officers.[11]

North or South, the average soldier of the 1860s was most likely an independent farmer or a farmer's son. His work had been regulated by the weather, the cycle of the growing year, and the remote but all-important authority of the market. The authority immediately over him was personal—not the "feudal" authority of the planter but the patriarchal rule of a father or an older brother who bossed him until such time as he could set up his own farm, and whose authority derived from his place in the family.

The American of the 1860s found military regimentation hard to accept not simply because of this relative freedom from discipline in the workplace. Americans of the antebellum period had been brought up on a republican ideology that celebrated personal automony and democracy. Thomas Jefferson had particularly stressed the need for independence among the citizens of a republic. The period before the war had seen the extension of the franchise (to free white males) throughout the United States; followers of Andrew Jackson were obsessed with the ways corruption might undermine free institutions. In the North, of course, the Republican party was based largely on the defense of free labor and free men; and in the South the Democratic party, with its sometimes paranoid denunciations of corruption and with its thoroughly egalitarian rhetoric outlived the commercially oriented Whig party. Finally, American political thinkers had always viewed the military with suspicion; a Confederate soldier could still use eighteenth-century terminology and refer to an officer as a member of the old "standing army."[12]

If regimentation was difficult for most Americans of the 1860s to bear, it was particularly hard for a southern white man. Subordination and regulation were not simply abstractions in a republican demonology. He had seen them during his life—perhaps had seen them every day. The rules and restrictions of the army reminded the Confederate of the humiliation of slavery and of the degraded position that blacks held in his society.[13]

Southerners of all classes referred to military discipline as a form of slavery. Edwin Fay, a Louisiana soldier and perpetual grumbler, had not been in the Confederate army long when he decided, "No negro on Red River but has a happy time compared with that of a Confederate soldier." One item in particular drew the ire of Fay and other Confederates as being to close to slavery: when a soldier wanted to leave camp he had to obtain a pass. The spectacle of white men carrying passes drew the amused attention of at least one southern slave and probably more. Sgt. C.E. Taylor wrote his father in July 1861 what a black in Corinth, Mississippi, said after he witnessed a guard demand to see Taylor's pass. "He said it was mighty hard for white folks now. He said he had quit carrying a pass and his master has just commenced to carry them." J.C. Owens summed up the resemblance between slavery and soldiering when he wrote, "I am tired of being bound up worse than a negro."[14]

It was not simply the lack of freedom inherent in military service that caused the Confederate to think of slavery. The physical condition of army life—living in filth, eating poor food and little of it, and dressing in rags—set the soldier apart from the more fortunate members of white society and made his position much more like that of southern blacks. Because of the deep-rooted racism of southern society, this experience humiliated the Confederate. One response to this was restiveness under authority. The other, possibly more important, response was a certain contempt for people back home—at least the speculators living in luxury.

This feeling of being set apart from the civilian population, combined with the shared dangers of battle and hardships of the march, helped produce the Confederate soldier's esprit de corps. His suffering proved his patriotism and thus raised his self-esteem.[15]

This esprit de corps held together an army that had been composed initially of volunteers. These men were willing to follow military rule because they believed in what they were fighting for—those never very precisely defined "Southern rights." H.C. Kendrick, who would later die at Gettysburg, wrote his family in June 1863, "I am perfectly resigned to higher authority, but while I am willing to submit to it for the good of my country, I feel my own importance no less. It is not through a depreciation of myself that I feel willing to submit to my superiors in military rank but it is alone from my deep conviction of the importance of my own obedience as an example to others." However, this same man who took such pride in performing his duties as a soldier was perfectly willing to violate orders if he thought they were not justified. In May 1863, for example, he deliberately went out of the lines to cross the Rapidan River and buy milk and butter despite strict orders to the contrary.[16]

Men like Kendrick were willing to obey orders when they could see the reason for them. It did not take long for such men to see the reason for military discipline. They voluntarily endured the status of a slave when they could see it was both temporary and necessary. Furthermore, it did not take long in the service to realize that discipline was in one's own best interest.

From volunteerism and the shared misery of combat and campaigning came another aspect of Confederate loyalty. With the exception of Jefferson Davis, the Confederate authorities who inspired the most devotion both during the Civil War and after were the army officers—and even Davis's popularity seems to have been more a product of his postwar imprisonment than it was of his service as the Confederate head of state. The military experience created loyalty in the soldier to those who suffered by his side, whether officers or common soldiers, and a corresponding distance from those civilians who stayed at home. During the war desertion did not simply mean desertion from some abstract entity called the Confederate States of America; it meant abandoning the men with whom one had fought. It meant becoming one of the stay-at-homes. And after the war, the veteran's loyalty often belonged to those who had served with him in the Confederate army.

Confederate loyalty was also based upon a distinctive world view. Nine-teenth-century Americans were committed to politics in a way almost in-comprehensible to twentieth-century Americans; they had not yet been taught cynicism. Nonetheless, the Confederate soldier's understanding of the political world—and of the world at large—was based on Christianity, and on a Christianity almost entirely conceived of as personal morality. Evangelical Protestantism, which produced the religious ethos of the South, placed individual salvation as the most important single goal of the religious life. Salvation was manifested through a conversion experience and through a subsequent godly life. The emphasis was on personal morality, not on larger social institutions. Sin, which would earn God's displeasure, was a personal matter.[17]

This emphasis on personal morality set many Confederates to searching their own souls in the dark years of the war rather than examining their institutions with a critical eye. A wave of revivals swept the Confederate armies during the winter of 1863-1864. Pious Confederates—like pious Yankees—could interpret the war as God's punishment for a guilty nation and hope that repentance would bring peace. And the hand of God could be seen in Confederate defeats. One soldier wrote his wife in July 1864, as Johnston's army faced Sherman's across the Chattahoochee River, "it seems like the Lord has turned his face from us and left us to work out our own destruction." But just as divine displeasure could explain military defeat, the possibility of divine favor could lead men to continue the struggle long after it seemed rational; this soldier went on to offer hope in the form of a prayer, "Oh that he would give the people to see the error of there ways as he did the children of Isreal and save us from everlasting destruction."[18]

As late as February 1865, a Confederate captain could write his wife that God would bring the South victory. He died on March 20, 1865, of wounds received at the battle of Bentonsville; his last words were a message for his wife and children: "Tell them I love them but must leave them. Tell them all to meet me in Heaven." Evangelical Protestantism's fascination with the children of Israel encouraged hope in ultimate victory no matter what the odds; its emphasis on personal morality encouraged men to look for the causes of misery and defeat in their own shortcomings and vices, not in social institutions. One soldier predicted there would be no peace until the Confederate army had become "soldiers of the cross."[19]

Another reason for the continued loyalty of the soldier to the cause was that of racial solidarity. Nervous politicians in the North had argued that the Emancipation Proclamation would help unite the white South; they were right. In particular, Confederate soldiers hated black troops and committed atrocities against them. While much had been made of the "revolutionary" proposals to arm Confederate blacks entertained and reluctantly acted upon in the final days of the war, it is not at all clear that the average Confederate soldier would have ever accepted these desperate measures. They certainly did not accept blacks as legitimate foes.

Private Smith of the 51st Illinois watched black troops charge the Confederate lines at the battle of Nashville. The Confederates, whom Smith thought to be wavering at the point when the black soldiers entered the fight, went into a "frenzy" at their approach. Smith said they fought "like demons, slaughtering the poor blacks fearfully." Reinforcements reached the Confederate lines and counterattacked, "yelling, no quarter—to niggers." The black troops were forced to retire "but brought some rebel prisoners back with them, and left behind a most unmerciful number of their dead."

"The rebels who were captured by the colored troops, gave up with a very bad grace," Smith observed, particularly the officers. Smith thought that the officers regarded it as a disgrace to be captured by men "who, perhaps were their former slaves, and whom may be, they had laid the lash over their black backs before the war." Smith observed an incident that confirmed his belief as to Confederate attitudes: "One rebel captain who was marching to the rear, siezed the gun from the hands of one of his guards and shot the negro down, but was promptly run through the body by a sword in the hands of a white officer just behind him."[20]

A similar incident occurred in a skirmish around Yazoo City. Black cavalry captured a Confederate soldier, who was ordered to the rear by the company's lieutenant. The prisoner refused to go under a black guard; the lieutenant "shot him dead."[21]

The massacres at Fort Pillow and the Crater are well-known examples of the Confederate soldiers' virulent hatred of black troops, but their steady hatred was revealed in unspectacular, day-to-day hostilities as well. In the lines around Petersburg, where black troops were used, a Pennsylvania regiment found it advisable, when replacing a black regiment on picket, to call over to the Confederates "that the 2nd Pa was back again." A soldier in that regiment explained to his mother that when white troops were on picket an informal truce was maintained, but when black troops were on picket the Confederates opposite kept up a constant fire. "[T]hey hate a niger worse than they hate a coperhead Snake." This should not have surprised her, as he had already told her that the Confederates took no prisoners when it came to black troops.[22]

The final reason for Confederate loyalty is the simplest. During the war the primary alternative to Confederate rule was Yankee rule. Whatever the sectional rancor before 1861, fighting a war does not engender love for one's opponents. Even if the sufferings of the white men and women might be traced ultimately to those who led them into secession, they were frequently inflicted by the soldiers of the North.

Racial prejudice, unit pride, the wartime experience itself all inspired Confederate loyalties among the white men of the South, slaveholder and nonslaveholder. And these loyalties held over into the postwar period, long after they had any immediate relevance—so long that they harmed those who held them. But the process by which a man formed these loyalties—the Confederate experience—was more complicated than any reference to "deference" or "planter hegemony" could suggest.

In the years after 1865, the Civil War dominated men's imaginations. The returning Confederate veteran had to make sense out of four and a half years of bloody war culminating in military defeat and social revolution. After Reconstruction the Confederate veteran demonstrated a loyalty to his former captains that became a hallmark of southern politics.[23] And yet the injustices perpetuated by the Confederacy had the potential, at least, to create another type of southern politics. This latter type of politics, one based on economic realities, came closest to its realization in the Farmer's Alliance and the People's Party.

The Confederate experience had been a terrible experience, despite the hundred and twenty years of celebration that began, apparently, with Appomattox—that began when General John Brown Gordon, who was to become an eminent Bourbon politician, railroad frontman, Ku Kluxer, and professional veteran, answered General Joshua Chamberlain's salute in a way that authentically bound up both the victor and the vanquished in a moment of beauty and dignity. After the war it was the Gordons and the Jubal Earlys of the South whose Lost Cause panegyrics and Confederate statuary defined the Confederate experience in such a way that its horror was forgotten. One of the many prices paid to the Gordons and Earlys for their services was the trivilization of the political role of the average southern white man.

In one sense, the veteran's loyalty to his captain is explained by the conjunction of evangelical moralism and the war experience. Leaders were to be men of good personal character. And men of good character were those who had gone to war, not those who had stayed at home. Good soldiering came to define good character; the most natural way of judging a leader was to evaluate his performance as a soldier. Almost by definition, postwar southern leaders would have to be veterans, with their Confederate loyalties in order.[24]

In the years after the war, the Lost Cause orators offered the veterans something more than a reactionary political program to support and to be betrayed by. They offered something required by all veterans: an ordering of experience which otherwise might overwhelm the soldier in images of random horror. The elegiasts of the cause answered the question, "Why had we suffered so?" The answer was not always coherent, but it was comforting: they had suffered in a righteous cause, opposing Yankee domination, although now, somehow, one should be a loyal citizen and admit it was—somehow—better that the South had been defeated. The perfect act of celebrating the cause demanded that its practitioner not be too much of a diehard—even Jubal Early had returned to the United States after deeply sworn vows to shake its dust forever from his sandals.

To ask the veterans to realize that their sacrifices could be ordered in another manner—that they were the products of an unjust social system that turned bravery against the best interests of the brave—would have been to ask too much. To fight for the cause was tragic and noble; it made suffering honorable. To suffer for a delusion and be defeated was to be tricked—this would have made suffering unbearable.

It was difficult to renounce the Lost Cause purely and simply and still lead politically. Renouncing the cause was tantamount to embracing the hated Yankee and the black. Even if one accepts that the average white southerner should not have followed the politicians into rebellion, it is hard to see what in the wartime experience would make him love the forces of the Union. Preserving the Union meant killing southern white men and inflicting suffering on their families.

And so the veterans attended reunions and voted Democratic. As Lawrence Goodwyn describes it, "a folk loyalty took rigid definition after the surrender at Appomattox: independent thought was unpatriotic. The rock foundation of racial hierarchy being sundered, the cause required the defense of hierarchy itself. One defended one's captain." Such defense became the easiest way for the veteran to accept the wartime experience.[25]

This was one direction in which the Confederate experience could lead, and it was the most common direction. The granite Confederate soldiers standing in courthouse squares bear mute testimony to this. But there was another kind of knowledge that the war could bring to men, one that the platitudes of the United Daughters of the Confederacy did not exhaust, one that might come to men who had seen authority corrupted and had suffered because of that corruption. Such knowledge was possessed by the organizers of the agrarian rebellion of the 1880s and 1890s.

When Farmer's Alliance lecturers recruited in the South, they called on their Confederate past to reassure the farmers that one could be both a good veteran and a good Alliance man. Displaying Confederate credentials in much the way Bourbon politicians did, they overcame suspicions the audience might have about their character and loyalty and persuaded their listeners to consider political and economic issues.

In Fulton County and elsewhere, Ben Terrell called upon common memories of the war to unite his Georgia audience and the Texas-born Alliance. He himself, he told Georgia farmers, was a veteran, having served in Hood's Texas brigade. In that same brigade there was a Georgia regiment; "better truer men never stood in line of battle." If Georgians and Texans fought side by side in the 1860s, they could do so again in the 1880s. The agrarian crusade demanded greater loyalty than the Confederate cause had: "We are fighting now against a foe more insidious [than the North] and if we lose, we shall sink lower and our condition will be more pitiable than when we lost the Southern cause." Terrell argued that courage and discipline in the struggle for farmer's rights was as necessary as courage and discipline were for the soldier in battle. The effectiveness of such appeals may be judged by Terrell's 1889 estimate that the Alliance was primarily composed of Confederate veterans. And the Tennessee

Alliance's paper, the *Nashville Toiler,* praised the farmer's crusade for making history—"history that will be a honor to the manhood, courage, and intellect of an army of veterans who are so nobly and determinedly resisting the effects of combined capital to enslave a free and independent people." It was not only possible to be a Confederate veteran and an Alliance man; at times it seemed impossible to be an Alliance man *unless* one was a Confederate veteran. No wonder in the first volume of the *National Economist,* the Alliance's national newspaper, the Western Maryland Rail Road ran advertisements for their route from Baltimore to the Gettysburg battlefield.[26]

When the Alliance lecturers went North to recruit midwestern farmers and Union veterans, the style of their appeal to the Civil War experience necessarily changed. In the North, the lecturers emphasized common military participation in the war as a bond between all veterans. They played upon the resentment that the Union soldiers had felt toward stay-at-homes. The interpretation favored by the Alliance in many ways foreshadowed that of the revisionist generation of Civil War historians: the war was a blunder brought about by unscrupulous politicians, who sent the honest men of the republic, North and South, off to suicidal battle while they reaped the profits of the war. The president of the Alliance, while making a speech in California, publicly thanked God for the abolition of slavery.[27]

While they do not directly testify to the bitterness that southerners may have felt because of the Confederate experience, such appeals for unity among veterans North and South suggest that Alliance members recognized that their participation in the service set them off from those who did not serve. Alliance lecturers commonly portrayed the shirkers as hypocrites who preached sectional hate both in 1860 and in 1890 for their own advantage.

The bitterness of the Confederate experience is best displayed not in the speeches of Alliance organizers but in a letter written by a woman in Tennessee in answer to Bourbon charges made against the Populist presidential candidate of 1892, the former Union general James B. Weaver. His Democratic enemies claimed that while he was stationed in the area around Pulaski, Tennessee, Weaver abused and robbed the citizens. Callie P. Wade, the daughter of a Pulaski shoemaker, wrote the *Southern Mercury* that the accusations against Weaver were false.

Wade's father had been working as a tanner when prominent local citizens persuaded him to enlist in the Confederate army in 1863. The wealthy of Pulaski assured Wade and others that their families would be cared for while they served. But during the harsh winter of 1863-64, the rich men ignored the poor.

"I recollect one cold winter day," she wrote, "having little or nothing to eat, and no fire, we sent my brother to Mr. S.E. Rose for some wood, and he very generously sent word for us to buy it, and what happened to our family happened to all, for they all refused to help us in any way." Callie P. Wade's mother was dying at the time. "Time and time again did we apply for relief," she remembered, but they were "always turned away with some insulting remark."

Wade's family was visited by the wife of a Union surgeon after Weaver's arrival in the area. This woman brought back stories of the destitution of the poor families of Pulaski; Weaver sent provisions and firewood to many families and instructed the doctors of the 111th Illinois to care for the sick.

"If he made Martin and Rose and others shell out and keep their faith with the men who were at the front fighting their battles for them, he should receive the plaudits of the whole people instead of being censured," she argued. She swore she herself would continue "to bless and pray for Gen. Weaver, for he not only saved my life, but the lives of hundreds of other families of Confederate soldiers such men as Rose, Martin, Batt, and Stacy left to the tender mercies of the federals."

The editor of the *Southern Mercury* printed this testimony with approval. He despised the "aristocracy North and South" that had brought on the war and then "sneaked out of it by hiring substitutes." Callie P. Wade's letter showed, he said, that the accusations against Weaver were made by "men who favored a 'rich man's war and a poor man's fight'—men who believed that the man who had twenty negroes should stay at home, and the 'poor trash,' with wool hat, coperas breeches and 'one gallus,' should do the fighting." The resentments and injustices of the 1860s were remembered with bitterness by men and women such as Caliie P. Wade in the 1890s. They could be enlisted to aid the Populist crusade.[28]

On the Fourth of July 1890, the president of the Farmer's Alliance—a North Carolinian, a Confederate veteran—spoke to an audience of farmers and Union veterans in Winfield, Kansas. Leonidas Lafayette Polk, the same man who helped impress his fellow North Carolinians in 1863, appealed to those Kansas farmers to join the agrarian crusade. He too was able to draw upon the experience of the war—and he did so in a way that suggested what the veterans of all wars always believe: that the man who has served has a special knowledge that those who stayed at home can never know. Polk argued that the Civil War experience had placed Union and Confederate veterans far beyond Lost Cause sentiments and Gilded Age political concerns. Such concerns were for cowards, men who had not passed through the maelstrom of the war:

Some people have stirred up sectional feeling and have kept us apart for twenty-five years. I tell you that I believe in my heart of hearts that the man, North or South, who urged on the war—I care not what his name may be, or what position he may hold—that man helped to light the flame of war, and when it was ablaze all around the horizon fired your mind and sent you to the front and then skulked out of it himself. And who in 1865 found out that we had a war, got mad, and has been mad ever since. . . . The man who never smelt gun powder or heard a minnie ball. The man who has to use the sacred dust of the grave and has scattered it to the winds, and tried to work upon our passions. . . . I say, and I have declared before, I believe him to be the worst of our enemies on the face of the earth![29]

The message was clear. Men on both sides who had been through the war were bound together by that experience. Polk called upon them as veterans to realize that they had been betrayed by their leaders. This too was a legacy of the Civil War experience, and surely Polk was not the only veteran to learn this lesson. The New South's tragedy was how few did.

I thank Robert Abzug, Robby Cohen, E.D. Mitchell, Martha Reiner, Charles Sellers, Nina Silber, and Harry Watson for their help.

1. For Lieutenant Polk's biography, see Stuart Noblin, *Leonidas Lafayette Polk: Agrarian Crusader* (Chapel Hill, 1949); for Polk's Civil War service see the L. L. Polk Papers, Southern Historical Collection, University of North Carolina, Chapel Hill, specifically his letters to his wife, Jan. 29, March 9, March 21, March 26, April 19, and July 23, 1863.

2. It is a common assumption, for example, that one advantage possessed by the Confederate army during the war was the fact that southern officers were used to command and that southern soldiers, trained by a pervasive class-and-caste system, were used to obedience. A recent and very explicit example of these attitudes is to be found in William L. Barney's *Flawed Victory* (New York, 1979). Barney describes Confederate officers as "members of a master class," accustomed to deference from both blacks and poor whites. Emory Thomas comments on the deference shown by poorer whites to their social betters in *The Confederate Nation* (New York, 1979) and argues that while planter hegemony was challenged during the war it emerged relatively unscathed. These are far from being the only historians who accept what might be called "the barbecue theory of social control," according to which the wealthy maintained their power by throwing an occasional sop to their poor kinsmen and neighbors. This interpretation of the antebellum South, which has developed hegemonic status of its own in the profession, is now being challenged by the growing body of literature dealing with antebellum politics and the role of the small slaveholder and the nonslaveholder in the South. Among these works are James Oakes, *The Ruling Race* (New York, 1982), Harry Watson, *Jacksonian Politics and Community Conflict* (Baton Rouge, 1981), and J. Mills Thornton III, *Politics and Power in a Slave Society* (Baton Rouge, 1978). The truth of the matter is that in a society as fluid as the antebellum South, there was sufficient possibility for upward mobility that even nonslaveholders might expect to own slaves sometime in the future—thus non-slaveholder support of slavery is perfectly rational if deplorable. After all, Thomas Sutpen, William Faulkner's embodiment of the Old South in *Absalom, Absalom!*, is the son of poor whites.

3. Michael P. Johnson, *Toward a Patriarchal Republic: The Secession of Georgia* (Baton Rouge, 1977), 63; Steven A. Channing, *Crisis of Fear: Secession in South Carolina* (New York, 1970), 155.

4. For a discussion of the economy of the Old South, see Gavin Wright, *The Political Economy of the Cotton South: Households, Markets, and Wealth in the Nineteenth Century* (New York, 1978). For the premarket sector, James A. Henretta, "Families and Farms: *Mentalitie* in Pre-Industrial America," *William and Mary Quar-*

terly 35 (Jan. 1978): 3-32; Michael Merrill, "Cash is Good to Eat: Self-Sufficiency and Exchange in the Rural Economy of the United States," *Radical History Review* 4 (Winter 1977): 42-71; Gavin Wright and Howard Kunreuther, "Cotton, Corn, and Risk in the Nineteenth Century," *Journal of Economic History* 35 (Sept. 1975): 526-51. See also Forrest McDonald and Grady McWhiney, "The South from Self-Sufficiency to Peonage: An Interpretation," *American Historical Review* 85 (Dec. 1980): 1095-1118.

5. Georgia Lee Tatum, *Disloyalty in the Confederacy* (Chapel Hill, 1934); Carl Degler, *The Other South* (New York, 1974); Kenneth M. Stampp, "The Southern Road to Appomattox," in *The Imperiled Union* (New York, 1980).

6. Charles Royster, *A Revolutionary People at War* (Chapel Hill, 1979). For the Confederacy's internal crisis, see Bell Wiley, *The Plain People of the Confederacy* (Baton Rouge, 1943), and Paul Escott, *After Secession* (Baton Rouge, 1978).

7. For an account of modernization in the Confederate state see Emory Thomas, *Confederate Nation;* it does not seem to me that Thomas appreciates the relationship between this modernization process—which he calls a "revolutionary experience"—and the prewar conflict between yeomen and planters. Escott, *After Secession,* has a useful account of the conflict between Davis and Vance and Brown; see also Frank Owsley, *State Rights in the Confederacy* (Chicago, 1925) and May Spencer Ringold, *The Role of the State Legislatures in the Confederacy* (Athens, Ga., 1966).

8. James M. Skelton to Emily Skelton, Feb. 11, 1863; A.H. Skelton to his sister, Jan. 10, 1863, Skelton Papers, Southern Historical Collection, University of North Carolina, Chapel Hill.

9. Charles A. Wills to Mary, June 12, 1863, Mary J. Wills Papers, Swem Library, College of William and Mary.

10. Paul Escott, "The Quiet Rebellion of the Common People," in *After Secession.*

11. The classic study of the Confederate soldier is Bell Wiley, *The Life of Johnny Reb* (Indianapolis, 1943). Having read hundreds of letters and diaries of Confederate soldiers, I am continually impressed by the honesty and insight of Wiley's work; it is a masterpiece of social history. The same can be said of his *The Life of Billy Yank* (Indianapolis, 1952).

12. Charles A. Wills to Mary, May 10, 1863, Mary J. Wills Papers, Swem Library, College of William and Mary.

13. Space does not allow a full discussion of Confederate insubordination. David Donald discusses this issue fully in his essay, "The Southerner as Fighting Man" in *The Southerner as American,* ed. Charles G. Sellers (New York, 1960), 72-88.

14. Bell Irvin Wiley, ed., *"This Infernal War": The Confederate Letters of Sgt. Edwin H. Fay,* (Austin, Tex., 1958), 51, 162; C.E. Taylor to his father, July 14, 1861, Confederate States of America Records, Barker Center, University of Texas; J.C. Owens to Susannah Owens, April 26, 1863, Confederate Papers (Miscellaneous), Southern Historical Collection, University of North Carolina, Chapel Hill.

15. The soldier's feeling of being set apart—liminality—has long been characteristic of the warrior experience. The soldier has long been seen as both the representative of his society and as a figure foreign to organized society. Traditionally, war is seen as teaching a knowledge which cannot be communicated. The best discussion of this is Eric J. Leed, "Structure of War Experience," in *No Man's Land: Combat and Identity in World War I,* (New York, 1979). Understanding the psychological impact of warfare upon men is crucial for understanding the Confederate soldier and veteran.

16. H.C. Kendrick to his family, June 2, 1863; May 28, 1863; H.C. Kendrick Papers, Southern Historical Collection, University of North Carolina, Chapel Hill.

17. For a fine analysis of evangelical Protestantism and its impact on southern culture, see Donald G. Matthews, *Religion in the Old South* (Chicago, 1977).

18. J.M. Davis to Miss Mary N. Davis, July 6, 1864, Malcolm Letters, University of Georgia. Confederate religion deserves more detailed study. A suggestive study of Yankee religion is James H. Moorhead, *American Apocalypse: Yankee Protestants and the Civil War, 1860-1869* (New Haven, 1978).

19. Thomas B. Hampton to Jestin C. Hampton, Feb. 26, 1865, in K.C. Phillips, "Reminiscences," Thomas B. Hampton Papers, University of Texas; H.C. Kendrick to mother and father, March 9, 1863, H.C. Kendrick Papers, Southern Historical Collection, University of North Carolina, Chapel Hill.

20. Clyde C. Walton, *Private Smith's Journal: Recollections of the Late War* (Chicago, 1963), 195-96.

21. Christopher Keller to George and Esther Keller, May 21, 1864, Christopher Howser Keller Letters, Schoff Collection, Clements Library, University of Michigan.

22. Henry Pippitt to Rebecca Pippitt, June 20, 1864, Dec. 5, 1864, Schoff Collection, Clements Library, University of Michigan.

23. For a discussion of the Civil War veteran, see David Herbert Donald, "A Generation of Defeat," in *From the Old South to the New: Essays on the Transitional South,* ed. Walter J. Fraser and Winfred Moore, Jr. (Westport, Conn., 1981), 3-20.

24. For a discussion, in a somewhat different context, of personal morality in later southern political thought, see Bruce Palmer, *"Man Over Money": The Southern Populist Critique of American Capitalism* (Chapel Hill, 1980), 4-5. There is congruency between the Populist conceptions of the role of the producer in society and of the role of the soldier in war. Both the producer and the soldier, as opposed to the capitalist and the stay-at-home, possess virtue and both are exploited.

25. Lawrence Goodwyn, "Hierarchy and Democracy: The Paradox of the Southern Experience," in Fraser and Moore, *From the Old South to the New,* 235.

26. *National Economist* 1, no. 2 (March 30, 1889): 31; 1, no. 6 (April 27, 1889): 83; 1, no. 12 (June 8, 1889): 189. For rhetoric similar to Terrell's from the son of a Confederate veteran, see C. Vann Woodward, *Tom Watson: Agrarian Rebel* (New York, 1963), 135. For a struggle in Georgia between General Gordon and the Farmer's Alliance as to the true loyalties of the veteran,, see Woodward, *Tom Watson,* 163-64, and the *National Economist* 4, no. 1 (Sept. 20,, 1890): 14-15, in which the president of the Georgia Alliance came out against what he called "the old soldier racket" in contemporary politics.

27. *National Economist* 1, no. 2 (March 30, 1889): 22; 1, no. 12 (June 8, 1889): 1; 2 no. 26, (March 15, 1890); 3 no. 15 (June 28, 1890): 227; 6, no. 9 (Nov. 14, 1891) 131-32.

28. The *Southern Mercury* (Dallas, Texas) November 3, 1892, pp. 13-15. Some of the families Wade complains about were also involved in the creation of the Ku Klux Klan after the war. See Mrs. S.E.F. Rose, *The Ku Klux Klan or Invisible Empire* (New Orleans, 1914).

29. Quoted in Stuart Noblin, *Leonidas Lafayette Polk,* 13.

6

"Blues Falling Down Like Hail": The Ordeal of Black Freedom

LEON F. LITWACK

With the passage of time, black men and women who had endured enslavement came to articulate a disillusionment that encompassed both their bondage and the tortured freedom they had enjoyed since emancipation. Patsy Mitchner was "'bout 12 years old" when the Union Soldiers passed through North Carolina. Taught by her master and mistress to fear the Yankees, she chose to hide. But when the other slaves left, she ran away and settled in a nearby town. "I have wurked for white folks, washin', cookin', an' wurkin' at a laundry ever since freedom come." Some seventy years after emancipation, when interviewed about her life, she had no reason to recall her bondage with any nostalgia. Her master had treated the blacks "mean," she had seen her mother beaten, the food, clothing, and sleeping quarters had been "bad," and her mother, brother, and sister had been sold to a slave speculator and shipped to Mississippi "in a box-car." Reflecting on her enslavement and freedom, she could talk only of different kinds of oppression. "Slavery wus a bad thing an' freedom, of de kin' we got wid nothin' to live on wus bad. Two snakes full of pisen. One lyin' wid his head pintin' north, de other wid his head pintin' south. Dere names wus slavery an' freedom. De snake called slavery lay wid his head pinted south an' de snake called freedom lay wid his pinted north. Both bit de nigger, an' dey wus both bad."[1]

What Patsy Mitchner suggested, the experience of four million black men and women after the Civil War confirmed: the theory and practice of white supremacy transcended regional boundaries, emancipation introduced still other forms of white duplicity and coercion, and the attitudes and behavior which had justified and underscored enslavement persisted in different guises. The governing class refused to rearrange its values and priorities to grant to black southerners a positive assistance commensurate with the inequalities they had suffered and the magnitude of the problems they faced. More than a century of black freedom has not significantly altered Patsy Mitchner's assessment, only sharpened it, only deepened its tragic implications, only underscored the terrible paradox of black men and women seeking admission into a society which refuses to recognize their essential humanity.

The death of slavery in the South is an episode as dramatic as any in the history of the American people. Few if any experiences in American lives have been felt so deeply, so intensely by so many. And few experiences in our history have been so replete with paradox, ambiguity, and irony, with both tragedy and triumph. From the moment the Civil War broke out, the nearly four million enslaved black men and women of the South were placed in an anomolous and precarious position. They constituted the muscle of a military and economic effort designed to perpetuate their bondage; they were both the cause of the war and indispensable to the Confederacy. But could they be trusted? The answer came slowly in some cases, quickly in others: the more desperate the Confederate cause became, the more the white South depended on the labor and loyalty of its blacks. And the more they were needed, the less they could be trusted.

Throughout the history of slavery, the attitudes blacks manifested toward their enslavers had varied considerably. The most loyal and devoted would be enshrined forever in white southern mythology—in story, in legend, even in statues and song. The deeds of a Nat Turner were equally well known. And one can only speculate as to how many slaves resembled the cook in a North Carolina family who spit in the biscuits and pissed in the coffee to get back at her white folks.[2] Every slave had the capacity for outrage and resistance. And no slaveholding family, especially one which thought it commanded the affection and loyalty of its blacks, could know for certain when any one of them might choose to give expression to his or her outrage and what form that expression might take.

The Civil War and emancipation swept away the pretenses, dissolved the illusions, and laid bare the tensions and instability inherent in the master-slave relationship. Neither whites nor blacks were untouched by the physical and emotional demands of the war. Both races suffered, and each evinced some sympathy for the plight of the other. But there was a critical difference, and that difference grew in importance with each passing month. If slaves evinced a compassion for beleaguered masters and mistresses, if they deplored the ravagement of the land and crops by Union soldiers who brutalized and looted whites and blacks alike, many of these same slaves and still others came to appreciate at some moment in the war that in the very suffering and defeat of their white folks lay their only hope for freedom. That revelation was no less far-reaching in its implications than the acknowledgment by white southerners that they were facing danger on both sides—from the Yankees and from their own black folk. "We have already been twice betrayed by negroes," Joseph LeConte noted, as he made his way to the safety of the Confederate lines, "we avoid them as carefully as we do Yankees."[3]

With emancipation, each black family, each black man and woman would need to determine the meaning, the dimensions, and the immediate implications of freedom. How would they now feed, house, and clothe themselves? Where could they go? To make certain of their freedom, would they need to separate themselves from those who had previously owned them? If they chose to remain, what relations would they sustain with their former owners? Whether they left or stayed, how could they safely manifest their freedom? And, perhaps most critically, what could they aspire to in a society in which whites commanded the land, the tools, the crops, and the law and in which the prospect of four million newly freed black men and women made it all the more imperative for whites to maintain their domination? George King, a former South Carolina slave, remembered having been raised on "two-hundred acres of Hell" ("the white folks called it Samuel Roll's plantation"). It was there that he had watched "the old she-devil Mistress . . . whip his mammy 'till she was just a piece of living raw meat." And he remembered as well how his master chose to tell the slaves they were free: "The Master he says we are all free, but it don't mean we is white. And it don't mean we is equal. Just equal to work and earn our own living and not depend on him for no more meats and clothes."[4]

Within such perceptions of reality, newly freed black men and women determined the content of their freedom. To experience "de feel of bein' free," they adopted different priorities and found themselves driven in many directions at the same time. Most often the difference between slavery and freedom could be perceived in the choices that became available to them, in the opportunities to expand their personal and psychological autonomy, to secure families, to locate loved ones, to formalize marital ties, to take new surnames or reveal old ones, to educate themselves, to withdraw the women from the white folks' kitchens and fields, to worship in their own churches, to assemble for political and community purposes, and to work at a pace and under terms commensurate with their new status.[5] For some, freedom took on meaning only when they left the places where they had worked as slaves; still others found sufficient satisfaction in abandoning only their slave domiciles. Even if they chose to work on the same place, many freedmen acted quickly to break up the slave quarter by removing their cabins from close proximity to the residence of the former master or by erecting a new one on the plot they now rented.

To suggest, as some contemporary observers did, that emancipation made no difference in the lives of black men and women is to judge emancipation solely by its economic content and to ignore how many blacks perceived their freedom. To those who had endured enslavement, even as they acknowledged the burdens of freedom, even as they conceded new insecurities in their day-to-day lives, even as they recognized the white man's superiority in rights, power, and resources, freedom made a difference. "Dere is sumpin' 'bout bein' free," a former Alabama slave recalled, "and dat makes up for all de hardships. I'se been both slave and free and I knows. Course, while I was a slave I didn' have no 'sponsibility, didn't have to worry 'bout where sumpin' to eat and wear and a

⁊ to sleep was comin' from, but dat don't make up for bein' free." Nor was ⁊ any ambiguity in the response of a former Florida slave when he observed that "even the best masters in slavery couldn't be as good as the worst person in freedom." Still another former slave placed even his circumscribed freedom above the security allegedly enjoyed in slavery: "Every time I think of slavery and if it done the race any good, I think of the story of the coon and dog who met. The coon said to the dog 'Why is it you're so fat and I am so poor, and we is both animals?' The dog said: 'I lay round Master's house and let him kick me and he gives me a piece of bread right on.' Said the coon to the dog: 'Better then that I stay poor.' Them's my sentiment. I'm lak the coon, I don't believe in 'buse."[6]

Whatever the frustrations, failures, and hardships black men and women experienced during and after the Civil War, they acted on the assumption that freedom made a difference. In doing so, they demonstrated unmistakably that the slavery they had endured, no matter how brutal and oppressive, had not succeeded in reducing them to docile, irresponsible, childish Sambos. The well-meaning missionaries and teachers from the North learned that lesson soon enough. So did the former slaveowning class, as it endured changes in the demeanor and behavior of former slaves that transformed faithful servants and workers—or so they had seemed—into unrecognizable men and women. The distance black men and women chose to place between themselves and their old status could not always be measured by how far they traveled from their place of bondage. As many former masters and mistresses came to discover, black men and women found ways to manifest their freedom even as they labored in the same fields and kitchens they had labored in as slaves. "Henney is still with me," a South Carolina white woman informed her niece, "but not the same person that she was."[7]

The transition from slavery to freedom took some ironic twists. The same class that had loved to boast of how it looked after old and decrepit slaves now beheld the spectacle of former slaves caring for and refusing to abandon old and decrepit whites who had recently been their masters and mistresses. The same class that had thought blacks to be tied to them by feelings of dependency found themselves painfully dependent on blacks, unable to look after themselves. The testimony of white mistresses forced to assume responsibility for the daily chores once undertaken by their black help is unanimous on this point; the cries of despair reflected both physical exhaustion and psychic humiliation. Yet, none of the many white women who testified to the agonies of performing such chores thought to ask how their black help had performed these tasks day after day, while at the same time in many instances caring for a husband and children. If few former slaveowning families ever paused to scrutinize their own lives and dependency, the blacks who worked for them knew only too well. "Dey was glad to have a heap of colored people bout dem," Josephine Bacchus recalled, "cause white folks couldn' work den no more den dey can work dese days like de colored people can."[8]

Nothing in the experience of the slaveowning class had prepared it to deal with blacks as free workers, and in many respects it was less equipped to make the transition to freedom than its former slaves. Few seemed capable of learning new ways and shaking off old attitudes. Whatever comfort and inspiration this class found in the aftermath of the Civil War seemed confined to an evocation, a celebration of the past, to an elaboration of myths about the Old South and the Lost Cause. In acknowledging emancipation, former slaveholders had not surrendered the convictions with which they had held black men and women as slaves, and they fully expected those men and women to maintain the old slave demeanor. The kinds of questions they chose to ask about the future revealed only a grim determination to recover the past, to find new ways of exploiting black labor and commanding black lives. "Can not freedmen be organized and disciplined as well as slaves?" a white South Carolinian asked. "Is not the dollar as potent as the lash? The belly as tender as the back."[9] Nothing in the postwar behavior and attitudes of the former slaveholders suggests that the ownership of slaves had compromised their values or tortured their consciences or made them feel morally reprehensible or guilt ridden. The only problem, some conceded, had been with those few slaveholders who had abused the institution. Like any northern employer, the former slaveholder insisted that the excesses of the few should not be visited upon the system itself, which had been essentially benign. If some felt a measure of guilt, none questioned the absolute necessity of maintaining the domination of the superior race.

After emancipation nearly every field hand aspired to work for himself on his own plot of land, to become the independent proprietor of a small farm. That was the most American of aspirations, the stamp of respectability in an agri-cultural society, the way to enter the mainstream of American life. For many former slaves, the certain confirmation of freedom was to own the very land on which they had been working and which they had made productive and valuable by their own labor. But such aspirations were not to be realized, at least not on any significant scale, as they conflicted with prevailing notions of how success ought to be achieved in a capitalist society. Such aspirations also conflicted with the perceived needs of the planter class, which wanted a black agricultural working class, not an independent black yeomanry. For blacks to succeed in becoming proprietors of small farms posed dangers as great as those raised by the specter of blacks succeeding as voters or legislators.

If emancipation created in the victorious North a rhetorical commitment to helping blacks help themselves, it was never translated into a significant measure of economic opportunity for the newly freed slaves. All too often, federal policies placed former slaves at work for the same men who had previously commanded their labor. In South Carolina, a federal official took pains to explain to a group of freedmen the meaning of free labor, what he chose to call "the price you pay for your freedom."

There are different kinds of work. One man is a doctor, another is a minister, another a soldier. One black man may be a field hand, one a blacksmith, one a carpenter, and still another a house-servant. Every man has his own place, his own trade that he was brought up to, and he must stick to it . . . . If a man works, no matter in what business, he is doing well. The only shame is to be idle and lazy.

You do not understand why some of the white people who used to own you, do not have to work in the field. It is because they are rich. If every man were poor, and worked in his own field, there would be no big farms, and very little cotton or corn raised to sell; there would be no money, and nothing to buy. Some people must be rich, to pay the others, and they have the right to do no work except to look out after their property. It is so everywhere, and perhaps by hard work some of you may by-and-by become rich yourselves. [10]

The message seemed clear enough, at least to the federal official and the government he represented, if not to the assembled freedmen. The federal government and the nation said in effect that special consideration did not need to be accorded the freed slaves to correct two centuries of special inequality and exploitation.

In the postwar South, the relationship of slave and master was transformed into that of tenant and landlord. Without land of his own, the question for the newly freed black and for the first generation born in freedom was the degree to which the white man's dependence on his labor could be transformed into a weapon with which to bargain and expand his autonomy, improve his day-to-day life, and enhance his prospects for the future. Few expressed the new relationship more eloquently or more cogently than Ned Cobb (Nate Shaw), the sharecropper born in Alabama in 1885 and made a part of our historical consciousness through Theodore Rosengarten's *All God's Dangers: The Life of Nate Shaw.*

In my condition, and the way I see it for everybody, if you don't make enough to have some left you aint done nothin, except givin the other fellow your labor. That crop out there goin to prosper enough for him to get his and get what I owe him; he's makin his profit but he aint goin to let me rise . . . . I learnt that right quick: it's easy to understand if a man will look at it. . . . You want some cash above your debts; if you don't get it you lost, because you gived that man your labor and you can't get it back.

Now it's right for me to pay you for usin what's yours—your land, stock, plow tools, fertilize. But how much should I pay? The answer ought to be closely seeked. How much is a man due to pay out? Half his crop? A third part of his crop? And how much is he due to keep for hisself? You got a right to your part—rent; and I got a right to mine. But who's the man ought to decide how much? The one that owns the property or the one that works it? [11]

Since both sides perceived their needs and rights in very different ways, conflict was inevitable in the postemancipation South. If the former slaveholders did not respond easily to the concept of free labor, neither did the freed blacks respond easily or passively to perceived limitations placed on their working lives and opportunities. They resisted contractual labor. They sought to reduce the hours they worked each day. They rejected working in gangs under white supervisors. They broke up the slave quarters. They demanded shares or wages that reflected their contribution to the making of the crop. Many of the women withdrew their labor from the fields and from the white family's kitchen. And in securing farms of their own and moving onto those farms, whether as purchasers or (more often) as renters, blacks achieved a certain kind of personal autonomy and forced upon the old ruling class a new organization and management of labor. [12]

Whether expressed collectively, as in tough bargaining sessions, plantation strikes and walkouts, or individually, as in the personal struggles waged by a Ned Cobb, the efforts of former slaves and the first generations born in freedom to use their labor to force concessions from white employers marked a break with the past. Even the sharecropping system was in many ways a compromise, since black workers achieved a semblance of autonomy while the landlord maintained control of the land. Freed from gang labor, the black tenant family worked to make the plot of land their own. For most of them, however, such triumphs were rare. Neither the illusion of autonomy imparted by the initial experiments in sharecropping nor hard work and frugality could overcome the cycle of debt that so sharply circumscribed their economic freedom. The fact remained that most black farmers enjoyed neither ownership of the land nor the full rewards of their labor. The bargaining power they wielded proved less formidable in practice than in theory, particularly after Reconstruction. The landlord ultimately used ownership of the land, control of credit, vagrancy laws, blacklists, the courts, and the police to reassert his authority over black labor.

No matter how often the black press and black orators celebrated the examples of economic success and land ownership, the great mass of black southerners remained landless agricultural laborers. The political and civil rights they won during Reconstruction failed to alter their economic lives. Heightened expectations gave way to a sense of personal betrayal. Whether they listened to their leaders, to their teachers, to their ministers, or to their professed white friends, southern blacks after the war had heard the same hopeful message of uplift and self-help, the same moral and economic injunctions. Through their industry, skill, enterprise, and frugality, they would some day command a place in the South commensurate with their numbers and their weight in the economy.

From virtually every source, these assurances were imparted and embellished. The freedmen's schools, even as they familiarized blacks with their civil rights, taught them to be diligent, faithful, and punctual in the work place, to respect property and authority, to cultivate the virtues of honesty, industry, and frugality. Frederick Douglass admonished his people: "If you would be prosperous, you must be industrious." Still another black leader assured freedmen that money commanded moral as well as material power: "The representatives of dollars and cents are always the most influential men in a community." The African Methodist Episcopal Church preached to southern blacks that the only way to win over the hearts and minds of white people was through their pockets: "If free black labor affects the pocket in any way, it will affect the heart." Commonplace, too, was advice to emulate the Jews: "They got wealth and education and kept together; they were patient; but ever toiling, hopeful, and ever watching, economical, saving, even penurious and mercenary." If any doubts remained about the rewards of materialism and the need to emulate successful whites, the Reverend Henry Highland Garnet, a veteran black aboli-tionist, assured a gathering of freedmen, "The more money you make, the lighter your skin will be. The more land and houses you get, the straighter your hair will be." Even as they found their economic opportunities sharply curtailed, even as the deepening agricultural depression of the post-Reconstruction years drove thousands off the land, southern blacks were asked to pay obeisance to the same materialist deities, values, and goals that motivated the larger society. Success came ultimately to the hardworking, the sober, the honest, and the educated, to those who served their employers faithfully, who respected property and the sanctity of contracts, who cultivated habits of thrift, cleanliness, and tem-perance, who led moral, virtuous, Christian lives.[13]

In the experience of black southerners, such advice was as naive and mistaken in its assumptions as it was persistent. Faithful adherence to the work ethic and to the shibboleths of capitalism and democracy brought most of them nothing. Having been told that his people needed only to improve themselves to win the respect of whites, John Randolph of North Carolina thought the evidence suggested otherwise. "It is not enough to tell us that we will be respected accordingly as we show ourselves worthy of it, when we know there are some worthy ones whose fate is just the same."[14] After all, if success came to the hardworking, why were black southerners not the most successful race on earth? How could they be frugal if they had no money to save? And if they did manage to save some money, how could they buy land if whites conspired to deny them ownership? Why should they strive to improve the white man's land, to make the crops, and to care for the stock when each year found them deeper in debt? "White man sit down whole year," a black Georgia farmer exclaimed; "Nigger work day and night and make crop; Nigger hardly gits bread and meat; white man sittin' down gits all. *It's wrong.*"[15]

The Negro as a buffoon, as a menial, as a servant was acceptable. Whites had come to accept irresponsibility, ignorance, and submissiveness as peculiar Negro traits. Consequently, those blacks who failed to fit the stereotype seemed somehow abnormal, even menacing. "The Negro as a poor ignorant creature," Frederick Douglass observed, "does not contradict the race pride of the white race. He is more a source of amusement to that race than an object of resentment . . . . If he comes in ignorance, rags, and wretchedness, he conforms to the popular belief of his character, and in that character he is welcome." While "in his downward course," Douglass perceived, the Negro "meets with no resistance," yet "his step upward is resented and resisted at every step of his progress." For blacks who aspired to better themselves, this posed an impossible dilemma. "The resistance we now meet," Douglass concluded, "is the proof of our progress." The resistance was aimed not at "the colored man as a slave, a servant or a menial" but "as a man . . . . It is only when he acquires education, property, and influence, only when he attempts to rise and be a man among men that he invites repression. It is not the Negro but the quality in which he comes which makes him an offense."[16]

To grapple with such a paradox could be a most frustrating and debilitating experience. While claiming that blacks were incapable of becoming their political, social, or economic equals, whites betrayed the fear that they might. If Reconstruction taught blacks any lesson, it was that many whites feared black success far more than black failure. The language used to describe black political participation, the violence meted out to black leaders, and the methods employed to undermine black voting and organizing revealed the very depths of white concern about the implications of a biracial democratic system. The white South was driven to violence, not because it had been dismayed by black failure in Reconstruction but by the spectacle of blacks learning the uses of political power. "There was one thing," W.E.B. Du Bois would write, "that the white South feared more than Negro dishonesty, ignorance and incompetency, and that was Negro honesty, knowledge, and efficiency." James Lynch, a black Reconstruction leader in Mississippi, suggested as much when he summed up the white creed used to justify racial repression: " 'We must proscribe the negro because he is inferior and incapable,' but when he attempts to be successful, it says, 'We must proscribe the negro, or he will equal us: he will become so refined, and strong in intellect, that he will win the hearts of our daughters and become our legislator.' "[17]

Even as whites dwelt on the ignorance and illiteracy of blacks, they did not necessarily welcome the emergence of a class of educated, literate, and ambitious blacks. Among some whites, it had long been an article of faith that an educated black man was a useless black man. Education spoiled the Negro as a laborer, developed in him wants that could never be satisfied, expectations that could never be realized. When the "new negro" reaches for "higher and better things than the old attained," a white woman warned, he gives up those very qualities that made "the dear old darkey" such a superior menial. Inevitably, it seemed, an educated Negro was bound to become a discontented Negro, and hence a danger to society. "Education brings light," an Atlanta newspaper editor explained, "and light perception, and with quickened faculties, the negro sees the difference between his real and his constitutional status in the republic. He sees that neither worth nor merit nor attainment can overcome the worldwide repulsion of type and color; and, seeing this, he is moved to rebellious protest and sometimes to violent revenge." That "violent revenge," some whites argued, had already begun to take the form of attacks on white women.[18]

Thirty years after the Civil War, Booker T. Washington, articulating classic petit-bourgeois aspirations to an overwhelmingly propertyless black laboring class, emerged as the preeminent black spokesman. He grounded his advice to blacks on the proposition: "It is not within the province of human nature, that the man who is intelligent and virtuous, and owns and cultivates the best farm in his county, shall very long be denied the proper respect and consideration." And he insisted as well, "The Negro merchant who owns the largest store in town will not be lynched." W.E.B. Du Bois, whatever his differences with Washington, articulated much the same position: "The day the Negro race courts and marries the savings-bank will be the day of its salvation."[19]

But Washington and Du Bois were wrong, tragically mistaken. Expectations were betrayed too often for most blacks to maintain the faith. Whatever else they learned in school, black children came to understand, as their parents had, that their color marked them as inferior in the eyes of whites, no matter how they conducted themselves. "We came to understand," a black woman would recall of her youth, "that no matter how neat and clean, how law abiding, submissive and polite, how studious in school, how churchgoing and moral, how scrupulous in paying our bills and taxes we were, it made no essential difference in our place." Some young blacks found themselves cheated, beaten, and kicked off jobs by white employees who resented their ambition, their eagerness to learn a trade.[20]

Even as Washington articulated his self-improvement creed, the violence inflicted upon blacks was at times quite selective, aimed at those who had succeeded, those in positions of leadership, those who owned the best farm in the county and the largest store in town, those perceived as having stepped out of their proper sphere. Washington had only to read his own mail to gain a sense of what was happening. Back in 1890, Isaiah Montgomery, the only black delegate to the Mississippi Constitutional Convention, proclaimed his faith in economic and educational progress as the key to race progress. He approved a reduction in black voting based on literacy and a poll tax, convinced that such qualifications would encourage blacks to improve themselves. By obtaining property and knowledge, blacks would win back the vote and gain acceptance by whites. Some fourteen years after the Constitutional Convention, an obviously shaken Montgomery wrote a discouraging letter to Washington in which he cited several incidents in Clay County—examples of "the depths to which Mississippi has descended":

Rev. Buchanan has the best appointed printing establishment of any colored man in the

State, and conducts a Baptist Newspaper, . . . and was no doubt prospering, his daughter was his cashier and Book-keeper, they kept a Horse and Buggy, which the young woman used frequently in going to and from work; they kept a decent house and a Piano; a mass meeting of whites decided that the mode of living practiced by the Buchanan family had a bad effect on the cooks and washerwomen, who aspired to do likewise, and became less disposed to work for the whites. [A mob subsequently forced Buchanan and his family from the town, not even permitting them to remove their possessions.]

Thomas Harvey runs a neat little Grocery, he kept a Buggy and frequently rode to his place of business, he was warned to sell his Buggy and walk. Mr. Chandler keeps a Grocery, he was ordered to leave, but was finally allowed to remain on good behavior. Mr. Meacham ran a business and had a Pool Table in connection therewith, he was ordered to close up and don overalls for manual labor. Mr. Cook conducted a Hack business between the Depots and about town, using two Vehicles, he was notified that he would be allowed to run only one and was ordered to sell the other.[21]

The examples might be multiplied many times over. The fears of black success and assertiveness that had provoked much of the violence of Reconstruction proved equally pervasive in the early twentieth century when blacks no longer posed a political threat. A black newspaper voiced despair over the "daily examples" of white men singling out for harassment "the black man who has something, who knows something and who stands for something." Not infrequently, the newspaper reported, successful blacks found themselves accused of improper relations with a white woman and were forced to sell their property at a loss and leave town. The lesson derived from these examples seemed obvious to the editor: if given a choice, white southerners clearly preferred the "shiftless, worthless, ignorant" Negro to the educated and ambitious Negro.[22]

The Class of 1886 at Tuskegee Institute felt sufficiently optimistic about their prospects to adopt as their motto "There Is Room at the Top." No doubt the school's principal, Booker T. Washington, encouraged the class in their lofty aspirations. But in the town of Tuskegee, the danger of success was readily acknowledged by a black resident: "I know men who won't keep a horse. If they get one they will sell it. If you ask such a one why he sold his horse he very likely will say: 'A white man see me in dat 'ere horse, he look hard at me. I make [up] my min' a mule good 'nugh for a ole nigger like me.'" A black farmer in Alpharetta, Georgia, knew that he "better not accumulate much," because, he explained, "no matter how hard and honest you work for it, they . . . well you can't enjoy it." Henry Baker, a black Alabama farmer, remembered the consternation with which a white neighbor greeted the news that he had "paid out" his mortgage. "He wuz the sickest man yuh evah seed 'cause he wuz a renter hisself en he jes couldn't stan' tuh see a 'nigger' git ahead uv him." In Mississippi, in the 1890s and in the early twentieth century, white farmers terrorized black farmers off land they rented or had purchased with money they had saved as tenants; the more fortunate blacks lost only their lands and crops. Incidents of white violence, in fact, had a way of increasing in the summer months, after blacks had planted their crops. "Now is the season," explained one newspaper, "when the tenant with the best crop gets run off the place."[23]

Few understood better than Ned Cobb, the Alabama sharecropper, how evidence of black success aggravated white fears and anxieties. Through persistence and hard work, and by drawing on his inner strength and refusing to submit to the whims of white men, Cobb managed to accumulate some property. But to keep the property was a continual struggle, demanding more resourcefulness and energy than he had expended to acquire it. "I had men to turn me down, wouldn't let me have the land I needed to work, wouldn't sell me guano, didn't want to see me with anything. Soon as I got to where I could have somethin for sure and was making somethin of myself, then they commenced a runnin at me." Nor did Ned Cobb's white neighbors appreciate his resourcefulness in stocking up an impressive supply of meat on his place. "They looked hard, didn't stop lookin . . . . They didn't like to see a nigger with too much; they didn't like it one bit and it caused em to throw a slang word about a 'nigger' havin all this, that, and the other. I didn't make no noise about it. I didn't like that word, but then that word didn't hurt me; it was some action had to be taken to hurt me."[24]

Public displays of success, such as Ned Cobb driving about town in a buggy, infuriated local whites even more. That was because, Cobb explained, white people "hated to see niggers livin like people." For blacks to accumulate property or money was to make them independent, and whites feared the consequences. "Afraid a nigger might do somethin if he got the money in his own hands, do as he please; might hold on to it if he wanted to hold it, might spend it accordin to his pleasure. The white people was afraid—I'll say this: they was afraid the money would make the nigger act too much like his own man. Nigger has a mind to do what's best for hisself, same as a white man. If he had some money, he just might do it."[25]

For some blacks, as Cobb came to realize, the way to survive in the South was not to accumulate enough to arouse white resentment. The unsuccessful black man posed no threat; he knew his place. Cobb described his own father as such a man. "He had money but—whenever the colored man prospered too fast in his country under the old rulins, they worked every figure to cut you down, cut your britches off you. So, it might have been to his way of thinkin that it weren't no use in climbin too fast; weren't no use in climbin slow, neither, if they was goin to take everything you worked for when you got too high." Ned Cobb's brother seemed to have adopted that lesson as a way of life, working precisely in that spirit. "He made up his mind that he weren't goin to have anything and after that, why, nothin could hurt him."[26]

Neither accommodation nor economic achievement guaranteed blacks their civil rights, not even their physical survival. How many black southerners were lynched, beaten, flogged, mutilated, or quietly murdered in order to enforce deference to whites will never be known. Nor could any accurate body count reveal the savagery, the sadism, the exhibitionism that, with increasing regularity in the late nineteenth and early twentieth century, characterized assaults on black men and women—the severed ears and entrails, the mutilated sex organs, the burnings at the stake, the public display of skulls and severed limbs as trophies. The ordinary modes of violence and punishment no longer satisfied the emotional needs of the mob. Newspapers supplied the lurid details, the photographers captured the carnival-like atmosphere, the expectant mood of the crowd, the men and women hoisting their children on their shoulders. Seldom did the participants seek to conceal their identity. The confident manner in which they went about their business was matched only by the complacency and arrogance with which they justified these rites of racial self-preservation. After a brutal lynching in Little Rock, the local newspaper observed, "This may be 'Southern brutality' as far as the Boston Negro can see, but in polite circles, we call it southern chivalry, a southern virtue that will never die."[27]

The degree, the intensity, the quality of the racial violence at the turn of the century made a mockery of the notion that racial progress would win the respect and recognition of whites. For four days in 1906, white mobs in Atlanta lynched, murdered, and assaulted blacks and plundered their homes and shops. "I knew then who I was," recalled Walter White, then a youth of thirteen. When the mob threatened to burn down his house, they shouted, "It's too nice for a nigger to live in!"[28] Much of the violence fell on the property-owning blacks, on the most industrious, the most respectable, the most law-abiding, the most accommodating, the most educated—teachers, physicians, lawyers, clergymen, merchants, businessmen, editors. The middle-class neighborhood in which they lived became a convenient target of the mob, the place to teach the "uppity, aloof, smart-ass niggers" lessons they would never forget. Among those driven from their homes was Dr. W. F. Penn, a prominent black physician, a graduate of Yale University, a man who commanded influence in the community. "What shall we do?" he asked Atlanta whites in the aftermath of the riot. "If living a sober, industrious, upright life, accumulating property and educating his children as best he knows how, is not the standard by which a coloured man can live and be protected in the South, what is to become of him? . . . When we aspire to be decent and industrious we are told that we are bad examples to other coloured men. Tell us what your standards are for coloured men. What are the requirements under which we may live and be protected?"[29]

No matter how many whites deplored lynching and white terrorism, the dominant racial views which fed the violence remained unchanged. Historians provided a version of Reconstruction that dramatized the need to repress blacks. The newly emerging social sciences provided scholarly footnotes to traditional racist assumptions about the character and capabilities of blacks. The dialect stories, the cartoons, the anecdotes, the caricatures that appeared regularly in newspapers and magazines—the pornography of race relations—reinforced the familiar image of the shiftless, improvident, irresponsible, immoral, and occasionally dangerous and threatening Negro. The minstrel show and vaudeville and soon the cinema depicted a race of buffoons and half-wits.

With equal forcefulness, dehumanizing images of black men and women were imprinted on the white mind in the commercial products sold to white America, in caricatures and objects which exaggerated and distorted the physical appearance of black people and mocked their lives and aspirations. The "picturesque" Negro, slow, stupid, and easily frightened, replete with banjo eyes, saucer lips, and an obsequious or leering grin, was packaged and marketed as a suitable household or yard adornment, even as racist tracts and political demagogues dwelt on the unrestrained savagery and sexual lusts of blacks.[30] Dehumanization and repression tended to reinforce each other. If the Negro was a source of contamination, the need to quarantine him, to segregate him, even to lynch him occasionally could hardly be questioned. "We whites," a Memphis merchant explained to a visitor, "have learnt to protect ourselves against the negro, just as we do against the yellow fever and the malaria—the work of noxious insects."[31]

In the estimation of many whites, the problem of racial control had been aggravated by a new generation of blacks unschooled in the discipline and demeanor of slavery. When they conformed to racial etiquette, they did not appear to do so with the same conviction; they did not play their roles with the same cheerfulness. "They don't sing as they used to," observed an Atlanta white woman to a northern visitor. "You should have known the old darkeys of the plantation. Every year, it seems to me, they have been losing more and more of their care-free good humour. I sometimes feel that I don't know them any more. Since the riot [of 1906] they have grown so glum and serious that I'm free to say I'm scared of them!"[32] The contrast suggested to many whites the need to impress upon this new generation, many of whom were flocking to southern cities and towns after being squeezed off the land, that there were clear limits to their freedom and aspirations.

Even as disfranchisement, segregation, and violence took their toll, some black southerners fought a lonely struggle to maintain their civil rights. Some focused on overcoming illiteracy, on building their own community institutions, and on shaping a culture that would provide the inner resources necessary for survival in a hostile society. But the odds were always formidable. Race relations in the South, a visitor declared in 1909, had become a "state of war." The whites owned the land, the law, the police, the courts, the government, and the press. Who can say what kind of violence took the largest toll in black minds and bodies—the violence inflicted by lynch mobs or the violence meted out by the landlord, the creditor, the judge, the sheriff, the policeman, the newspaper editor, and the politician. Born in Natchez in 1908, Richard Wright spent his childhood in Mississippi, Tennessee, and Arkansas. He was deeply impressed with the mechanisms and pervasiveness of white repression and control, and with the extraordinary ways those mechanisms shaped his day-to-day behavior. The anticipation of violence, he recalled, was often far more terrifying than the violence itself. "The things that influenced my conduct as a Negro did not have to happen to me directly; I needed but to hear of them to feel their full effects in the deepest layers of my consciousness. Indeed, the white brutality that I had not seen was a more effective control of my behavior than that which I knew."[33]

The black thinkers, the editors, the preachers, the leaders thrashed about with their programs, manifestos, and sermons. The success ethic persisted into the twentieth century as "race uplift." And some blacks managed to move into the lower middle class, or even higher, capitalizing on the special business opportunities created by segregation. But the great mass of southern black men and women, trapped in an exploitative economic system that encouraged neither initiative nor hope, knew that they had been done in. Most struggled as best as they could and tried to suck whatever joy they could out of a bad situation. Some found a refuge of sorts in the church. Some took out their frustration and anger in alcohol and drugs, some in violence against other blacks. Numbers of young blacks opted to live by their wits on the fringes of society, in a kind of underworld emerging in the 1890s, mostly in the cities and towns, where they carried on what Ralph Ellison later described as "an unceasing psychological scrimmage with the whites."[34]

With most of the normal outlets for expression closed to them, unable to exercise any influence at the polls, blacks found other ways to articulate their feelings. The bluesmen and blueswomen gave perhaps the fullest voice to the unfairness blacks sensed about their day-to-day lives and future prospects. More directly than the spirituals, more personalized and individualistic than the work songs, black music around 1895 began to reflect a growing alienation, a growing separation from the norms and values of white and black society, a growing separation from church, from school, from family. The blues had its roots in the hollers, shouts, chants, and work songs of black field hands. But it expressed to a larger degree the consciousness, the day-to-day experiences, the frustrations, the anxieties, the despair, and the values of a new generation of blacks, as in the bluesy dirge sounded by Charlie Patton, born near Edwards, Mississippi, in the mid-1880s;

> Ev'ry day, seems like murder here
> Ev'ry day, seems like murder here
> I'm gonna leave tomorrow, I know you don't want me here.[35]

or in the defiance found in the songs of Furry Lewis, born in 1900 and raised in the Delta at Greenwood:

> I believe I'll buy me a graveyard of my own,
> I believe I'll buy me a graveyard of my own,
> I'm goin' kill everybody that have done me wrong.[36]

Few exceeded in intensity the tormented cry of Robert Johnson, who spent his youth in the upper Mississippi Delta. To hear him is to sense some of the terrors, tensions, and betrayals that pervaded the lives of blacks coming of age in the South in the early twentieth century. In "Crossroads Blues," for example, he finds himself in a predicament every black youth is taught to avoid. He is at a rural crossroads trying to flag a ride. Night is approaching, he is in a place he should not be, where no one knows him, and where the common expression is, "Nigger, don't let the sun go down on you here." He doesn't know which way to run, and he suspects it will make no difference.

> I went to the crossroads, fell down to my knees.
> I went to the crossroads, fell down on my knees.
> I asked the Lord above, have mercy, save poor Bob if you please.
> Uumh, standing at the crossroads I tried to flag a ride.
> Ain't nobody seems to know me, everybody pass me by.
>
> And the sun going down, boys, dark gone catch me here.
> Uumh, oh dark gone catch me here.
> I haven't got no loving sweet woman, that love will be near.
>
> You can run, you can run, tell my friend poor Willie Brown.
> You can run, tell my friend, poor Willie Brown
> Lord, that I'm standing at the crossroads, babe,
> I believe I'm sinking down.[37]

On the eve of World War I, tens, soon hundreds of thousands of blacks began to move out of the South. Within two decades, they would change the racial map of the United States. But in the Promised Land, in places like Chicago and New York, Cleveland and Detroit, they would come to learn that racial privilege knew no Mason-Dixon line and that racial injustice did not always manifest itself in lynchings, Jim Crow, or disfranchisement. For many of the migrants, the basic rules did not change. There was no way to assimilate. There was no way to separate. There was no way to win.

> I got to keep moving, I got to keep moving
>   blues falling down like hail
>   blues falling down like hail
> Uumh, blues falling down like hail
>   blues falling down like hail
> And the days keeps on 'minding me
>   there's a hellhound on my trail,
>   hellhound on my trail,
>   hellhound on my trail.[38]

I am grateful to Greenwood Press and to Walter J. Fraser and Winfred B. Moore, Jr., for permission to draw from some material which appeared in my essay "The Ordeal of Black Freedom" in *The Southern Enigma: Essays on Race, Class, and Folk Culture* (1983).

1. George P. Rawick, ed., *The American Slave: A Composite Autobiography* (Westport, Conn., 1972), vol. 15, North Carolina Narr. (Part 2), 117-23.

2. Pauli Murray, *Proud Shoes: The Story of an American Family* (New York, 1956), 159-60.

3. Joseph LeConte, '*Ware Sherman: A Journal of Three Months' Personal Experience in the Last Days of the Confederacy* (Berkeley, 1938), 125.

4. Rawick, *The American Slave*, vol. 7, Okla. Narr., 165-67.

5. See Leon F. Litwack, *Been in the Storm So Long: The Aftermath of Slavery* (New York, 1979), especially chapter 5, "How Free is Free?"

6. Rawick, *The American Slave*, vol. 4, Texas Narr. (Part 2), 204; vol. 17, Florida Narr., 182; vol. 7, Oklahoma Narr., 209. For other examples, see vol. 2, South Carolina Narr. (Part 1), 335; vol. 4, Texas Narr. (Part 1), 153, 262; vol. 5, Texas Narr. (Part 3), 153, 161; Vol. 8, Arkansas Narr. (Part 1), 105; Vol. 12, Georgia Narr. (Part 1), 8, (Part 2), 279; Vol. 13, Georgia Narr. (Part 3), 65, 293; Vol. 14, North Carolina Narr. (Part 1), 460; *Christian Recorder*, Jan. 16, 1864; M. Waterbury, *Seven Years Among the Freedmen*, 3d. ed. (Chicago, 1893), 76; David Macrae, *The Americans at Home* (New York, 1952; reprint), 133, 210, 213; Whitelaw Reid, *After the War: A Southern Tour, May 1, 1865, to May 1, 1866* (Cincinnati, 1866), 272-73; J. T. Trowbridge, *The South* (Hartford, 1867), 151.

7. Mrs. William Mason Smith to Mrs. Edward L. Cottenet, July 12, 1865, in *Mason Smith Family Letters, 1860-1868*, ed. Daniel E. Huger Smith, Alice R. Huger Smith, and Arney R. Childs (Columbia, S.C., 1950), 221.

8. Rawick, *The American Slave*, Vol. 2, South Carolina Narr. (Part 1), 22. For freedmen and freedwomen who remained to assist former owners, see Litwack, *Been in the Storm So Long*, 330. For the postwar experiences of white women forced to assume household tasks, see pp. 354-58 of the same work.

9. Lacy Ford, "Labor and Ideology in the South Carolina Upcountry: The Transition to Free-Labor Agriculture" (Paper presented at The Citadel Conference on the South, April 25, 1981), 16-17. I am grateful to Dr. Ford for permission to cite this quotation.

10. "To the Freed People of Orangeburg District," in Capt. Charles Soule to O.O. Howard, June 12, 1865, Records of the Subordinate Field Officers for South Carolina, Bureau of Refugees, Freedmen and Abandoned Lands, National Archives, Washington, D.C.

11. Theodore Rosengarten, *All God's Dangers: The Life of Nate Shaw* (New York, 1974), 108. Nate Shaw is the fictitious name of Ned Cobb, who died on Nov. 5, 1973. The author chose to use the alias "as a measure of protection and privacy"; his real identity was subsequently revealed and in future references in this essay Nate Shaw will appear as Ned Cobb.

12. See Litwack, *Been in the Storm So Long*, especially 392-99, 420-25, 430-45.

13. S.S. Ashley to Col. N.A. McLean, Feb. 7, 1866, American Missionary Assn. Archives, Amistad Research Center, New Orleans; *The Black Republican* (New Orleans), April 29, 1865; *Christian Recorder*, Aug. 25, Aug. 18, March 17, 1866, Sept. 30, 1865. For advice to the freedmen, see *The Black Republican*, April 15, 1865 ("The Duty of Colored Men in Louisiana"); *The Colored American* (Augusta, Ga.), Dec. 30, 1865

("What Is a Man?"), Jan. 6, 1866; *The Free Man's Press,* Aug. 1, 1868 ("Learn a Trade");
Christian Recorder, April 8, 1865 ("What Shall We Do To Be Respected?"); June 3, 1865
(R.H. Cain); Aug. 26, 1865 (R.H. Cain); Dec. 9, 16, 23, 1865 ("Advice from the Editor
. . . To the Many Freedmen Throughout the South"); Feb. 3, 1866 (J.C. Gibbs); March
10, 1866 ("Trying Moment for the Colored People"); March 24, 1866 ("Emigration of
Colored People"); April 21, 1866 (R.H. Cain); May 19, 1866 ("Get Land"); May 26, 1866
(Bishops of the AME Church, "Address to the Colored People"), Sept. 22, 1866 ("Our
Great Need"); Jan. 5, 1867 (Editorial), Sept. 14, 1867 (J.M. Langston); Nov. 30, 1867
("Self-Reliance the Key to Success"); *The Louisianian* (New Orleans), April 6, 1871
("Self-Reliance").

 14. *Christian Recorder,* May 21, 1864.

 15. W.E.B. Du Bois, *The Souls of Black Folk* (Chicago, 1903), 151.

 16. *The Life and Writings of Frederick Douglass,* ed. Philip S. Foner, 4 vols. (New
York, 1950-55), 1: 414; 4: 195, 378; Waldo E. Martin, Jr., "The Mind of Frederick
Douglass" (Ph.D. diss., Univ. of California, Berkeley, 1980), 397-99. I am grateful to Dr.
Martin for calling my attention to the last quotation.

 17. W.E.B. Du Bois, "Reconstruction and Its Benefits," *American Historical
Review* 15 (1910): 795; *Christian Recorder,* March 3, 1866.

 18. Myrta L. Avary, *Dixie After the War* (New York, 1906), 401-2; *The Possibilities
of the Negro in Symposium: A Solution of the Negro Problem Psychologically Considered* (Atlanta, Ga., 1904), 21, 147-53. See also Ray Stannard Baker, *Following the
Colour Line* (New York, 1908), 84-85, 241-42; Booker T. Washington and W.E.B. Du
Bois, *The Negro in the South* (Phiadelphia, 1907), 180; and Clifton Johnson, *Highways
and Byways of the South* (New York, 1904), 82, 358.

 19. Booker T. Washington, *Future of the American Negro* (Boston, 1899), 176;
Robert L. Factor, *The Black Response to America* (Reading, Mass., 1970), 253; Francis
L. Broderick, *W.E.B. Du Bois: Negro Leader in a Time of Crisis* (Stanford, 1955), 66.

 20. Murray, *Proud Shoes,* 270; Richard Wright, *Black Boy* (New York, 1945),
160-69.

 21. *The Booker T. Washington Papers,* ed. Louis R. Harlan and Raymond W.
Smock, 11 vols. (Urbana, Ill., 1972-81), 8:61-63.

 22. Quoted in Robert T. Kerlin, *The Voice of the Negro* (New York, 1920), 131.

 23. C. Vann Woodward, *Origins of the New South, 1877-1913* (Baton Rouge, 1951),
218; letter to the editor, *Chicago Defender,* April 28, 1917; " 'The Money Ralley' at
Sweet Gum: The Story of a Visit to a Negro Church in the Black Belt, Alabama,"
typescript, n.d. (circa 1912), Robert Park Papers, box 1, folder 10, p. 11, University of
Chicago (I am grateful to Dr. James Grossman for bringing the last two items to my
attention); John W. Blassingame, ed., *Slave Testimony* (Baton Rouge, 1977), 664;
Jacquelyn Dowd Hall, *Revolt against Chivalry* (New York, 1979), 140. On white ter-
rorism in Mississippi, see William F. Holmes, "Whitecapping: Agrarian Violence in
Mississippi, 1902-1906," *Journal of Southern History* 35 (1969): 165-85, and Dept. of
Justice records in the National Archives, Washington, D.C.

 24. Rosengarten, *All God's Dangers,* 544, 192.

 25. Ibid., 193, 264.

 26. Ibid., 27, xxi.

 27. Quoted in *The Crisis,* April 1918.

 28. Walter White, *A Man Called White* (New York, 1948), 11. On the Atlanta riot,
see also Charles Crowe, "Racial Violence and Repression in the Progressive Era,"
Journal of Negro History 53 (1968): 234-56, and "Racial Massacre in Atlanta, September 22, 1906," *Journal of Negro History* 54 (1969): 150-73.

29. Baker, *Following the Colour Line,* 19-20.

30. On the artifacts of racism, see Janette Faulkner and Robbin Henderson, *Ethnic Notions: Black Images in the White Mind* (Berkeley, 1982).

31. William Archer, *Through Afro-America* (London, 1910), 60.

32. Baker, *Following the Colour Line,* 28.

33. Archer, *Through Afro-America,* 234; Wright, *Black Boy,* 150-51.

34. Ralph Ellison, *Shadow and Act* (New York, 1964), 83.

35. "Down the Dirt Road Blues," in *Charley Patton: Founder of the Delta Blues* (Yazoo Records L-1020).

36. "Furry's Blues," in *Furry Lewis: In His Prime, 1927-1928* (Yazoo Records L-1050). On the blues, see also Lawrence W. Levine, *Black Culture and Black Consciousness* (New York, 1977); LeRoi Jones, *Blues People* (New York, 1963); and Robert Palmer, *Deep Blues* (New York, 1981).

37. "Crossroads Blues," in *Robert Johnson: King of the Delta Blues Singers* (Columbia Records, CL-1654).

38. "Hellhound on My Trail," in ibid.

7

Grant and the Freedmen

ARTHUR ZILVERSMIT

The eight years of Grant's presidency were crucial years for American blacks. The election of 1866 marked the repudiation of Andrew Johnson's efforts to restore the South with little change in racial relations; the election of 1868 gave Grant and the Republican Congress the opportunity to work together to establish a new place for the Negro in American life. Grant's policies toward the freedmen and the South—the so-called Southern Question—earned Grant a poor reputation among contemporary intellectuals as well as historians. Early historians of Reconstruction blamed Grant for carrying out a misguided and cruel policy that subjected the better classes of the South to the rule of their inferiors. Yet revisionist historians, who have pointed out the merits of Radical Reconstruction, have not added luster to Grant's reputation.[1] Now, as we note the end of the "Second Reconstruction," we might reexamine Grant's policies toward the freedmen, for it was during Grant's presidency that black Americans made their last significant gains in the nineteenth century, and when he left office blacks faced the long period that Rayford Logan has aptly called "the Nadir."

Grant's prewar career gives no hint of his future role in helping to determine the fate of blacks toiling on southern plantations. Growing up in the virulently anti-Negro Middle West, Grant married into a slaveowning family and at one time even owned a slave (whom he eventually freed).[2] Politically, Grant avoided even the mildly antislavery position of the Republican party—supporting Buchanan in 1856 and Douglas in 1860. As Grant later noted, he had never considered himself to be an antislavery man before the war.[3]

The attack on Fort Sumter evoked Grant's deep feeling of loyalty to the Union, but like most northerners he did not see the war as an antislavery struggle. In fact, Grant predicted that the war might lead to slave rebellions, which Union armies would be forced to subdue, and he gave no indication that he would object to helping to suppress slave revolts.[4] During the early years of the war there was little to distinguish Grant's policies and attitudes towards the slaves from those of other generals—he calmly carried out the government's shifting policies, avoiding both the radicalism of Frémont and the foot-dragging of McClellan. When Gen. Frémont established martial law in Missouri, emancipating the slaves of all rebels, Grant instructed his officers to "carry out \ proclamation of Genl Fremont" in all particulars. A few months later, howev\ Grant ordered his subordinates to be diligent in carrying out Gen. Henry W. Halleck's notorious General Order number three, requiring all commanders to expel fugitive slaves from their camps. Grant recognized that Halleck's orders were unpopular in some quarters but, he pointed out, "No matter what our private views may be on this subject . . . these orders must be obeyed."[5]

This theme—a soldier's duty to obey orders and to execute policy rather than develop it—formed a constant thread in Grant's policies towards the blacks during the war and even after. As he wrote to his mentor, Congressman Elihu B. Washburne: "So long as I hold a commission in the Army, I have no views of my own to carry out. Whatever may be the orders of my superiors, and law, I will execute. No man can be efficient as a commander who sets his own notions above law and those he is sworn to obey. When Congress enacts anything to [o] odious for me to execute I will resign."[6]

Following orders on matters relating to blacks was not difficult for Grant, for his views were clearly in the mainstream of northern public opinion. Writing to his father in the first autumn of the war, Grant said that his major aim was to defeat the rebellion and to restore the Union but, "If it is necessary that slavery should fall that the Republic may continue its existence, let slavery go." But slavery was not a major issue. As he told his father, "I have no hobby of my own with regard to the negro, either to effect his freedom or to continue his bondage. If Congress pass any law and the President approves, I am willing to execute it." Until that happened, however, Grant did not believe that it was right for soldiers to even discuss "the propriety of laws and official orders."[7]

As Grant moved south in 1862, mere obedience to orders became increasingly difficult as he met an unprecedented situation. Thousands of black refugees came into the Union lines in search of freedom. As Chaplain John Eaton recalled, "Their comings were like the arrival of cities . . . . There was no Moses to lead, nor plan their exodus."[8] Faced with the logistical problems of this great migration, Grant's first inclination was to move many refugees out of the war zone and he sent hundreds to Cairo, Illinois, where they were made available to midwestern employers. But the region's well-known hostility to black immigration soon put a stop to this.[9] In August 1862 the administration had ordered commanders to make use of Negro laborers who came within their lines, but this was hardly a comprehensive solution and Grant was forced to seek alternative ways of caring for the refugees, the sheer number of whom threatened the effectiveness of his army.[10]

Grant's close friend and political sponsor, Congressman Elihu B. Washburne, advised the general that the time was ripe for a changed policy in regard to the Negro: "The administration has come up with what the people have long demanded—a vigorous prosecution of the war by all means known to civilized warfare. The negroes must now be made our auxiliaries in every possible way they can be, whether by working or fighting." He shrewdly added: "That General who takes the most decided step in this respect will be held in the highest estimation by the loyal and true men in this country."[11]

In November Grant took action. He appointed John Eaton to take charge of the refugees, putting those who were able to work in the cotton fields and providing food, clothing, and shelter for all blacks within the camp.[12] Despite Washburne's prediction, however, Grant was still on his own; the administration was not ready to give him an unequivocal directive. Several days after appointing Eaton, Grant told Halleck that he had put refugee blacks to work picking cotton and asked Halleck for further guidance. In reply, Halleck merely reiterated the administration's policy on "contrabands"—that is, to make use of the refugees as laborers.[13]

In long discussions with Eaton, Grant revealed a deep, humane interest in the plight of the blacks. He considered the care of the refugees a program of high priority and Eaton enjoyed easy and frequent access to his commander, who carefully studied the detailed reports that Eaton prepared. In many ways, large and small, Grant made it easier for Eaton to carry out his monumental task in the midst of an army that was indifferent if not hostile to blacks.[14]

In the absence of clear policy directives from Washington, and without being aware of plans developed in other sectors, Grant took the initiative and developed his own policy for refugees.[15] His choice of Eaton (who had been an educator as well as a chaplain) and his close supervision of Eaton's work show that when directly confronted with the black refugees, their needs and miseries as well as their hopes, he established an imaginative and humane program. Grant acted without knowing whether his policy would be supported by the War Department. Faced with the hungry, sick, and needy, Grant ordered his quartermaster to issue government supplies to the former slaves, even though the government had not authorized the use of supplies for blacks who were not directly employed by the army.[16]

The administration approved most of these policies but, in January 1863, when Grant sought to ease the constant pressure of caring for more and more former slaves by sending some of them to Ohio to a philanthropist who had agreed to provide for them, Grant faced opposition. The War Department, sensitive to the Democrats' argument that the Emancipation Proclamation would lead to large-scale Negro migration to the Midwest, told Grant to countermand his orders.[17] In another effort to reduce the flow of refugees, who he believed were hampering the effectiveness of the army, Grant told his subordinates not to entice slaves to leave their plantations, but to allow the blacks to stay at home and "labor faithfully for reasonable wages."[18] In response, Halleck (author of the orders that had positively barred fugitive Negroes from the camps in his command) took an avuncular tone and lectured Grant on the government's new policy—"to withdraw from the use of the enemy all the slaves you can." As Halleck pointed out, "The character of the war has very much changed within the last year."[19] Grant knew this, of course. Taking slaves away from the enemy did undermine the South's capacity to wage war; six months earlier he had made the same point in a letter to his sister. But he had been weighing those considerations against the necessity for maintaining the mobility of the forces he commanded. For Grant, "the contrabands" had become a most "troublesome" question although he was "not permitted to send them out of the Department, . . . [with] such numbers as we have it is hard to keep them in."[20]

Nonetheless, he quickly brought his command into line with the policy Halleck had transmitted. He told his subordinates to "encourage all negroes, particularly middle aged males, to come within our lines." In words reminiscent of Halleck's letter, Grant pointed out that the "Rebellion has assumed the shape now that it can only terminate by the complete subjugation of the South."[21] Faced with the necessity of caring for an ever-increasing number of newly-freed blacks, without the option of sending them to the North, Grant continued to support Eaton's valiant efforts to meet their needs and he sent another chaplain, Asa Fiske, to collect desperately-needed clothing and money from charitable northerners. After leaving the Mississippi Valley, Grant continued to take an interest in the freedmen. A representative of the Western Freedmen's Aid Commission reproted that he had gotten little help from Union officers in Tennessee until Grant took over.[22]

According to Eaton, Grant understood that this work with the freedmen had important implications for the future; if the Negro demonstrated that he could be a reliable free worker, then "it would be very easy to put a musket in his hand and make a soldier of him and if he fought well, eventually to put the ballot in his hand and make him a citizen."[23] Accordingly, when the time came, Grant lent his full support to raising black troops. On April 22, 1863, Grant's aide, Lt. Col. John A. Rawlins, ordered commanding officers to "afford all facilities for the completion of the Negro regiments now organizing in this Department." He pointedly noted that "It is expected that all Commanders will especially exert themselves in carrying out the policies of the Administration, not only in organizing colored regiments and rendering them efficient, but also in removing prejudice against them."[24]

Grant told the president that he accepted the policy of arming blacks first of all because he believed that he should support all the decisions of the government whether or not he personally agreed with them. But, he added, in this case his personal views were in complete agreement with the new policy: "by arming the negro we have added a powerful ally. They will make good soldiers . . . . I am therefore most decidedly in favor of pushing this policy to the enlistment of a force sufficient to hold all the South falling into our hands and to aid in capturing more."[25]

In his letter to Lincoln, Grant emphasized once again his view that the duty of a soldier in a democracy is the execution of policies developed by the duly-elected civilian authorities. Obedience to orders was the primary determinant of Grant's policies towards the freedmen during the war. Yet, as the letter also demonstrates, Grant's personal views continued to be in accord with northern public opinion which, by the summer of 1863, favored the use of Negro soldiers. Like Lincoln, Grant's major Civil War aim was the preservation of the Union and he supported emancipation as a war measure, not as an independent goal. Yet, once emancipation was an established policy, Grant did not merely accept it, he welcomed it.[26]

Similarly, Grant welcomed the use of blacks as soldiers, praised them for their valor in combat and insisted that the Confederates treat captured black soldiers in the same manner as white prisoners of war.[27] When faced directly with the problems of the freedmen, as he was in the Mississippi valley, Grant's policies went beyond mere obedience to orders and revealed a generous and humane concern for blacks. Yet these concerns occupied a subordinate position in his hierarchy of values. Grant's major concerns were military, not humanitarian or political.

In the period of the Johnson presidency, Grant was largely silent on racial issues. At the president's request, he visited the South and issued a report which placed him in the middle of the road on the "southern question." While testifying that "the mass of thinking men of the South" acquiesced in the results of the war, Grant urged that troops be kept in the South for some time to protect both races. He recommended that only white troops be assigned garrison duty in the South because this would arouse less antagonism and also because the presence of black troops might distract the freedmen from their work and encourage them to believe that their former masters' estates would be divided among them. On the other hand, Grant recognized that the attitudes of whites would not change over night and that the blacks would therefore require the protection of the Freedmen's Bureau for several years.[28]

Although Grant undoubtedly would have preferred avoiding political conflict, the increasingly acrimonious struggle between Johnson and Congress over who would control Reconstruction pushed Grant into a position where he had to make choices. Distrusting Johnson, Congress assigned Grant a major role in supervising military reconstruction. In his role as commanding general, Grant's policies increasingly allied him with the Radicals. As one of Grant's subordinates confided to his diary: "The General is getting more and more Radical."[29] Grant supported Gen. Philip Sheridan, whose radical acts aroused the ire of both the whites of Louisiana and the president and, in a series of General Orders, he instructed southern commanders to protect the rights of the freedmen when they were threatened.[30] Even before he formally broke with the administration, Grant had come to the conclusion that the results of the war could not be protected by following Johnson's policy of conciliating the South. According to

Adam Badeau, who was close to Grant during the Johnson years, Grant urged southerners to accept the fourteenth amendment (to avoid even harsher terms for readmission) and he came to support Negro suffrage (reluctantly) in order to provide a loyal electorate in the South. Grant was slow to convert to this position "but when he once accepted the new faith, he remained firm."[31]

It was when Grant himself assumed the presidency, of course, that he had the greatest opportunity for affecting the future of the freedmen. At his inauguration it was not clear what his policies would be. The election had failed to clarify the meaning of Grant's increasingly close identification with the radical opponents of Andrew Johnson. In order to predict Grant's presidential actions it would have been necessary to pay close attention to one of the few statements he did make during the campaign. In his letter accepting the nomination, Grant told the Republican convention that it was impossible to state a clear line of policy for his four years as president because new issues would arise and, more important, "the view of the public on old ones are constantly changing." Therefore, the president as *"a purely administrative officer* should always be left free to execute the will of the people."[32] As president, no less than when he was a general, Grant defined his role as executing rather than developing policy. In his inaugural address, a perceptive listener could have heard the same theme in Grant's pledge to execute all the laws "whether they meet my approval or not." He went on to say, "I know of no method to secure the repeal of bad and obnoxious laws so effective as their stringent execution."[33] Although Grant would suggest policies to the legislature, he clearly believed that it would be his role as president to carry out the will of the people as expressed in the legislation of their representatives.

This is not to say that Grant had no ideas of his own about Reconstruction— the most pressing issue of the day. By the time of the inauguration, he had come to support the vote for blacks. In his inaugural address he urged the ratification of the Fifteenth Amendment, and to speed its ratification he asked the governor of Nebraska to call a special session of the legislature.[34] Moreover, when it was ratified, Grant took the unusual step of sending a special message to Congress in which he described the amendment as "a measure of grander importance than any other act of the kind from the foundation of our free government to the present day." He called upon the freedmen to make intelligent use of the ballot and urged whites to "withhold no legal privilege of advancement to the new citizen." He asked Congress to take all constitutional measures available to provide the popular education necessary for a government based on universal male suffrage.[35]

Although Congress failed to enact Grant's recommendations on education, it moved swiftly to pass an "Enforcement Act" to implement the new suffrage amendment and protect the freedmen.[36] Within a few months, however, it became painfully clear that the white South would not heed Grant's request to "withhold no legal privilege" from the former slaves. Instead, the whites of the South embarked on a campaign of barbaric violence and cruelty, designed to prevent the freedmen from exercising their newly-won rights. Grant and his attorney general, E. Rockwood Hoar, were slow to implement the new powers to protect the rights of the freedmen that Congress had given the executive, but southern intransigence and graphic reports of violence and intimidation in the South led Grant to proclaim in his annual message to Congress that it would be the administration's policy to allow all men to vote "without fear of molestation or proscription."[37] A few months later, Grant asked the newly-assembled Forty-Second Congress for additional powers to combat southern intimidation of blacks. Even before Congress acted, Grant threatened military intervention in South Carolina, using his constitutional powers to protect states against domestic violence.[38]

But as a military man, Grant was especially sensitive to charges that he sought military solutions to political problems, and he wanted Congress to clarify his role in enforcing the Fourteenth and Fifteenth Amendments.[39] The "Ku Klux" Act of April 1871, which authorized the president to suspend the writ of habeas corpus in those areas in which intimidation and violence were widespread, enabled Grant and his new attorney general, Amos Akerman, to carry out a systematic campaign against the Ku Klux Klan—a campaign that was initially quite successful in limiting organized violence against the freedmen.[40] Thousands of Klansmen were arrested and hundreds of others fled their homes to escape arrest. As a result, the election of 1872 was "the fairest and most democratic election in the South until 1968."[41]

Although Grant's enforcement policy of 1871-72 succeeded in overcoming the Klan's systematic program of terror, the policy was hampered from its very inception. From the moment the Ku Klux bill was introduced, it was clear that the Republican coalition that had (briefly) supported the rights of the freedmen was falling apart. The first enforcement act had had the united support of the party—moderates as well as radicals; when the Ku Klux bill was before Congress, however, such prominent Republicans as Lyman Trumbull and Carl Schurz were in the opposition.[42] A year later the opposition had increased to the point that a bill to continue the president's authority to suspend the writ of habeas corpus was defeated in the House. The shift in congressional sentiment became even clearer as Congress, anxious to cut spending, failed to provide adequate funds for the Justice Department to execute those enforcement statutes that were still in effect. At the same time, the courts seriously undermined the federal program to protect Negro rights by casting grave doubts on the constitutionality of the enforcement acts. Northern public opinion, Congress, and the courts were beginning that ominous shift from supporting the rights of the freedmen that was to bring the first Reconstruction to such an unhappy end.[43]

As Grant continued to attempt to protect the rights of the freedmen, he found himself increasingly isolated, executing a policy developed by men who no longer believed in it themselves. As the Republican party deserted the Negro, Grant continually found himself on the defensive when discussing the administration's southern policies. After sending troops to Louisiana, for instance, Grant patiently explained to Congress that "colored laborers" who had refused to accede to their employers' coercion had been executed. If such conditions did not justify federal intervention, then the Fifteenth Amendment and the enforcement acts were meaningless and "the whole scheme of colored enfranchisement is worse than a mockery and little better than a crime." Although he was aware that many now believed the North should sit back and quietly allow white southerners to disenfranchise blacks, Grant pointedly announced that as long as he was president, "all the laws of Congress and the provisions of the Constitution, including the recent amendments thereto, will be enforced with rigor."[44]

For the most part, Grant fulfilled this pledge. In the fall of 1875, it is true, Grant refused to aid the embattled regime of Governor Adelbert Ames of Mississippi. Determined to regain control of the state and to eliminate the integrated Reconstruction government, white supremacists had launched a campaign of intimidation and violence aimed at destroying the Republican party and winning the election at any cost.[45] Ames realized that the militia could not protect black voters. As he wrote to his wife, "So far has this intimidation gone that I cannot organize a single company of militia."[46] Recognizing the desperation of his situation, Ames asked for federal troops.

Grant later explained to Congressman John R. Lynch that his first impulse had been to send the troops that Ames requested. As Lynch related the story many years later, Grant told him that he had given orders to the War Department to send troops to Mississippi, but that before the orders were executed he was persuaded by a group of Ohio Republicans that such action would be so unpopular it would lead to the party's defeat in Ohio. "The President assured me," Lynch recalled, "that it was with great reluctance that he yielded,—against his own judgment and sense of official duty." Lynch recalls that he delivered a stinging rebuke to the president, saying that this was "the first time I have ever known you to show the white feather." According to Lynch, Grant admitted that he had been wrong. "I should not have yielded. I believe that at the time I was making a grave mistake. But as presented, it was duty on one side, and party obligation on the other. Between the two I hesitated, but finally yielded to party obligation."[47] In addition to the pressure of northern party members, moreover, Grant was faced with the fact that even the members of the Republican party in Mississippi were seriously split on the wisdom of intervention. In the absence of any strong countervailing influences, Grant yielded.[48]

At first, Grant's cautious policy seemed to pay off when Ames and the Mississippi Democrats, brought together by an agent of the attorney general, reached a compromise. Ames was optimistic. With less than three weeks to go before the election, he wrote to Attorney General Edwards Pierrepont, praising his envoy's "timely and skillful intervention" and claiming that "a bloody revolution has been averted." He predicted that "we will have peace, order and a fair election."[49] A week before the election, however, it became clear that the Democrats had no intention of honoring their agreement to end the campaign of terror. Pierrepont's agent in Mississippi, George K. Chase, bluntly told the attorney general: "It is impossible to have a fair election on November 2d without the aid of U.S. troops." By this time, however, it was too late to send the troops which might have afforded some protection for black Republicans.[50]

Grant regretted his failure to combat the violence of 1875 in Mississippi, and the next year, in the wake of renewed violence in South Carolina, he responded quickly, stripping garrisons on the eastern seaboard of all available troops in order to send them to the scene of the trouble. By election day, there were more federal soldiers in South Carolina than at any other time since the end of the war.[51] Even after Congress had lost interest in supporting the Fifteenth Amendment, Grant continued to regard it as the law of the land.[52]

But Grant's enforcement policy was fatally limited by the fact that northern public opinion had become increasingly critical of federal intervention to protect southern Republican regimes. As one radical newspaper pointed out, the "overwhelming public sentiment *at the North*" was now opposed to using federal authority for "the protection of life at the South." And as public opinion shifted, members of Congress, some of whom had initially devised the policy of enfranchising the freedmen, now had grave doubts about the wisdom of Radical Reconstruction, leaving Grant to execute laws that they no longer supported.[53] Having come to the presidency believing that it would be his duty to carry out the will of the people by enforcing the laws enacted by their representatives, Grant found that his efforts to enforce the laws led only to increased public criticism and political isolation. But the man who had once announced that he would "fight it out on this line if it takes all summer," was not easily swayed from his course.[54] Grant had come to radical republicanism relatively late, but he found himself (ironically) to be among the last of the Radicals.

In enforcing the reconstruction acts and implementing the new amendments to the constitution, Grant was hewing closely to his traditional role of carrying out policies originally formulated by others; his persistence reflected his characteristic stubborness. Yet Grant's comments on southern atrocities reveal a concern that went deeper than that of a man who considered himself only an agent and whose persistence was based on more than mere stubborness. For example, Grant displayed a deep concern for the abused freedmen when he denounced the Hamburg, South Carolina, massacre of blacks as "cruel, bloodthirsty, [and] wanton" but nonetheless typical of white oppression of Negroes throughout the South. He denounced the redeemer government of Mississippi as having been chosen "through fraud and violence such as would scarcely be accredited to savages," and, with bitter sarcasm, pointed out that the only right the redeemers were fighting for was the right "to kill negroes and republicans without fear of punishment."[55]

Grant's conviction that blacks were entitled to all the rights granted them by the Constitution was reflected in his actions in social matters as well as political decisions. President Grant's racial views were tested at his first New Year's reception. It had been traditional (since the days of Lincoln) for Negroes to attend the White House New Year's reception but they had been admitted separately.[56] When Grant was asked about his plans for the reception, he agreed to follow precedent. Somehow, however, blacks had gotten the idea that they would now be admitted to the reception on an equal basis and they crowded up to the gates. When Grant heard about it, he ordered that the crowd be admitted without separating people by race.[57] Although he was subject to criticism for allowing blacks to mix with whites, Grant persisted and at the ball celebrating his second inauguration white and black couples mixed freely on the dance floor. In the days of Grant's presidency the social life of the capital was more nearly integrated than it had ever been before (or would be again for several generations).[58] Blacks recognized that Grant played an important role in this. According to Washington's Negro newspaper, "No man need be afraid now since the Chief Magistrate of the nation receives all alike at his levees—since, in fact, the chief men of Washington society invite colored men to their receptions."[59]

Frederick Douglass gave high praise to Grant's racial attitude, pointing out that except for Lincoln and Sen. Charles Sumner "no man in high position has manifested in his intercourse with me upon all occasions and in all places more entire freedom from vulgar prejudice of race and color than Ulysses S. Grant." Grant's relatively unprejudiced racial views are also evidenced by his genuine concern for the fate of American Indians and his appointment of a native American as Commissioner of Indian Affairs.[60]

Although Grant had not been an opponent of slavery before the war, he had been kind to the individual blacks who had worked for him and a former slave, "Old Uncle Jason," recalled that Grant was the kindest man he had ever worked for.[61] In his private life, Grant treated blacks as individuals, judging them by the same standards as whites. The contrast between Grant and his wife is striking in this respect. According to the picture drawn by their son Jesse, who grew up in the White House, Julia Grant, who came from a slaveholding family, treated blacks with a blend of paternalism and indulgence. Her parting words to her favorite Negro coachman were, "You rascal!" On the other hand, despite the example of those around him, Grant was neither paternalistic nor indulgent. One of Jesse's anecdotes reveals something of Grant's personal relations with blacks. Bill Barnes, who had been Grant's personal servant since Vicksburg, continued to serve the general after the war and enjoyed a high place in the servant hierarchy. Periodically, however, Barnes would go on a drunk and Grant would dismiss him. After some time, "father would soften and secure another job for Bill," but shortly thereafter Grant would find that Barnes was back in his own service. Jesse recalled that "It amused us all greatly and completely baffled father." In due time the cycle would be repeated—Grant would fire Barnes and the rest of the family would quietly reinstate him. Finally, when Grant was about to embark on his world tour in 1877, he discovered Bill Barnes (whom he had fired once again) on board, busily unpacking. At this point Grant called the captain and insisted that Barnes be removed from the ship. Significantly, he added that Julia Grant should not be informed until it was too late to bring Barnes back. Although the dismissal of a servant who had been in his service for a long time was a harsh act, it showed greater respect for Barnes as a man than Julia Grant's paternalistic indulgence of the foibles of a member of a lower class. This anecdote, one of the few pictures we have of the private life of Ulysses S. Grant, reveals a man who was capable of transcending the racism that pervaded the society around him.[62]

Most American blacks and the old abolitionists who were their allies recognized that Grant supported their interests. Frederick Douglass was one of Grant's strongest supporters. For Douglass, the issue was clear: "If we stand by President Grant and his administration, it is from no spirit of hero worship or blind attachment to mere party, but because in this hour there is no middle ground." Douglass argued that a refusal to support Grant in the election of 1872 was "the surest way to undo the work of the last ten years, and remand the Negro to a condition in some respects worse than that from which the Union delivered him."[63] Sella Martin, who edited the black newspaper *New Era,* praised Grant because both he and the members of his cabinet had "shown a willingness to put colored men in any place they have the ability to fill, whenever there has been a vacancy." This was remarkable, in view of "the old conservative sentiment of the country." Robert Brown Elliott, a black congressman from South Carolina, put it clearly when he told Grant that blacks would support him in the election: "We stand by you because you have stood by us."[64]

Although Douglass not only campaigned for Grant but virtually turned his newspaper into an instrument of the 1872 Grant campaign, he knew that Grant and the Republican party had not transformed America and that the blacks were still not getting what in justice was due to them. As a political realist, however, Douglass understood the choice: "Whatever else may be said of the Republican Party and of General Grant, they are now the only visible hope of the colored race in the United States. Outside of these we see no power that is likely to stand between the Negro and murder."[65] Within this context, the Democratic charge that Grant had snubbed Douglass by not inviting him to dinner with the rest of the Santo Domingo delegation seemed unimportant to Douglass. In public, he denied that there had been any snub.[66] In private he admitted that the president should have invited him, "But the President was not educated in the Gerritt Smith school and I judge him by his opportunities, in this light he is a good and noble man."[67]

Grant's actions as president had earned Douglass's respect, but by the end of the second term it had become much more difficult to defend the rights of the freedmen. In 1875 Congress had refused to give Grant a new enforcement act and in the next year an openly hostile Congress tried to use the army appropriation bill to force Grant to withdraw the troops from the South.[68] By 1876 the Supreme Court had undermined enforcement of the Fourteenth and Fifteenth Amendments by its decision in the Cruikshank case.[69] Although Grant had continued to support the rights of the freedmen long after most of the "Best Men" had given up on Radical Reconstruction, by the last winter of his presidency he was tired.[70] Subject to merciless abuse for his southern policy and faced once more with a request to bail out the Republican party of Louisiana, Grant was ready to surrender. His sleep disturbed by worries about the turmoil in Louisiana, appalled at the sheer incompetence of the Louisiana Republicans, Grant told Secretary of State Hamilton Fish that he was now "opposed to the fifteenth amendment" and thought "it was a mistake, that . . . had done the Negro no good, and had been a hindrance to the South, and by no means a political advantage to the North."[71] Although Grant sustained the Republican regimes of South Carolina and Louisiana to the end, he endorsed his successor's decision to withdraw the federal troops from the South, thereby ending the experiment of reconstructing the South on a biracial basis.[72]

By 1877, then, Grant's attitude towards the freedmen had come full circle. He had started out with views that differed little from those of his neighbors. Under the prodding of the Radicals and in response to southern intransigence, Grant had moved to the defense of black rights. Having come to this position slowly, he was also slow to abandon it. Moved by a combination of an intense sense of loyalty and commitment to principle (as well as sheer stubbornness), Grant continued to defend the freedmen after his tutors had changed their minds. Eventually, however, Grant found himself back in the mainstream, ready to give up on radical social change. He had come to the presidency believing that he would be called upon to "execute the will of the people." This limited view of the role of the presidency left Grant with few resources to resist drifting with the tide.

Revisionist historians (such as Grant's most recent biographer, William McFeely) are disappointed in the failure of the Radical Republicans to build a genuine racial democracy in the South and they hold Grant at least partly responsible for this failure.[73] If he had pushed harder, they argue, perhaps the first Reconstruction would have been more successful. But the problem was not one of presidential leadership. Given the temper of the nation in 1876 and the wholesale desertion of the cause of black freedom by the members of the

Republican party, no president, no matter how deep his personal commitment to racial justice, could have accomplished more than Grant. McFeely views Grant as the typical American of his age—no worse, but certainly no better—and his attack on Grant for his failure to pursue racial justice with greater force is therefore an indictment of the American people. But in his commitment to protecting the freedmen Grant was not a representative American. What is truly remarkable is that Grant did continue to support the rights of the freedmen after Congress and the people had given up on the first Reconstruction. It was to his credit that he held out as long as he did—that he followed rather than led the retreat from principle.

1. For example, William A. Dunning characterized Grant as "narrow, headstrong, and politically untutored," lacking the "ability to judge men" (*Reconstruction: Political and Economic, 1865-1877*, vol. 22 of *The New American Nation: A History* [New York, 1907], 165, 178, 192). William Gillette sees Grant's southern policy as "a study in incongruity: a curious, confusing, changeable mix of boldness and timidity, decision, activity and passivity" (*Retreat from Reconstruction, 1869-1879* [Baton Rouge, 1979], 166-67).

2. William S. McFeely, *Grant: A Biography* (New York, 1981), 12, 22, 62-63; *The Papers of Ulysses S. Grant*, ed. John Y. Simon, 17 vols. to date (Carbondale, Ill., 1967-   ), 1: 347, 347n. John A. Carpenter argues that since Grant "could have sold the Negro for badly needed cash, but did not, the manumission must have been done out of principle" (*Ulysses S. Grant* in *Twayne's Rulers and Statesmen of the World Series* [New York, 1970], 12). Julia Grant continued to own slaves as late as the summer of 1863 and General Grant apparently raised no objections (Jesse R. Grant, *In the Days of My Father, General Grant* [New York, 1925], 17).

3. McFeely, *Grant*, 69-70; Grant to Elihu Washburne, Aug. 30, 1863, *Grant Papers*, 9: 217-18.

4. Grant to Jesse Grant, May 6, 1861, *Grant Papers*, 2: 22; Grant to Julia Grant, May 6, 1861, Ulysses S. Grant Papers; Library of Congress, Presidential Papers, microfilm (Washington, D.C., 1964), reel 1.

5. Grant to Col. John Cook, Sept. 12, 1861, *Grant Papers*, 2: 243-44; Grant to Col. John Cook, Dec. 25, 1861, ibid., 3: 342.

6. Grant to Elihu B. Washburne, March 22, 1862, ibid., 4: 408.

7. Grant to Jesse R. Grant, Nov. 27, 1861, ibid., 3: 227; Grant to Jesse R. Grant, Aug. 3, 1862, ibid., 5: 264.

8. John Eaton, *Report of the General Superintendent of the Freedmen, Department of the Tennessee and State of Arkansas for 1864* (Memphis, 1865), 4.

9. V. Jacque Voegeli, *Free but Not Equal: The Midwest and the Negro during the Civil War* (Chicago, 1967), 60-61, 107; J.M. Tuttle to Edwin Stanton, Cairo, Ill., Sept. 18, 1862, in *War of the Rebellion: . . . Official Records of the Union and Confederate Armies*, 120 vols. (Washington, D.C., 1890-1901, hereafter cited as *O. R.*) 3d ser., 2: 569, and Edwin Stanton to J.M. Tuttle, Sept. 18, 1862, *O.R.*, 3d ser. 2: 569.

10. Voegeli, *Free but Not Equal*, 96.

11. Washburne to Grant, July 25, 1862, *Grant Papers*, 5: 226n.

12. John Eaton, *Grant, Lincoln, and the Freedmen* (New York, 1907), 5.

13. Grant to Halleck, Nov. 15, 1862, *Grant Papers*, 6:315; Halleck to Grant, Nov. 16, 1862, *O. R.*, 1st ser., 17 (part 1): 470-71, and *Grant Papers*, 6: 315-16n.

14. Eaton, *Grant and the Freedmen*, 12, 20, 44, 86, 107-11, 119; Ulysses S. Grant, *Personal Memoirs of U.S. Grant*, 2 vols. (New York, 1885-1886), 1: 424-25.

15. Eaton, *Grant and the Freedmen*, 13n.

16. Ibid., 21-22.

17. Grant to Halleck, Jan. 6, 1863, *O. R.*, 1st ser., 17, (part 1): 481; Halleck to Grant, Jan. 19, 1863, *O. R.*, 1st ser., 52 (part 1): 323.

18. Special Field Order No. 12, Feb. 12, 1863, *O. R.*, 1st ser., 24 (part 3): 46-47; Grant to Halleck, Feb. 18, 1863, *Grant Papers*, 7: 338-39.

19. Halleck to Grant, March 31, 1863, *O. R.*, 1st ser., 24 (part 3): 156-57.

20. Grant to Mary Grant, Aug. 19, 1862, *Grant Papers*, 5:310-11; Grant to Gen. James B. McPherson, March 13, 1863, *Grant Papers*, 7:415.

21. Grant to Major General Fred. Steele, April 11, 1863, *O. R.*, 1st ser., 24 (part 3): 186-87. Cf. Halleck's letter (cited above in note 19): "There is no possible hope of reconciliation with the rebels . . . . There can be no peace but that which is forced by the sword."

22. Eaton, *Grant and the Freedmen*, 222-23n, 121.

23. Ibid., 14-15.

24. *Grant Papers*, 8: 94n.

25. Grant to Abraham Lincoln, Aug. 23, 1863, Abraham Lincoln Papers, Library of Congress, Presidential Papers, microfilm (Washington, D.C., 1959), reel 1, document no. 25799.

26. Bruce Catton, *Grant Moves South* (Boston, 1960), 388-89; Lincoln to Grant, Aug. 9, 1863, printed in Arthur Zilversmit, ed., *Lincoln on Black and White* (Belmont, Calif., 1971), 144.

27. Bruce Catton, *Grant Takes Command* (Boston, 1969), 23, 374, 389, 404; Grant to Halleck, Aug. 19, 1864, Library of Congress, Presidential Papers, reel 3; Grant to Gen. Robert E. Lee, Oct. 20, 1864, *O. R.*, 2d ser., 7: 1018-19.

28. "Letter of General Grant Concerning Affairs at the South," Dec. 18, 1865, *Senate Executive Documents*, 39th Cong., 1st sess., no. 2, 106-08. Cf. McFeely, *Grant*, 238-40.

29. C.B. Comstock, March 1, 1867, quoted in William B. Hesseltine, *Ulysses S. Grant, Politician* (New York, 1935), 81. Harold Hyman argues that Grant was radicalized by his perception that the southern governments recognized by Johnson presented a threat to army personnel in the South. "Johnson, Stanton, and Grant: A Reconsideration of the Army's Role in the Events Leading to Impeachment," *American Historical Review* 66 (Oct. 1960): 85-100.

30. Joseph G. Dawson III, "General Phil Sheridan and Military Reconstruction in Louisiana," *Civil War History* 24 (1978): 134, 135, 136, 143, 146; Martin E. Mantell, *Johnson, Grant, and the Politics of Reconstruction* (New York, 1973), 28.

31. Ibid., 68; Adam Badeau, *Grant in Peace* (Hartford, 1887), 43-45, 57-59.

32. Grant to Joseph R. Hawley, May 29, 1868, printed in John Hope Franklin, "Election of 1868," in *History of American Presidential Elections*, ed. Arthur Schlesinger, Jr., and Fred L. Israel, 4 vols. (New York, 1971), 3:1274.

33. James D. Richardson, ed., *A Compilation of the Messages and Papers of the Presidents, 1789-1908*, 11 vols. (n.p., 1908), 7:6.

34. Ibid., 8; Carpenter, *Grant*, 85. As late as January 1867, Grant had supported Johnson's veto of a bill giving freedmen the vote in the District of Columbia, but his reasons were not that he was generally opposed to Negro suffrage. According to Gideon

Welles, Grant argued that it was "very contemptible . . . for members of Congress whose states excluded negroes, to give them suffrage in the District." Howard K. Beale, ed., *Diary of Gideon Welles, Secretary of the Navy under Lincoln and Johnson,* 3 vols. (New York, 1960), 3:5.

35. Richardson, *Messages and Papers,* 7: 55-56; *New Era,* April 7, 1870.

36. James Ford Rhodes, *History of the United States from the Compromise of 1850 to the Final Restoration of Home Rule at the South in 1877,* 7 vols. (New York, 1893-1904), 6:294; Gillette, *Retreat from Reconstruction,* 25-26; James M. McPherson, *Ordeal by Fire: The Civil War and Reconstruction* (New York, 1982), 566.

37. McPherson, *Ordeal by Fire,* 564-66; McFeely, *Grant,* 364, 365-66; Richardson, *Messages and Papers,* 7:96, 112.

38. Richardson, *Messages and Papers,* 7:127-28, 132-33.

39. George F. Hoar, *Autobiography of Seventy Years,* 2 vols. (New York, 1903), 1:205; McPherson, *Ordeal by Fire,* 567; McFeely, *Grant,* 369. Grant's fears that he would be denounced for using the military proved to be accurate. A North Carolina newspaper denounced him as "a dictator" and the *New York Herald* accused him of not recognizing that he was no longer a general in the field. See Allen W. Trelease, *White Terror: The Ku Klux Klan Conspiracy and Southern Reconstruction* (New York, 1971), 415-16.

40. Kenneth M. Stampp, *The Era of Reconstruction, 1865-1877* (New York, 1965), 200-201; J.G. Randall and David Donald, *The Civil War and Reconstruction,* 2d ed. (Lexington, Mass., 1969), 683-684. Historians have differed on the effectiveness of the Grant administration's enforcement activities. William McFeely maintains that the period of stringent enforcement of the anti-Klan laws ended in December 1871 when Grant dismissed Attorney General Akerman *(Grant,* 369-73). John Hope Franklin argues that the campaign against the Klan achieved very little *(Reconstruction After the Civil War* in *The Chicago History of American Civilization* [Chicago, 1961], 167-68). John Carpenter argues that in its enforcement policy "the record of the Grant administration falls far short of what it should have been. Instead of too much interference, there was too little" *(Grant,* 86-90). On the other hand, William C. Harris argues that in Mississippi by early 1872, the enforcement campaign "had the desired effect"; as a result, the fall 1872 elections were conducted with relative security for the Republicans *(The Day of the Carpetbagger: Republican Reconstruction in Mississippi* [Baton Rouge, 1979], 404-5).

41. McPherson, *Ordeal by Fire,* 567.

42. Rhodes, *History of the U.S.,* 6:294, 314-16; Ellis P. Oberholtzer, *A History of the United States since the Civil War,* 5 vols. (New York, 1917-1937), 2:381.

43. Rhodes, *History of the U.S.,* 6:331; Everette Swinney, "Enforcing the Fifteenth Amendment, 1870-1877," *Journal of Southern History* 28 (May 1962): 211-13, 207-9; McPherson, *Ordeal by Fire,* 593.

44. Richardson, *Messages and Papers,* 7:297-99; see also Grant's message to the Senate, Jan. 13, 1875 in ibid.

45. Harris, in *Day of the Carpetbagger,* the most recent account of Mississippi politics during Reconstruction, makes clear that race was not the only issue. Governor Ames had alienated many members of his own party by his failure to carry out his promised policies of reform. By 1874, Harris points out, Ames "was losing interest in Mississippi affairs" and sought "to escape the responsibilities of governing a society that he disdained" (622; see also 623-90 *passim*).

46. Ames to Blanche Butler Ames, Sept. 2, 1875, quoted in McFeely, *Grant,* 419.

47. Congressman Lynch met with Grant in November 1875. John R. Lynch, *The Facts of Reconstruction* (New York, 1913; reprint, New York, 1968), 147-55.

48. William C. Harris points out that "the force of the materials that Grant saw was

clearly on the side of those seeking to prevent federal interference" *(Day of the Carpet-bagger*, 658, 665-66, 669-70. See also James W. Garner, *Reconstruction in Mississippi* (New York, 1901), 381, 381-82n.

49. Ames to Pierrepont, Oct. 16, 1875, *Chronicles from the Nineteenth Century: Family Letters of Blanche Ames and Adelbert Ames*, ed. Blanche Butler Ames, 2 vols. (n.p., 1957), 2: 256-57n.

50. *Mississippi in 1875: Report of the Select Committee to Inquire into the Mississippi Election of 1875, with the Testimony and Documentary Evidence, Senate Reports*, 44th Cong., 1st sess., no. 527, part 2, 92. The date of Chase's letter was probably Oct. 27. By then Ames thought it was too late for troops to be useful (Ames to Blanche Butler Ames, Oct. 27, 1875, *Ames Family Letters*, 2: 240-41). Nonetheless, on Oct. 28, Secretary of War Belknap told Gen. C.C. Augur to be prepared to suppress disorder during the election in Mississippi. But when Augur asked who would have the authority to call for troops, Belknap, after showing the telegram to Grant and Pierrepont, cagily replied: "further instructions are not deemed necessary. You are expected to do your duty discreetly. Order must be preserved and bloodshed prevented if possible" (James Sefton, *The United States Army and Reconstruction, 1865-1877* [Baton Rouge, 1967], 231). The dates of Belknap's order and Augur's reply were supplied to me by the National Archives. In the fall of 1875, both Grant and Pierrepont were preoccupied with the rapidly-developing Whiskey Ring scandal (McFeely, *Grant*, 410-12, 416).

51. Joel Williamson, *After Slavery: The Negro in South Carolina During Reconstruction, 1861-1877* (Chapel Hill, N.C., 1965), 270, 270n. Williamson points out that, in the wake of Custer's defeat, the government did not have sufficient troops to afford the blacks adequate protection.

52. Richardson, *Messages and Papers*, 7: 418-21.

53. Chicago *Inter-Ocean*, Jan. 19, 1875, quoted in Gillette, *Retreat from Reconstruction*, 184; John G. Sproat, *The Best Men: Liberal Reformers in the Gilded Age* (New York, 1968), 12-44. C. Vann Woodward, argues that the Radicals' policies on race were flawed from the very beginning. ("Seeds of Failure in Radical Race Policy," in *New Frontiers of the American Reconstruction*, ed. Harold Hyman, [Urbana, Ill., 1966] 125-47.

54. Grant to Halleck, May 11, 1864, *O. R.* 1st ser., 26 (part 2):627.

55. Grant to D. H. Chamberlain, July 31, 1876, Grant Letter Book, vol. 3, Library of Congress, Presidential Papers, reel 4, pp. 105-6.

56. Benjamin Quarles, *The Negro in the Civil War* (Boston, 1953), 253.

57. The savagely anti-Negro *New York Herald* reported the story under the headline "The Niggers Insulted" (Jan. 2, 1870). George Downing, president of the National Council of Colored Men, wrote to Grant about the incident and Grant replied through Gen. O.E. Babcock. The reply was apparently satisfactory since neither Downing nor the National Executive Committee raised the issue again and a few weeks later the committee praised Grant highly for his special message announcing passage of the Fifteenth Amendment (Babcock to Downing, Jan., 1870, Grant Letter Book, Library of Congress, Presidential Papers, reel 3). The National Executive Committee's praise of Grant is in the *New Era*, April 7, 1870. See also George Sinkler, *The Racial Attitudes of American Presidents from Abraham Lincoln to Theodore Roosevelt*, Anchor ed. (Garden City, N. Y., 1972), 154.

58. Constance McLaughlin Green, *The Secret City: A History of Race Relations in the Nation's Capital* (Princeton, N. J., 1967), 109. Green points out that "In 1932 the Young Communist League sponsored the first biracial dance to be held in Washington since President Grant's inauguration in 1873" (218).

59. *New Era*, Feb. 24, 1870.

60. Frederick Douglass, *U.S. Grant and the Colored People* (n. p. [1872]), 7; McFeely, *Grant*, 305-18.

61. McFeely, *Grant,* 62.

62. Jesse Grant, *Days of My Father*, 63, 210-11.

63. April 6, 1871, in Phillip S. Foner, *The Life and Writings of Frederick Douglass,* 4 vols. (New York, 1950-1955), 4: 242. *The New National Era*, edited by Douglass, was a continuation of the *New Era*. James McPherson points out that most of the abolitionists supported Grant despite Sumner's well-publicized defection. ("Grant or Greeley? The Abolitionist Dilemma in the election of 1872," *American Historical Review* 71 [October 1965]: 43-61).

64. *New Era*, Jan. 20, 1870; Robert B. Elliott to Grant, Sept. 19, 1872, quoted in Peggy Lamson, *The Glorious Failure: Black Congressman Robert Brown Elliott and the Reconstruction of South Carolina* (New York, 1973), 151-52. Cf. Gillette, *Retreat from Reconstruction,* 195-96, who argues that the Grant administration did not give jobs to blacks.

65. *New National Era*, March 30, 1871, in Foner, *Douglass*, 4: 72. James T. Rapier, black Congressman from Alabama, also founded a newspaper to support Grant's reelection (Loren Schweninger, *James T. Rapier and Reconstruction* [Chicago, 1978], 107). Given the fact that the other candidate, Horace Greeley, clearly identified himself with those hostile to their interests, blacks did not have any real alternative to supporting Grant in the election.

66. Douglass says that "These gentlemen [the commissioners and one secretary] called in a body upon the President and were invited in an informal way to dine with him. I was not in company with the Commissioners when this call was made, and did not see the President until afterward. Had I been in company with the Commissioners at the time of their visit, I have no question but that an invitation would have been extended to me. (*Grant and the Colored People,* 7).

67. Douglass to Gerritt Smith, Sept. 11, 1872 in Foner, *Douglass*, 4: 297. In another letter to Smith, Douglass had said that he did not consider the president "a great sinner" for having failed to invite him, but he would have welcomed the invitation as "a reproof of the insult" offered him when, on returning to Washington, the captain of a Potomac mail packet refused to seat him in the dining room with the other members of the Santo Domingo commission (Douglass to Smith, Aug. 15, 1872, printed in Foner, *Douglass,* 297. Previously, Douglass had not suffered any acts of discrimination and, according to the *New York Times*, Grant had given specific orders to assure Douglass equal treatment (*New York Times*, Aug. 6, 1872).

68. Oberholtzer, *History of the U.S.*, 3: 195-96; Stampp, *Reconstruction,* 209.

69. Swinney, "Fifteenth Amendment," 209.

70. Sproat, *Best Men,* 12-44. James McPherson publishes a letter to William Lloyd Garrison from his son, Wendell Phillips Garrison, which exemplifies the shift in view among reformers: "You see in every Southern issue a race issue, and your sympathies are naturally with the (nominally) weaker race. I try to judge each one according to the facts and principles involved, holding fast to this maxim: that good government is first to be thought of and striven for, and that the incidental loss which it may occasion either race is less mischievous than the incidental protection accorded to either by bad government." ("Coercion or Conciliation? Abolitionists Debate President Hayes's Southern Policy," *New England Quarterly* 39 [December 1966]: 481-82).

71. "Hamilton Fish Diary," Jan. 17, 1877, Allan Nevins, *Hamilton Fish: The Inner History of the Grant Administration*, 2 vols., rev. ed. (New York, 1957), 2: 835. Fish's version of this conversation must be read in the context of the fact that he had long been

hostile to Negro suffrage. See his speech of June 1874 quoted in Gillette, *Retreat from Reconstruction*, 215.

72. Stanley Hirshson, *Farewell to the Bloody Shirt: Northern Republicans and the Southern Negro, 1877-1893* (Bloomington, Ind., 1962), 35, 60; Vincent P. De Santis, *Republicans Face the Southern Question, 1877-1897*, Johns Hopkins University Studies in Historical and Political Science series 77, no. 1 (Baltimore, 1959), 124.

73. McFeely, *Grant*, throughout, but especially p. xiii.

PART IV

Past in Present:
The Long Aftermath of War

8

The Present Becomes the Past: The Planter Class in the Postbellum South

JAMES OAKES

Buried in the sixteenth chapter of Ulrich B. Phillips's monumental study of *American Negro Slavery* is an extraordinary footnote. To document his rhapsodic account of "plantation life" in the antebellum South, Phillips cited his "own observations in post-bellum times in which, despite the shifting of industrial arrangements and the decrease of wealth, these phases have remained apparent." He bolstered his case with two additional postwar memoirs, a traveller's account and the journal of an eighteenth-century plantation tutor. Thus Phillips violated the rule he had set down in the preface a few hundred pages earlier. "Reminiscences are . . . disregarded, for the reason that the lapse of decades has impaired inevitably the memories of men." Instead he would rely on the "contemporary records of slaves, masters, and witnesses." With one stroke Phillips disregarded his own sage advice in three different ways; first by relying on memoirs, second by citing his own recollections of plantation life, and finally by failing to cite even a single "contemporary" source from an antebellum master or slave.[1]

There is more involved here than mere inconsistency. What Phillips "observed" in the late nineteenth century was a radically transformed social hierarchy topped by a distinct planter class that had no clear parallel in the Old South. Yet Phillips's interpretation assured readers that the postwar elite was continuous with its antebellum counterpart. In so doing he contributed, albeit inadvertently, to the very process by which a new planter class consolidated and legitimized its economic and political influence in the late nineteenth and early twentieth centuries. It is not enough to say that Phillips observed southern history from the perspective of a Progressive. For southern progressivism was itself the culmination of a profound social and political transformation that was set in motion by the Civil War. The connections between what Phillips and his contemporaries wrote and the world they observed at close range are far more intimate and deserve far more attention than most historians have allowed.[2]

Certainly there were planters in the Old South, but it is not clear that they constituted a discrete "class." The proliferating definitions of the words "planter" and "plantation" among scholars of the antebellum South suggest the nature of the problem. In the absence of any clearcut, qualitative definition, most historians fall back on quantitative criteria that are hopelessly varied. Was a planter the owner of ten slaves? Fifteen slaves? Twenty? Thirty? Fifty? Each figure has its advocates. Or was a plantation defined by its acreage? If so, do we count improved acreage, unimproved acreage, or both? And how many acres? If we fall back on some combination of land and slaves, the possibilities are virtually limitless. A more useful dividing line may be the point at which a master ceased to be directly involved in the production process. As Kenneth Stampp has argued, masters who "had at their command as few as a half dozen fieldhands . . . were tempted to improve their status by withdrawing from the fields and devoting most of their time to managerial functions."

But if we assume that the master-slave relationship was the distinguishing characteristic of antebellum southern society, it follows that the planters were only one part of a much larger class of slaveholders. Whatever the cultural, political, and economic differences separating wealthy planters from small slaveholders, all shared a powerful social identity as masters. All enjoyed the extraordinary legal privileges that were activated with the ownership of a single slave. All faced the problem of motivating a labor force that lacked the intrinsic incentives associated with economic independence or the extrinisic incentives that were part of a wage labor system. Thus the Old South had a slaveholding class which included, at its smallest, one out of four white families. The majority of masters controlled the labor of between one and five slaves. A much smaller proportion of the master class can be called planters, who were distinguished not by their unique relationship to the means of production but by their sheer wealth and the political influence that wealth has always commanded in American politics.[3]

The broad spectrum of slave ownership played an important role in the political conflict between slaveholders and yeomen. In a democracy of white men, it mattered that the slaveholding class included between 25 and 50 percent of the free families. In a polity severely divided over the proper relationship between government and the economy, it mattered that the commercial interest was not limited to a tiny planter elite. And in a society where economic opportunity for most white men was defined as the acquisition of land and slaves, the prevalence of small slaveholdings was an important source of legitimacy for the master class, just as the precipitous decline in slave ownership was a potential threat. How the southern social structure changed after the Civil War was therefore bound to have a corresponding influence on postwar politics and ideology.[4]

Emancipation was only the beginning. A bloody war that often had the character of a social revolution was followed by several years of tension and suspicion between the freed slaves and the former masters. With the free people now in possession of their own labor and their old masters still in control of the land, the stage was set for a substantial reorganization of labor relations. Eventually, they reached a compromise known as sharecropping. Landlords and sharecroppers confronted one another in a manner that was fundamentally new to the history of southern labor relations. The new arrangement gave most blacks far more autonomy than did slave labor. Croppers usually worked their own plots in family-sized units rather than in large gangs. As free laborers, they had the right to move about in search of whatever opportunities were available. By one estimate, as many as one in three sharecropping families changed employers each year.[5]

In practice, however, there were few alternatives for blacks in the postwar South. In mill towns and cities they were locked out of the best jobs; in the countryside black farmers found it all but impossible to purchase their own homesteads. The majority who remained in agriculture had no choice but to continue working for those who owned the land. For while emancipation had destroyed the master class, it had not significantly altered land ownership patterns. Because the planters still owned the land, they retained substantial control of a thoroughly reorganized labor force as well. After several generations of freedom, most black farmers remained dependent for their livelihoods on the South's white landowning class. In this paradox of persistence amid transformation rests the first and most important element in the emergence of a planter class after the Civil War.[6]

Yet the persistent concentration of land ownership masks a more fundamental change. The fact that most blacks now lived and worked in family units implied a critical transformation in the distribution of the black labor force among white landowners. Before the war, the majority of masters had owned five slaves or fewer, and more owned a single slave than any other number. But postwar labor arrangements required most landowners to employ a minimum of one complete family, and the average number of blacks in each sharecropping family was probably about five. Where half of all slaveholders had owned between one and five slaves, only 25 percent of postwar landlords employed the minimum of one sharecropping family. Thirty percent employed between two and four families, while another 17 percent employed between five and nine families.[7]

Thus while postwar landlords had far less power over their black workers than the slaveholders once had, the typical landlord in the late nineteenth century employed far more black workers. In 1860, 75 percent of the slaveholders owned under ten slaves. In 1900, 75 percent of the landlords in the cotton South employed at least two sharecropping families—probably ten or more blacks. If we ignore the fundamental change in labor relations and argue that the planters survived the Civil War, the nearly complete disappearance of the small slaveholders still suggests a dramatic discontinuity in the social structure. In a sense *only* the planters survived, and because of that it may be proper to speak of a distinct "planter class" only in the postwar South. That class constituted a much smaller proportion of the white population than the slaveholders had, yet it exercised authority over a larger proportion of black agricultural workers than had antebellum planters.

Control of both land and labor was hardly an assurance of social consensus. On the contrary, the planters were repeatedly confronted with political and economic challenges to their authority. One of the gravest threats planters faced came from the dramatic increase in the number of merchants. Devastated by the war, many landlords were in no position to provide credit and supplies to the freed people. Local merchants quickly filled the void, taking their business directly onto the plantations and thereby dividing authority over black share-croppers with the landlord class. Croppers contracted with local merchants who loaned the food and other necessities over the course of the year. After the harvest the merchants claimed payment from the freedmen's "share" of the crop. This arrangement was fraught with potential conflicts between planters and merchants, both of whom claimed a lien on the crops produced by the black workers. By the 1880s, landlords and merchants reached a working arrangement by two distinct means. First, potential conflicts were resolved in favor of the planters, who won the legal right to the prior lien on the sharecroppers' harvest. Second, the two classes effectively merged into one as merchants became landlords and landlords became merchants. Thus a consolidated land-lord-merchant class—a planter class—dominated the rural economy of the black South by the end of the nineteenth century.[8]

By an entirely different process of economic development a landlord-merchant class emerged and expanded its influence among white farmers after the war. With the spread of transportation, credit, and marketing facilities into "upcountry" areas, an increasing number of yeomen lost their land and fell into tenancy. This gave the landlord-merchants more direct economic influence over whites than the slaveholders had ever enjoyed. Market integration therefore involved a significant loss of independence for many white farmers. Indeed, tenancy rates are merely the statistical manifestation of a profound and disruptive transformation of the social relations that had long shaped the history of the southern yeomen. With the spread of the cotton economy into the heavily white areas after the Civil War, yeoman farmers came increasingly under the sway of their merchant-creditors. Local artisans could no longer compete with the flood of cheaper manufactured goods that flowed into their communities as they were absorbed into the national market. And with the breakdown of a local economy of farmers and artisans, traditional patterns of exchange could no longer be sustained.[9]

Locked into the market by a largely irreversible process of economic development, the yeomen steadily lost their independence to an increasingly powerful landlord-merchant class. The size of the average family farm shrank dramatically while the number of white farmers who lost their land altogether rose steadily. The social character of tenancy changed from a temporary stage in a life-cycle to a permanent condition. By 1900 a tenant farmer was as likely to fall into wage labor as he was to rise into landed independence. This was a dramatic departure from antebellum conditions. Until 1850 perhaps 70 percent of white farmers owned their own land. In the late nineteenth century, especially after 1880, the proportion of family-owned farms dropped precipitously. By 1910 nearly half of the South's white farmers no longer owned all of the land they worked. Here again a landlord-merchant class emerged *after* the Civil War and by the turn of the century exercised significant and unprecedented social and economic influence among whites who remained in the agricultural economy.

The social structure that Phillips observed in the rural South of the late nineteenth century bore only slight resemblance to its prewar antecedent. There is no discounting the poverty and oppression that still marked black life after emancipation. But it was not slavery. No landlord in the late nineteenth century enjoyed the legal right to break up a black family, to buy and sell a human being, or to extract labor by sheer physical force. Blacks worked not in slave gangs but as sharecropping families in a free-labor system with its own structure of incentives, its own relations of production and exchange, and its own economic consequences. Nor was white society untouched by this transformation. Small slaveholders no longer filled the gap between large planters and slaveless yeomen. Economic opportunity for white farmers, however narrowly defined before the war, had virtually disappeared by the end of the century. Enticed into the staple economy by the spread of transport and credit facilities, yeomen farmers steadily lost control of their economic lives to powerful men and seemingly impersonal institutions that had threatened but never overwhelmed them in antebellum years. The planter class and the plantation system that Phillips saw were not the remnants of the prewar South but the products of a fundamental restructuring of the social order.

As with the slaveholders, the postwar planter class was defined more by its power than its wealth. In many cases postwar planters were poorer than their antebellum counterparts; and they could scarcely claim the kind of authority over their employees that masters had once exercised over their slaves. Yet as the decades passed and the legal nature of sharecropping was settled in southern courts and legislatures, it was clear that while the slaveholders lost a great deal with emancipation the postwar planters nevertheless enjoyed considerable legal authority. And legal authority implied political influence. At every point in its rise to power, the postwar planter class had to translate its economic interests into legal doctrines, making the social transformation a political as much as an economic process.[10]

For this reason the political power of the planters was a critical part of what defined them as a class. Who controlled the legislatures, how judges were selected and who had the right to vote would all determine how effectively the planter class could consolidate its power. Who would write the lien laws that established whether sharecroppers, tenants, merchants, or landlords could make a legal claim on the crops? Who would write the fence laws that could protect or destroy the security of propertyless farmers? Who sat in the appellate courts that arbitrated the disputes between tenants and landlords, sharecroppers and planters?[11]

Not surprisingly, the political transformation of the postwar South was as dramatic as the social upheaval it accompanied. At their worst, New South politics were a national disgrace. When the transformation was complete, for example, the votes of only 5 or 6 percent of Virginia's adults were enough to win election to the governorship. A paltry electorate and grossly malapportioned legislatures preserved the domination of the black belt. Landlord-merchants and a shrunken class of independent farmers formed a tacit alliance against the majority of landless southerners, urban and rural, black and white. In those states that granted suffrage to the descendants of Civil War veterans, the right to vote became, in effect, a hereditary privilege. In some ways the South was closer to oligarchy than it had ever been.[12]

The means by which the planter class achieved such power were many and varied, but all depended in the end on the failed efforts to build a biracial alliance among white and black farmers. Having won the right to vote, the freed people quickly discovered that this was in many ways a Pyrrhic victory. To begin with, the black vote profoundly disrupted the class relations that had long shaped the white polity. The Old South's "dual economy" had physically separated most yeomen from most slaveholders, making geographical and class divisions coincide. Before the war, therefore, when the yeomen pushed for democratic reform, they generally aimed at taking power from the black belt. This they achieved through the steady elimination of property requirements for voting and officeholding and by the repeated reapportionment of the state legislatures. Once blacks secured formal admission to the polity, however, the same reforms had radically different consequences. Indeed, they implied a wholesale realignment of political power, for universal male suffrage in the postwar South gave heavily populated black belt counties unprecedented influence. For many white yeomen, the enfranchisement of the freedmen meant not black power but planter power.[13]

The political rise of the planter class therefore began with the reapportionment of the state legislatures under the terms laid down in the Reconstruction constitutions. The more democratic the prewar political structure the more dramatic were the effects on the postwar legislatures. Mississippians, for

example, had apportioned their prewar legislatures on the basis of white population, leaving the wealthiest plantation district along the Mississippi River with
surprisingly few seats in the state legislature. The Natchez region was overwhelmingly black; three out of four residents of Adams County were slaves,
who therefore counted for nothing in the apportionment of legislative seats. But
the Reconstruction constitution of 1868 defined the state's adult black males as
"qualified electors," instantaneously doubling the size of the voting population.
Accordingly, Mississippi's black belt reaped the political harvest from this
deceptively simple constitutional readjustment.[14]

The effects were visible in the actual distribution of legislative seats in
Mississippi. Today every district elects a single representative, and district
boundaries are periodically redrawn to assure that each representative has
roughly the same number of constituents. But in the nineteenth century the most
common method of apportionment was to give heavily populated counties more
seats in the legislature than sparsely settled counties. Mississippi's Reconstruction constitution gave three or more seats to only thirteen of the state's sixty
counties. Every one of the thirteen most favored counties had a black majority in
1860, and seven of those thirteen could not have qualified for so many seats
under prewar rules. Tishomingo County is a classic example. With 879 adult
white males in 1860, it had only one legislator in the state's House of Representatives. But when its 4,300 adult black males were added to the ranks of the
country's "qualified electors," Tishomingo automatically earned the right to a
second representative. Other heavily black counties—Adams, Lowndes, and
Warren, for example—increased their representation in the lower house of
Mississippi's General Assembly in 1868, reversing a process that had prevailed
for decades. By the second decade of the twentieth century most southern
legislatures were apportioned in favor of black-belt counties where the influence
of the planter class far outweighed the significance of the black electorate.[15]

Where fraud, terror, and manipulation reduced the political significance of
the black vote, the collapse of competitive party politics effectively narrowed the
political options open to white voters. Until the crisis of the 1850s, two-party
politics had provided an important mechanism for expression of the political
differences that separated yeomen from slaveholders. After the war, however, the
Republican party became the virtually exclusive voice of the freedmen, while
the Democratic party could organize itself around no principle greater than
white supremacy. Sustained political competition within the white South declined substantially, even as the potential for class conflict swelled. Some whites
continued to vote Republican; others enlisted in Independent or Greenback
movements. But by the 1880s radicalized southerners began to step outside the
confines of the major parties altogether. Across much of the South, whites and
blacks joined Farmers' Alliances and the Knights of Labor, and both organizations soon translated economic needs into political demands.[16]

Nervous reformers reacted by promoting a structural change even more significant than legislative malapportionment: the systematic disfranchisement of blacks. Some advocates of disfranchisement argued that suffrage restrictions were necessary in order to restore healthy political competition to the white South. In the words of one Alabama disfranchiser, the "grant of unrestricted suffrage to the negroes . . . has prevented any division of our people on economic or political questions." In the face of radical third-party threats from incipient coalitions of blacks and whites, constitutional reformers asserted that the revival of stable party politics among whites hinged on the elimination of the black voter.[17]

But the constitutional reform movement of the late nineteenth century, while aimed primarily at the disfranchisment of blacks, often solidified the political power of the planter class. In some states constitutional changes combined legal disfranchisement of blacks with legislative reapportionment. But this did not necessarily return power to heavily white counties. In states like Alabama, where legislative apportionment was based on total population, the disfranchisement of blacks simply enhanced the power of black-belt whites. And although its effects varied from state to state, certain forms of disfranchisement—especially poll taxes—effectively reduced the voting power of the poorest whites along with most blacks. Blacks loudly protested these constitutional "reforms." But even among whites there were objections from those who understood that disfranchisement threatened the voting power of the growing body of propertyless whites. In the end, disfranchisement gave tiny white minorities in the black belt political power equal to that of overwhelming white majorities elsewhere in the South.[18]

Other reforms simultaneously limited the growing influence of the urban electorate. As the black-belt elite increased its control of state legislatures, the legislatures in turn stripped city voters of their electoral influence. Appointed commissions replaced popularly elected city councils. Unelected controllers assumed the budgetary powers that had previously been the preserve of local legislators. Management of city services was turned over to professional experts whose claim to power rested precisely on their isolation from the influence of the electorate.[19]

By the end of the nineteenth century, when U.B. Phillips looked about his native Georgia and formulated his interpretation of the Old South, he was bound to be misled by what he witnessed. For his was a South transformed in fundamental ways. The prewar planters whose papers he so diligently uncovered did not constitute the discrete class Phillips observed in his youth. They had lost the power and much of the wealth of slave ownership, but in their place the postwar planters claimed broad economic influence. In the Old South the formal exclusion of blacks from the polity and the growing threat to slavery at the national level had compelled slaveholders to seek the support of white yeomen by acceding to their demands for democratic reform. In sharp contrast, postbellum planters had every incentive to undermine all political opposition, black and white. By playing on pervasive racial prejudices, the postwar elite successfully defended the enhanced power of the black belt and at the same time prevented fundamental issues from arising within the omnipotent Democratic party.

For a generation after Appomattox southerners rarely doubted that the prewar order had been thoroughly smashed. Defeated planters and postwar propagandists disagreed among themselves over the value of the changes the Civil War had brought to the South—but most agreed that things had changed dramatically. The advocates of the "New South Creed" openly repudiated the past and argued that the death of the Old South was an advantageous invitation to progress and prosperity. "The Old South . . . has gone 'down among the dead men,' and on its head-stone we see not the word 'Resurgem,' " Edwin Deleon wrote in 1870. "For that vanished form of society there can be no resurrection. . . . But the New South—its child and legitimate successor—sits in the seat of the dethroned king, exhibiting a lustier life, and the promise of greater growth and strength, than did its predecessor." Even those who acknowledged the seamier aspects of postbellum life attributed them to the departing legacy of the antebellum years.[20]

Memoirists agreed that something fundamental had changed, that "the soul is fled" from the southern plantation. The question was whether this was for better or for worse. Far less optimistic than the New South boosters, memoirists poured out their nostalgic reminiscences of a lost world in a host of published recollections. In the opening paragraph of *Memorials of a Southern Planter*, published in 1887, Susan Dabney Smedes explained her desire to preserve for her children the memories of a world that was irretrievably gone. "They will come to mature years when slavery will be a thing of the past," Smedes wrote. Nor did she conceal her polemical purposes. "They will hear much of the wickedness of slavery and of slaveowners. I wish them to learn of a good master." Several hundred pages of purple prose followed, replete with implausible anecdotes and flagrant self-contradictions, all of them reinforcing Mrs. Smedes's idyllic vision of the antebellum plantation.[21]

This emphasis on historical discontinuity was by no means universal in the decades following Reconstruction. The rhetoric of the Redeemers, like the Redemption constitutions, was an ambiguous mixture of resignation, resentment, and restoration. On the one hand, Redeemers, who often traced their roots to the defeated Whig unionists of the 1850s, had no interest in restoring the prewar balance of political power. Such men had both ideological and political affinities with the spokesmen for the New South Creed. On the other hand, Redeemers had to portray themselves as saviors of the South, men who overthrew the corrupt carpetbagger regimes and restored clean government and fiscal sanity. And as the violence and intimidation of black voters proved steadily more effective, as southern politics once again became white politics, the emphasis on historical discontinuity lost much of its urgency. Nevertheless, as long as white politicians relied on black votes—as they did even into the 1880s—they were compelled to acknowledge, however grudgingly, the reality of the changes wrought by Civil War.[22]

Far more than the Redeemers, Progressive reformers turned the postwar theme of radical transformation on its head. They invoked an interpretation of southern history that shifted the earlier emphasis in two distinct ways. First, they argued that the social order of their own age was largely continuous with its antebellum counterpart. They did this by defining slavery not as a labor system that had clearly been destroyed, but as a system of "race control" that was now being restored. Second, they defined the Civil War as a *political* rebellion whose termination required only that the seceded states be reincorporated into the Union. By this reasoning, the central theme of Reconstruction was not the transformation of labor relations but the political interference of the Radical Republicans in the government of the defeated states. The end of Reconstruction was thus marked by the restoration of the *status quo ante bellum*. To be sure, there were precedents for Progressive thought in both Redeemer rhetoric and antebellum proslavery ideology. Conversely, the theme of discontinuity would recur even in twentieth-century memoirs. Nevertheless, by stressing the continuity of political and racial hierarchies, Progressives broke from the emphasis on social change that had infused the polemical literature of the immediate postwar decades.

This intellectual shift was clearly discernible in the rhetoric of southern Progressivism, beginning with the disfranchisement conventions that swept through the region between 1890 and 1910. Progressive historical revisionism began with a wholehearted repudiation of the voting regulations established during Reconstruction and only partially adjusted by the Redeemer constitutions of the 1870s and 1880s. The delegates to the disfranchisment conventions made repeated reference to the "dark and perilous days of the Reconstruction period" when a " 'Congressional Aristocracy' . . . in its imperious, disdainful and revengeful legislation, absorbed all executive and legislative powers." At Louisiana's 1898 constitutional convention, Dr. J.L.M. Curry tied disfranchisement directly to the repudiation of the Reconstruction Acts. "These acts annulled the State government," Curry told the assembled delegates, "enfranchised the Negro and disfranchised the largest and best portion of the white people."[23]

A year before Curry spoke, as the disfranchisment movement in the South reached its peak, William Archibald Dunning at Columbia University gave his scholarly imprimatur to the Progressive interpretation of Reconstruction history. Dunning defined the Reconstruction years almost exclusively in political terms, stressed the "revolutionary" nature of the black franchise, and assured his readers that the protracted experiment of Radical dominion—"seven u wholesome years"—was doomed to fail on racial grounds alone. If whites were destined to rule, blacks were destined to lose the vote. And if the black vote was the chief legacy of Radical Reconstruction, it followed that disfranchisement was the final phase in what Dunning called "The Undoing of Reconstruction."[24]

That was the urgent message Dunning sent in the closing chapter of his influential *Essays on the Civil War and Reconstruction.* Fully aware of the immediate significance of his writings, Dunning interjected into historical essays arguments countering those white southerners who saw that disfranchisement would eliminate poor, uneducated white voters along with blacks. As reformers in several southern states prepared to launch their campaign for disfranchisement, Dunning reinforced their sense of historical purpose. "With the enactment of these constitutional amendments by the various states," he wrote in 1897, "the political equality of the negro is becoming as extinct in law as it has long been in fact, and the undoing of reconstruction is nearing completion."[25]

By defining Reconstruction as an abhorrent interruption, Progressive disfranchisers portrayed their own reforms as a restoration of sorts. But restoration implied a vision of the Old South that was compatable with the realities of the New South. Accordingly, the movement to disfranchise blacks was necessarily tied to a specific understanding and defense of the prewar social structure. Here, too, the relentless emphasis on white supremacy became a rhetorical device for discounting the centrality of slavery in antebellum society. By focusing on the attitudes that persisted rather than on the social structure that had been overturned, Progressives backed into a revisionist interpretation of the entire sectional crisis. "The ultimate root of the trouble in the South had been, not the institution of slavery, but the coexistence in one society of two races so distinct in characteristics as to render coalescence impossible," Dunning wrote. Slavery had merely been a *"modus vivendi* through which social life was possible," he concluded, and "after its disappearance, its place must be taken by some set of conditions which, if more humane and beneficent in accidents, must in essence express the same fact of racial inequality."[26]

The same set of assumptions infused the rhetoric of educational reformers in the Progressive South, for their goals were inseparable from those of the disfranchisers. "Ignorance at the ballot box" was the ostensible enemy of good government, and so literacy tests and better schools sprang from the same reformist impulse. Not surprisingly, educational experts were conspicuous at many of the disfranchisement conventions. They reassured delegates that a good education was the best guarantee of the right to vote wherever literacy was the standard. But it was a guarantee offered only to white children. Taking their cue from recent Supreme Court decisions that legalized segregation, reformers set out to build an educational system suitable for whites, secure in the conviction that what was best for black children was best determined by white planters. Their logic was simple, and like so much of Progressive ideology it rested on a particular vision of southern history. The same themes of restoration and continuity were evident in the words of a distinguished educational reformer at the turn of the century:

> I find in the State men who think that the negro has gone backward rather than forward and that education is injurious to him. Have these men forgotten that the negro was well educated before the War? Do they not recall that he was trained in those things essential for his life work? He has been less educated since the War than before. It is true that he has been sent to school, but his contact with the old planter and with the accomplished and elegant wife of that planter has been broken. This contact was in itself a better education than he can receive from the public schools, but shall we, for this reason, say that he is incapable of training? Ought we not, on the contrary, to study the conditions and realize that the training which he needs has not been given to him since the war?[27]

It was left to Dunning's most prominent student, Ulrich B. Phillips, to complete the circle of logic embedded in this view of history. More than anyone else, Phillips provided his contemporaries with an interpretation of the Old South that progressive-minded Southerners would find comfortably familiar and strikingly useful. In language that closely paralleled the words of educational reformers, for example, Phillips explained how in the antebellum South "the plantation was a school." He went so far as to compare the plantation schools to the settlement houses established by urban reformers in the early twentieth century. "The white household taught perhaps less by precept than by example," Phillips explained. "It had much the effect of a 'social settlement' in a modern city slum, furnishing models of speech and conduct along with advice on occasion, which the vicinage is invited to accept."[28]

Phillips's discovery of the "civilizing" function of the plantation "school" was less the product of his manuscript research than of the Progressive ethos of his age. Nevertheless, it would be a mistake to see Phillips's work as a self-conscious apologia for the status quo, much less a deliberate misrepresentation of what he knew to be the truth. Rather, Phillips saw the present within the past. And like Dunning before him, he added footnotes to the collective wisdom of his fellow Progressives—those he observed in his youth and who trained him at Columbia University. Yet Phillips's genius lay not simply in his scholarly ratification of Progressive prejudices, but in his ability to do so while at the same time preserving the values that had animated both the New South Creed and the nostalgic memoirists. What is true now was true then, Phillips wrote: the planter class was politically omnipotent and economically progressive, the planters themselves were at once benevolent and firm, and the blacks were ideally suited to their situation. White supremacy was, Phillips finally concluded, the "central theme" of southern history. If nothing else, this placed his fellow Progressives well within the great historical tradition established by his beloved slaveholders.[29]

It is no small irony that the myth of an omnipotent antebellum planter class emerged as part of the same intellectual impulse that would substantially reduce the significance of slavery in southern history. But that impulse was only the most extraordinary manifestation of a more generalized urge to minimize the centrality of social structure in historical development. This is not to discount the long and tragic influence of white racism, a history that is in many ways amenable to an emphasis on continuity. But the Progressives put white supremacy at the center of their conceptual universe precisely because it provided them with the evidence of continuity they were looking for to begin with. In this sense the discovery of the power of white supremacy was more important for what it allowed Progressives to obscure than for what it made them see. If the "central theme" of southern history was white supremacy, the postwar rise of the landlord-merchants was no more consequential than slavery had once been. History itself had become a weapon in the planters' struggle for political power and ideological legitimacy in the postbellum South. Continuity was their ultimate vindication.

For their helpful comments and suggestions, I would like to thank Deborah Bohr, Eric Foner, James Goodman, Louis Masur, Reid Mitchell, Daniel Rodgers, and the participants of the Shelby Cullom Davis Center seminar.

1. Ulrich B. Phillips, *American Negro Slavery* (New York, 1918; reprint, Baton Rouge, 1966), 313.

2. For Phillips' life, see John Herbert Roper, *U.B. Phillips: A Southern Mind* (Macon, Ga., 1984); Daniel Joseph Singal, *The War Within: From Victorian to Modernist Thought in the South, 1919-1945* (Chapel Hill, N.C., 1982), 37-57.

3. Otto H. Olsen, "Historians and the Extent of Slave Ownership in the Southern United States," *Civil War History* 18 (1972): 101-11.

4. James Oakes, *The Ruling Race: A History of American Slaveholders* (New York, 1982).

5. Leon F. Litwack, *Been in the Storm So Long: The Aftermath of Slavery* (New York, 1979); Jay R. Mandle, *The Roots of Black Poverty: The Southern Plantation Economy after the Civil War* (Durham, N.C., 1978), 20.

6. Roger L. Ransom and Richard Sutch, *One Kind of Freedom: The Economic Consequences of Emancipation* (Cambridge, 1977), 86-87; Leon F. Litwack, "The Ordeal of Black Freedom," in *The Southern Enigma: Essays on Race, Class, and Folk Culture,* ed. Walter J. Fraser, Jr., and Winifred B. Moore, Jr. (Westport, Conn., 1983), 5-24; John W. Cell, *The Highest Stage of White Supremacy: The Origins of Segregation in South Africa and the American South* (Cambridge, 1982), 103-70.

7. Ransom and Sutch, *One Kind of Freedom,* 79. The statistics on postwar tenancies apply only to the cotton South.

8. Harold D. Woodman, "Post-Civil War Southern Agriculture and the Law,"

Agricultural History 53 (1979): 319-38; Harold D. Woodman, "Postbellum Social Change and its Effects on Marketing the South's Cotton Crop," *Agricultural History* 56 (1982): 215-30; Jonathan Wiener, *Social Origins of the New South* (Baton Rouge, La., 1978); Ronald L.F. Davis, *Good and Faithful Labor: From Slavery to Sharecropping in the Natchez District, 1860-1890* (Westport, Conn., 1982); Michael Wayne, *The Reshaping of Plantation Society: The Natchez District, 1860-1800* (Baton Rouge, La., 1983).

9. Forrest McDonald and Grady McWhiney, "The South from Self-Sufficiency to Peonage: An Interpretation," *American Historical Review* 85 (1980): 1095-1118; Steven Hahn, *The Roots of Southern Populism: Yeoman Farmers and the Transformation of the Georgia Upcountry* (New York, 1983). But see also Lacy K. Ford, "Rednecks and Merchants: Economic Development and Social Tensions in the South Carolina Upcountry, 1865-1900," *Journal of American History* 71 (1984): 294-318; David Weiman, "The Economic Emancipation of the Non-Slaveholding Class: Upcountry Farmers in the Georgia Cotton Economy," *Journal of Economic History* 45 (1985): 71-93. The latter two place far less emphasis on the immediate dislocations of the Civil War than do Hahn or McDonald and McWhiney.

10. Eric Foner, *Nothing But Freedom: Emancipation and Its Legacy* (Baton Rouge, 1983), 39-73; Wayne K. Durrill, "Producing Poverty: Local Government and Economic Development in a New South County, 1874-1884," *Journal of American History* 71 (1985): 764-81. See also Charles L. Flynn, Jr., *White Land, Black Labor: Caste and Class in Late Nineteenth Century Georgia* (Baton Rouge, La., 1983).

11. J. Crawford King, Jr., notes that "the planter class did not get what it had been seeking until *after*" the Civil War, ("The Closing of the Southern Range: An Exploratory Study," *Journal of Southern History* 48 [1982]: 53-70).

12. V. O. Key, Jr., *Southern Politics in State and Nation* (New York, 1949), 513-17 *passim*. In the absence of a complete study of the origins of legislative malapportionment, the argument that follows must remain tentative.

13. On the disruptive influence racism had on class-based political insurgency in the postwar South, C. Vann Woodward's *Origins of the New South* (Baton Rouge, La., 1951) remains unsurpassed. See also the important essay by Armstead L. Robinson, "Beyond the Realm of Social Consensus: New Meanings of Reconstruction for American History," *Journal of American History* 68 (1981): 276-97.

14. Francis Newton Thorpe, comp., *The Federal and State Constitutions, Colonial Charters, and other Organic Laws of the States, Territories, and Colonies Now or Heretofore Forming the United States of America*, 7 vol. (Washington, D.C., 1909), 4: 2049-63, 2069-89. For useful background information, see D. Clayton James, *Antebellum Natchez* (Baton Rouge, La., 1968).

15. Thorpe lists the number of representatives per county (*Constitutions*, 4:2083-84). Adult male population is derived from Joseph C.G. Kennedy, comp., *Population of the United States in 1860* (Washington, D.C., 1864), 264-69. These statistics include twenty year olds who could not vote; but this should have no significant effect on the conclusions.

16. Lawrence Goodwyn, *Democratic Promise: The Populist Moment in America* (New York, 1976); Leon Fink, *Workingmen's Democracy: The Knights of Labor and American Politics* (Urbana, Ill., 1983), 149-77.

17. *Official Proceedings of the Constitutional Convention of the State of Alabama, May 21st, 1901, To September 3rd, 1901* (Wetumpka, Ala., 1940), 3:2780.

18. J. Morgan Kousser, *The Shaping of Southern Politics: Suffrage Restriction and the Establishment of the One-Party South* (New Haven, 1974). For a useful explanation of

the variations from state to state, see Joel Williamson, *The Crucible of Race: Black-White Relations in the American South Since Emancipation* (New York, 1984), 225-46.

19. Samuel P. Hays, "Social Analysis of American Political History, 1880-1920," *Political Science Quarterly* 80 (1965): 373-94; Jon Teaford, *The Unheralded Triumph: City Government in America, 1870-1900* (Baltimore, Md., 1984); James M. Russell, "Elites in Municipal Politics and Government in Atlanta, 1847-1890," in *Toward a New South,* ed. Orville Vernon Burton and Robert C. McMath, Jr. (Westport, Conn., 1982), 37-70.

20. Paul M. Gaston, *The New South Creed: A Study in Southern Mythmaking* (New York, 1970), 15; see also 56, 79.

21. Susan Dabney Smedes, *Memorials of a Southern Planter* ed. Fletcher M. Green (Baltimore, 1887; reprint, Jackson, Miss., 1981); James L. Roark, *Masters Without Slaves: Southern Planters in the Civil War and Reconstruction* (New York, 1977), 156-209.

22. Woodward, *Origins of the New South*, 1-22.

23. *Official Journal of the Proceedings of the Constitutional Convention of the State of Louisiana held in New Orleans, Tuesday, February 8, 1898* (New Orleans, 1898), 31. Similar attacks on the Reconstruction constitutions as a pretext for disfranchisement can be found in Alabama and elsewhere: *Address of Hon. Jon. B. Knox on his Installation as President, May 22, 1901* (Montgomery, Ala., 1901), 1; J.N. Brenaman, *A History of Virginia Conventions* (Richmond, Va., 1902), 80-81 (Brenaman was assistant secretary to Virginia's 1901-1902 Constitutional Convention); *Journal of the Constitutional Convention of the State of South Carolina* (Columbia, S.C., 1895), opening remarks by Robert Aldrich.

24. William Archibald Dunning, *Essays on the Civil War and Reconstruction and Related Topics* (New York, 1897), 249-52, 353-85. See also Dunning, *Reconstruction Political and Economic, 1865-1877* (New York, 1907), 109-23.

25. Dunning, *Essays,* 383.

26. Ibid., 384. For a devastating refutation of the Dunning interpretation, see Kenneth M. Stampp, *The Era of Reconstruction, 1865-1877* (New York, 1965), 3-23.

27. Quoted in Dwight B. Billings, Jr., *Planters and the Making of the 'New South': Class, Politics, and Development in North Carolina, 1865-1900* (Chapel Hill, N.C., 1979), 210.

28. Ulrich B. Phillips, *Life and Labor in the Old South* (Boston, 1929), 198-201.

29. Ulrich B. Phillips, "The Central Theme of Southern History," *American Historical Review* 34 (1928), 30-43. See also, Signal, *The War Within,* 37-57; Woodward, *Origins of the New South,* 142-74.

9

"Firm Flexibility": Perspectives on Desegregation in South Carolina

JOHN G. SPROAT

In South Carolina, as in the other states of the Deep South, the potential for violence existed throughout the racial crisis of the 1950s and 1960s. Unlike such strife-torn states as Alabama, Arkansas, Georgia, Louisiana, and Mississippi, however, the Palmetto State managed to integrate its public facilities without suffering the trauma of a major confrontation between blacks and whites. Tensions ran high throughout the period and localized incidents threatened regularly to erupt into major encounters. But the one manifestly exceptional incidence of violence—the bloody clash at Orangeburg between state police and black students from South Carolina State College—took place in 1968, well after the inevitability of desegregation had been acknowledged within the state's white power structure. Three students were killed at Orangeburg, twenty-eight others were wounded, and the tragedy left ineradicable scars in race relations. But it neither halted nor appreciably slowed down the demise of legalized segregation. Indicative of the state's acceptance of a changing social order was the entirely uneventful integration in 1963, first of the land-grant college at Clemson, then of the state university at Columbia. Desegregation of the public schools and other public facilities followed thereafter in relative good order.

For all practical purposes, then, the machinery for an accommodation between the races in accord with federal mandates was in all but irreversible operation in South Carolina barely a decade after the Supreme Court's historic ruling in the *Brown* v. *Topeka Board of Education* case in 1954. Black leaders working to effect compliance with the ruling in the face of massive resistance from whites, doubtless found the delay frustrating. For liberals outside the South, many of whom expected the ruling to "change the hearts and minds" of white racists overnight, the pace of change in such states as South Carolina seemed inexcusably slow. Considered in historical perspective, however, ten years is a very short period of time in which to effect social change of any sort and perhaps especially in the area of human relations.

Given South Carolina's long record of slavery and separation of the races, its deep-rooted traditions of caste and class, and its evident affinity for particularism in politics, the state's evolution from total segregation to even grudging acceptance by whites of measurable racial integration in such a brief period of time constituted a transformation of extraordinary proportions, both in public policy and in popular perceptions. Moreover, the fact that this radical shift became apparent publicly only after years of massive, undeviating resistance to change, and then took place figuratively overnight, made it all the more remarkable. Clearly, for all the massive resistance South Carolina proclaimed as its official response to the civil rights movement, other forces were at work simultaneously in the state to promote some sort of new accommodation between the races.

The word *accommodation* is used here advisedly, for it best defines the process by which whites, especially in the Deep South states, came to terms with social changes which most of them deplored but which none of them could ignore in the two decades following the Second World War. In a work marked otherwise by a dogged adherence to racial shibboleths of a bygone era, one close observer of these changes in South Carolina concluded perceptively in 1960 that "there is no *solution* to the problem of race relations: there can only be continual adjustment and readjustment of relationships."[1] The record of desegregation in the South reveals few instances of whites anywhere welcoming integration as a just and reasonable improvement in relations between the races. Rather, most whites adjusted to changes they perceived as having been imposed upon them by outside forces and unwise law, or in which they detected some derivative benefit to themselves. Where there was a sense of relief when "integration" came, it derived chiefly from an expectation that the constant "agitation" of the race question would at last cease.

For some whites, of course, religious conviction or a simple concern about the morality of the issue were motive enough to seek racial accommodation; and among southern liberals, who had worked for change long before it actually came, these considerations were of primary importance. But most whites, especially those in the power structures where the hard decisions on race relations were made, saw desegregation essentially as a matter of a practical adjustment in relationships between the races, which hardly affected the racial perceptions that had traditionally informed their attitude toward blacks. If "solving" the race problem meant reconciling the anomolies in three centuries of institutionalized separation and injustice, integration was no solution. But the adjustment in race relations that came with the downfall of legalized segregation was no less momentous for that failing.

This was especially true for South Carolina, which had long been at the center of the southern movement to resist change in the racial status quo. Well before the decision of 1954, the state had marshalled its forces to thwart any possible move by the federal courts or Congress to alter the existing relationship. Even during the Second World War, when South Carolinians were fighting on the battlefields of Europe against an enemy that had raised racism to the level of a religion, the state sought to preserve "racial purity" in politics by prohibiting blacks from voting in party primaries. When a federal judge in 1948 ordered a stop to what he called this "clear and flagrant evasion of the law," the rebuff only deepened the resolve of segregationists to "hold the line" in race relations.

Of supreme importance in determining their course of action thereafter was the return of James F. Byrnes to South Carolina from Washington and his decision to seek the governorship in 1950. Not since John C. Calhoun had any South Carolinian achieved the political prestige and national stature that Byrnes enjoyed at the time. When he aligned himself on the side of resistance to all federal intercession in civil rights matters, the segregationist cause gained a leader against whom it was all but impossible for accommodationists to prevail.

Precisely why Byrnes took this extreme position is not altogether clear. To be sure, in his long career of public service he had paid scant attention to the needs and aspirations of his black constituents and, in common with most southern politicians of his generation, he had never hesitated to exploit the race issue for political benefit. But he was no stranger himself to bigotry and prejudice, having been born and raised a Catholic in a fundamentalist Protestant society.[2] His experience in foreign affairs had exposed him to the most cosmopolitan influences, and he could not have been unaware of the momentous changes taking place after the war in race relations throughout the world. Perhaps his defense of segregation was dictated, as he always claimed, by his devotion to states' rights and fear of centralized power at Washington—although he himself had been highly instrumental in expanding the power and reach of federal authority during his long tenure in Congress and in his role as "assistant president" during the war. Perhaps it stemmed from bitterness about the Democratic party's treatment of him in 1944, when he had been denied the vice-presidential nomination Roosevelt had all but promised him. Doubtless, it had much to do with his recent sharp break with President Harry S. Truman—and with Truman's expressed intention to pursue significant civil rights reform.

In any event, Byrnes understood well from long experience in all three branches of government that change was in the air with respect to race relations. Indeed, it was already in the courts of South Carolina at the time he became governor, in the form of a suit brought by black parents in Clarendon County to gain admission of their children to the public schools on an unsegregated basis (a case that ultimately became part of the *Brown* decision).

As a prominent school administrator recalled later, most people at the time believed that "whatever the problem was, Governor Byrnes could solve it."[3] Byrnes himself believed that he could not only slow the pace of change but control its direction as well. As governor, he confronted the issue squarely, calling for undeviating resistance throughout the South to any further federal "encroachment" in the area of civil rights. By the end of his four-year term, South Carolina had prepared itself well to avoid compliance with any possible federal move to intervene in race relations, going so far as to relieve itself of the constitutional responsibility to provide a free public school system and to give the governor authority to close the schools at his discretion.

At Byrnes's urging, the General Assembly also created a special School Committee to coordinate all further efforts to maintain the racial status quo. Chaired by L. Marion Gressette, an orthodox segregationist senator from an overwhelmingly rural and black district, this "Segregation Committee," as some called it, consisted of both legislators and gubernatorial appointees, backed by a staff that included some of the ablest lawyers in the state. Over the years the committee screened all proposed legislation on racial matters; and in the end, ironically, it may have served the cause of accommodation better than that of segregation, by becoming something of a "legislative trashcan," in which the more bizarre proposals of the "fire-eating" racists quietly disappeared. Still, in 1951 it was an explicit manifestation of the state's determination to resist federal authority, and it permitted a number of oppressive laws to get onto the books during its relatively brief history.[4]

Byrnes also undertook a sweeping overhaul of the state's dual school system, in a hurried effort to make "separate-but-equal" education a reality and thereby convince the federal courts that further action was unnecessary. The sales tax that financed this costly program was a heavy burden on one of the poorest states in the Union; and in presenting his plan to the General Assembly, Byrnes justified it on the grounds that "it is right."[5] Never before, not even in the days of Radical Reconstruction, had white South Carolinians been asked to spend their tax dollars to benefit black people because it was the "right" thing to do, and Byrnes's appeal marked a slight, but significant, change in the tone of racial politics. It indicated as well that the governor and his advisors recognized both the inevitability of change and the vulnerability of South Carolina to federal action in support of change. The massive school building program that followed did not prevent desegregation, of course, but it had the salutary side effect of providing the physical base for a subsequent general improvement of education in the state.

In his belated attempt to salvage the "separate-but-equal" doctrine, the governor doubtless believed he was promoting better race relations, as well as protecting states' rights. Given his overall record in the statehouse and the "hard line" he clung to after he left office, however, James F. Byrnes unquestionably was the prime mover in South Carolina's massive resistance effort. Moreover, his unyielding opposition to racial accommodation had an effect well beyond the borders of his home state. For the failure of Byrnes—and such other "elder statesmen" of the South as Harry F. Byrd of Virginia and Richard B. Russell of

Georgia—to accept the Supreme Court's ruling as the law of the land and to counsel peaceful, orderly compliance all but insured that the region's movement toward racial accommodation would be a difficult and prolonged ordeal.

More to the point, Byrnes had the opportunity and regional stature at the time he became governor in 1951 to initiate a voluntary, gradual scrapping of the Jim Crow system, which almost certainly would have forestalled significant federal intervention. Instead, he became the very symbol of resistance, and it was not until well into the 1960s that other politicians in South Carolina found it "safe" to deviate publicly from his basic position on race relations, even though some of them, at least, perceived from the start that massive resistance must fail.[6]

Ironically, when the federal government did indeed move to end legalized segregation, much of what its message said—and failed to say—played into the hands of the massive resistors. As Numan V. Bartley has observed, the *Brown* decision was drafted in a manner to attract a consensus on the court; hence, it relied not upon the considerable body of legal precedent that had accumulated in recent years, but instead upon sociological and psychological arguments that ranged from the plausible to the theoretical.[7] Spokesmen for continued segregation, from powerful southern legislators in Washington to local rabble-rousers, had no difficulty in interpreting these arguments as "liberal jargon"—abstractions that had no relation to the realities of life in the South.

In that the justices failed to include an implementation decree or to lay down a precise timetable for compliance, their ruling in 1954 (and, more especially, the second *Brown* ruling the following year) invited delay at best, defiance at worst. The court's intent was to separate the constitutional issue of racial segregation from the delicate question of how southern whites would respond to a federal mandate on the issue. But the effect was to confuse the court's intent in the minds of moderates, as well as of racial extremists. Cyril Busbee, who would become South Carolina's Superintendent of Education during the years when desegregation actually took place, thought the *Brown* decision a reasonable one. In terms of "sheer human rights, to say nothing of civil rights, there was no other decision you could come up with," he noted some years later. Still, "no one knew exactly what the impact was when it came." Even the enjoinder in the second ruling to proceed with "all deliberate speed," Busbee recalled, was taken generally to mean "Well, take your time . . . but begin to look to see if there's something you can do."[8]

In acknowledging that local conditions might affect the pace and perhaps the terms of implementation, the court paid heed to the "delicacy" of the situation and countenanced a gradual approach to dealing with it. In so doing, however, it also put the burden of compliance upon those who were least prepared or suited for the responsibility: local officials and school board members. In rural areas, especially, most of these people were unabashed racists who had never given even a passing thought to altering the status quo. In effect, state officials were relieved of direct, categorical responsibility for bringing their constituencies into prompt compliance with an order of the supreme tribunal of the nation. This shift of responsibility gave opponents of the decision additional time and opportunity to develop strategies of resistance at the local level throughout the state. Worse, it had a shattering effect on the efforts of racial moderates to undercut the appeal of massive resistance among state officials, with whom, naturally enough, they had assumed responsibility for compliance with a federal order must rest.[9]

In South Carolina, the elaborate preparations to resist desegregation even before the courts ordered it would have delayed compliance under any circumstances. The will to resist was strong, as was a doctrinaire attachment to states' rights within a white establishment whose conservatism had deep roots. But the state might well have found itself quickly isolated and subject to strong regional pressures to conform, had the language and context of the court's decision been direct and specific enough to persuade other southern states to begin immediate "good faith" compliance. South Carolina could no more have stood alone in defying federal authority in 1954 than it could a century earlier.

In this regard, one of the most significant aspects of the entire desegregation crisis was the South's failure as a section to undertake a genuinely determined, coordinated, and sustained defense of segregation. In South Carolina, Byrnes and his successor, George Bell Timmerman, Jr., tried mightily to weld a southern front on the issue, but with little success. One of Timmerman's "keenest disappointments in public life," according to an admirer, was his inability to bring southern Democrats together in "sincere and genuine cooperation" on the racial and other national issues. Too many politicians had personal ambitions, it seemed, which undercut every effort to bring about "mutual trust and concerted action."[10]

Some political realignments took place in South Carolina as elsewhere, but the race issue alone was not enough to sustain them; and indeed they would have come in due time had race never been a major sectional issue. Moreover, even when the issue was bruited in a manner calculated to trigger a "fear of Washington" alarm, as it usually was, the realignments seldom affected state and local politics. Resistance could never have been massive for very long anywhere in the South, because it entailed resistance to much more than integration. In every southern state, the race issue was entangled with a host of other concerns, which made it impossible for politicians to single it out for prolonged special treatment, however successful some were in using it to momentary advantage. It carried more weight among whites in Deep South states than elsewhere, doubtless; but even there, the continuous interplay among other social, political, and, above all, economic factors prevented all but the most fanatical segregationists from paying it constant homage.

Massive resistors perceived correctly that *any* change in the existing pattern of race relations would jeopardize the whole structure of segregation. But they were helpless to control developments in other areas of southern life that impinged upon race relations and thereby inexorably changed the pattern. Too many people and interests in the South had differing impressions of the race issue for it ever to be ordered by any single, straightforward "solution," whether segregation or integration.

To affirm the ultimate futility of massive resistance is by no means to slight its oppressiveness or the outrages committed in its name. Timmerman kept South Carolinians preoccupied with the "race question" throughout his term as governor and very nearly took the state down the road Alabama and Mississippi were traveling at the time to ultimate civil disorder. It is a moot question as to how he would have responded to a court-ordered effort by blacks during his term to integrate the universities or public schools. That no such effort was forthcoming at the time may have been due to a perception among NAACP strategists that at least some of South Carolina's white leaders were working behind the scenes to dampen the appeal of the more fiery racists and move the state toward some form of accommodation, however slowly. Still, the period was a dangerous one, in which black colleges were systematically harassed, academic freedom was violated at the state university and elsewhere, and dissenters from the prevailing wisdom on racial matters were indiscriminately smeared as "reds," badgered into silence or ineffectiveness, and, in some instances, hounded out of the state.[11]

Under Timmerman's successor, Ernest F. Hollings, the racial temperature began to cool. As lieutenant-governor, "Fritz" Hollings had rung all the changes on massive resistance with other members of the political establishment, and his inaugural address was a classic defense of segregation. Once into his governorship, however, he toned down the rhetoric coming from the statehouse and quietly set about preparing the state to come to terms with change. Time and events turned Hollings into a realist on the question, and the virulence of some white racists genuinely alarmed him. "People thought I ought to have some magic to stop the monster that was about to gobble us up, or else they expected me to go to jail," he observed after touring the state in 1961. "It looked to me like it was high time we started sobering people up before it turned out to be too late."[12] Early in 1962, he told a group of reporters, off-the-record, that South Carolina's legal defenses against desegregation would "fall like a house of cards" before the year was out. "You might as well start preparing for the inevitable," he advised them. "We are not going to secede."[13]

Thereafter, the press began to alert the state to its fate. As one reporter informed his readers, "We are going to integrate. And the total force of legal minds the state can assemble won't change it. It's political dynamite, so don't ask a politician. But they're of one mind now: the end is near." Hollings would not have to supervise the changeover during his last months in office, he predicted; rather, it would be incoming governor Donald S. Russell who would have to "bear the brunt of the action."[14]

Still, throughout his last year as governor Hollings continued to nudge the state closer to "the inevitable." South Carolina, he declared, had a "firm policy of flexibility" with respect to desegregation and each new day brought a "new look" at the situation. Addressing the General Assembly for the last time as governor early in 1963, he formally alerted the state to the impending arrival of desegregation and asked people to accept the change "with dignity." A few days later, Donald Russell confirmed Hollings's message by opening his own inaugural fete, a barbecue on the grounds of the governor's residence, to "all of the people of South Carolina." Within a matter of another few days, the peaceful integration of Clemson University took place—the first open, unmistakable acknowledgment by the state's power structure that a momentous change was under way in relations between the races in South Carolina.[15]

As with massive resistance, the elements of peaceful accommodation in race relations had been at work long before the *Brown* decision, although always in a much less apparent and forceful manner. Of central importance were the peculiar dynamics of class in South Carolina. In comparison with other southern states, the Palmetto State's white population was a small, economically stable, relatively unified group, confronting a large, economically deprived, politically impotent population of blacks. The possibilities for control from the top were very different than, say, in North Carolina, where a large "middling" class of whites was not necessarily amenable to the leadership of an establishment.

Closely related were a legacy of paternalism and an aristocratic tradition—parochial and largely self-conceived, to be sure, but nonetheless real—especially among whites with deep family roots in the state. From the time of Wade Hampton and the conservative overthrow of Radical Reconstruction, these elements translated into a determination among established white leaders to put social stability above all other considerations: to insure that relations among classes and between races should never "get out of control." In the late nineteenth and early twentieth centuries, this control by a conservative elite suffered several glaring breakdowns. But the old Bourbon notion that some are born to rule, others to be ruled, survived the demagogic splurges of the Tillmans and Bleases to become of evident value as an instrument of control within the white community during the desegregation crisis. In a sense, the bizarre spectacle furnished by the race-baiters of an earlier day spurred white leaders in the years after the Second World War to prevent, almost at all costs, any revival of such populistic outbursts. A sense of deference generally among whites facilitated leadership efforts to divert virulent racism among lower-class rural whites, especially, into relatively harmless displays of defiance and to bottle up the occasional outburst of violence.

The essential conservatism of South Carolina's black people was equally central to the success of racial accommodation. The struggle for racial justice in the state was, of course, intimately related to the national civil rights movement, whose unrelenting pressure ultimately had much to do with persuading all but the most diehard segregationists that change was inevitable. Within each part of the South, however, distinctive local conditions affected the particular strategies activists developed to attain their goals. Black leaders in South Carolina were tough-minded realists, who held tenaciously to their goals in an atmosphere fraught with racial tension, where a single misstep could produce a catastrophe. Their demands, the manner in which they presented them, and the timing and tactics they used to press them, were always conditioned by intimate knowledge of the whites with whom they had to coexist.

They claimed their basic civil rights and sought some further accommodation that would insure, as well, the future nourishment of their broader human rights. But the message they repeated throughout the struggle was that change must come *within the system*—from a willingness on the part of white South Carolinians to accept the legitimate claims of black South Carolinians. They turned to the federal courts and other "outsiders" when they had to; but their primary effort was directed at persuading white leaders that their demands were just, reasonable, and clearly in the best interests of South Carolina. Above all, they emphasized their aversion to violence and their determination to see change come in an orderly, peaceful manner.[16]

Black activists elsewhere sometimes scorned this caution and deliberateness as Uncle Tom-ism. More accurately, it reflected the deep-rooted conservatism of the state as a whole, which affected the settled black population as well as the dominant whites, for all the misery the latter had inflicted upon the former over the years. James McBride Dabbs, author, minister, and long-time advocate of change, recognized this phenomenon for what it was and reminded his fellow whites that blacks, after all, were southerners, too. Blacks had shared the same region with whites for 300 years. Was it not reasonable to expect that they also shared many of the same values and aspirations? Blacks were as committed as whites to the worth of family, religion, community, and tradition—and as distrustful of abstractions, Dabbs noted. The value of the "concrete community" was of fundamental importance to black people, who wanted only therefore "to be accepted more completely within that community."[17]

Once a breakthrough in racial accommodation occurred in the early 1960s, the growing realization among whites that black goals were indeed "reasonable" and that their attainment would not mean the destruction of the social order facilitated the ensuing dialogue between the races. When Gov. Robert E. McNair, under whom accommodation proceeded rapidly in the mid-sixties, sat down to talk with the Reverend I. DeQuincey Newman, field secretary for the NAACP, the two men found that they could, indeed, *talk* with each other, because they shared so many of the same values and assumptions about what was right for their state.[18]

Black leaders further resembled their white counterparts in exerting a strong measure of control over their followers. Historians have only begun to delineate, much less to analyze, the class structure in the black communities of such cities as Charleston, Columbia, and Orangeburg, that produced over the years leaders to whom the masses deferred in matters of racial strategy and tactics. In Charleston, for example, the descendants of antebellum free blacks comprised a middle class whose influence had long been tacitly (and sometimes openly) acknowledged by white leaders. Analogous situations existed in other localities, even small towns in some of the most virulently racist areas of the state. Generalizations about these relationships can only be tentative at this time; but it is likely that the dynamics of class were of importance in influencing the behavior of many black South Carolinians in the civil rights struggle. Traditional black leadership did not go unchallenged, especially in the 1960s; but the success of young activists in South Carolina was markedly less apparent than in most other southern states.[19]

Also of critical importance in facilitating change was the dramatic reduction in the proportion of blacks to whites in the total population, resulting from the black exodus that reached a peak in the two decades following the Second World War. This emigration was a permanent departure that stripped entire rural areas of their population and radically altered the demographic profile of the state. It also coincided with an appreciable influx of whites from the North and West into the middle and upper strata of society. Together with the movement of both blacks and whites from the country to the cities, the revolution in the size, density, and distribution of the black population changed the perception of many whites about the "threat of Negro domination" that had long been one of the most formidable impediments to a rational dialogue between the races. The rhetoric was slow to change; but demagogues found its appeal less and less effective as the state moved toward accommodation. The significance of this phenomenon became all the more evident as demographic changes resulting from shifts in racial ratios in the northern and western states began to produce tensions once thought to be exclusive to the South.[20]

A strong commitment to "law and order" among both blacks and whites, plus a resolve—even among most massive resistors—to avoid any breakdown in law enforcement, also served the interests of racial accommodation. With few exceptions, white politicians tempered their wildest diatribes against desegregation and "outside interference" with assurances or warnings that violent actions would not be tolerated. Unlike their counterparts in many other parts of the South, moreover, the state's white Citizens' Councils stayed generally aloof from violence or even the sanction of violence, and, indeed, may have served as something of a "safety valve" in some rural communities. The line between runaway demagoguery and outright physical violence was a very thin one, and calls for "all-out defiance" of federal mandates could be heard in local and statewide election campaigns as late as 1970. But the examples of futile violence in other states, plus the general determination to maintain social order even in the face of "outrageous provocation" helped significantly to discourage direct racial confrontations.

Of singular importance in this regard was the State Law Enforcement Division (SLED), South Carolina's local equivalent of the FBI. Under the firm direction of J. Preston "Pete" Strom, SLED operated independently of other lawmen, yet exerted a strong influence over police throughout the state. It was especially adept at infiltrating extremist groups, and it is still "folk knowledge" in the Palmetto State that the Ku Klux Klan does not make a move without Chief Strom knowing about it. The relative weakness of the modern Klan in the state is attributable in large measure to SLED's effectiveness in monitoring its activities.

One particularly bizarre episode in 1956 reveals the manner in which SLED operated to short-circuit trouble. SLED agents unearthed a KKK plot to assassinate Bernard Baruch on one of the noted financier's periodic visits to his home state. Not wishing to alarm the ailing Baruch with such distressing intelligence and lacking sufficient hard evidence to make any arrests, Strom handled the matter simply by dispatching two of his agents to confront the Klan leader he suspected of hatching the plot with word that SLED was "on to him." Naturally, the Klansman denied everything—except to admit that "It would be a pretty good idea if somebody did kill the old Jew son of a bitch." The threat to Baruch's life was real enough, but as one of Strom's agents observed later, "Who would be foolish enough to kill somebody if the police knew about it?" Throughout the period of the desegregation crisis, blacks could feel reasonably confident that SLED—and, by extension, other law enforcement agencies— would hold the Klan and similar extremist groups in check, and this sense was important in keeping racial tensions under control.[21]

SLED worked closely with governors Byrnes and Timmerman in enforcing massive resistance—and with governors Hollings, Russell, McNair, and John C. West in effecting peaceful accommodation. After James Meredith had his historic confrontation with the state of Mississippi in 1962, Hollings sent Chief Strom to Oxford to investigate what had gone wrong at "Ole Miss," with a view to preventing a comparable eruption of violence when South Carolina's inevitable turn came to integrate its universities. One observer called the result of Strom's mission "probably the most complete and carefully thought-out [plan] ever drawn up in the United States to meet the threat of racial violence." In fact, the plan evolved from the thinking of several Hollings aides and reflected the growing determination of the state's more realistic leaders that South Carolina had the opportunity—and necessity—of profiting from the mistakes of other Deep South states. Strom's own account of events in 1963, especially at Clemson, suggests the wisdom of their judgment:

We had our plan set, we knew exactly what every man was going to do, where he was going to be placed, and every responsibility of each agent. That included SLED, the highway patrol, the campus police, and the whole police community. So . . . when Harvey Gantt came to Clemson [as the first black student to gain admission] you could hear a pin drop. I mean, we didn't have one bit of trouble, none whatsoever. Of course, we didn't have any at the University of South Carolina [in September] and did the same thing. It was all a matter of a well-executed plan.

SLED agents played important roles in policing the desegregation of local school districts and other public facilities, as well.[22]

Racial accommodation was also, of course, a matter of bedrock politics, and here the legacy of the New Deal was especially important. Conservative white South Carolinians had always disliked the New Deal's social reforms and expansion of federal authority, and from 1933 on they kept a sharp eye on everything coming out of Washington to discern the slightest hint of a challenge to the racial status quo. In "Cotton Ed" Smith, moreover, they had an irascible watchdog on hand in the Senate until 1944, representing not only unvarnished racism but also deep distrust of New Deal liberalism generally. Even without the civil rights issue, doubtless, many South Carolina whites would have been in revolt against the national Democratic party after the war on a variety of issues, especially the New Deal's alleged "coddling" of organized labor. James F. Byrnes's break with Truman and subsequent support of the Republican Eisenhower was a clear indication that old political allegiances were in flux.

On the other hand, South Carolina was never an indiscriminate foe of the New Deal. From 1930 to 1941, Byrnes was one of FDR's key men on Capitol Hill—an indispensable ally of the president's in getting crucial legislation through the Congress—and his appointment to the Supreme Court was deserved recognition of his loyal service. More important over the long term, New Deal liberalism took firm hold among many young whites, whose allegiance to the party of Franklin D. Roosevelt proved to be remarkably durable after the war, even as the party began to champion civil rights. Indeed, the generation of leaders that moved the state from massive resistance to peaceful accommodation in the 1960s received its earliest political nourishment from the New Deal.[23]

Politics in the Palmetto State in the postwar years has been studied extensively by others, and only a few developments relating to racial accommodation need be noted here.[24] For one thing, the national Democratic party's appeal remained surprisingly strong, despite the civil rights issue and the emergence of a viable modern Republican party in the South. Strom Thurmond's leadership of the States' Rights Democratic party in 1948 would appear to belie this generalization, and it is true that the "Dixiecrat" movement attracted sufficient support among grass roots Democrats with its racist appeal to carry the state in the presidential election that year. But that victory owed much to the archaic structure of the state Democratic party at the time and, ironically, stimulated reforms aimed at broadening the party's electoral base and modernizing its organization. Few of South Carolina's other political leaders participated in the "Dixiecrat" movement or gave Thurmond active support in his campaign. Moreover, just two years after running for the presidency, Thurmond was convincingly defeated at home when he tried to unseat Olin D. Johnston from the Senate.

To be sure, Thurmond's political fortunes ultimately soared, although not in any sure sense until he became the state's "elder statesman" in the late 1970s. Thurmond was always a political loner and never the sure captive of any party or ideology.[25] Perhaps no southern politician was more adept at using the race issue to personal advantage than this resourceful Democrat turned Dixiecrat turned Independent turned Republican. He entered politics in the 1930s as a populistic "radical" and something of a racial moderate, became a national symbol of racism in the 1950s, and began wooing black voters in his home state almost before the ink was dry on Lyndon B. Johnson's signature on the Voting Rights Act of 1965. His inconsistency on the issue served him well politically; but it also indirectly served the cause of accommodation by weakening the segregationist front against change and depriving South Carolina's racial extremists of a potentially powerful leader.[26]

Also arising out of the New Deal heritage was the voting power and political allegiance of South Carolina's black people. Even when the state Democratic party was doing its best to keep blacks out of its affairs in the 1940s, voices of common sense were warning party leaders that they were doing themselves a disservice. As one newspaper put it in 1948, "Why should the Democratic party of South Carolina find itself forced to run around like a hound dog with a can tied to its tail seeking a way to do what every member of the party knows must be done, if not today, then tomorrow?" That same year, the commencement speaker at the University of South Carolina—a prominent local attorney and civic leader—warned his listeners of the harmful effects the "race problem" was having on American foreign policy and counseled them on the voting issue that "common impulses of humanity demand that we cease to humiliate a large part of the population." Black people had a legal right to vote and they could be denied it only by deceit and corruption. "Are we to rear a generation of white tricksters and set an example of dishonesty to eight hundred thousand Negroes and expect our state to prosper in the way of right thinking and right living?" he asked the graduates.[27]

Sentiments such as these were straws in the wind that were almost blown out of the state during the ensuing years of massive resistance. But as a revitalized Republican party began to cut into the traditional Democratic voting base, the black vote became increasingly important in the thinking of younger Democrats especially—people such as Donald L. Fowler, a professional political scientist who would lead the party as its executive director, then as state chairman, during the years when racial accommodation was most fully realized. No Democrat could ignore the steady rise in black voter registration in the 1960s, and no Democratic candidate for governor after 1958 failed to make a special effort to win black votes. Beginning with Hollings, moreover, the state benefited from the leadership of four strong Democratic governors, all of whom were accommodationists elected with evident black support and all of whom remained generally on good terms with the national party despite occasional differences on issues and candidates. As one cogent analysis of recent southern politics confirms, this Democratic party readiness to assimilate blacks in order to offset defections to the Republicans meshed entirely with the strategy of black leaders to seek accommodation and change "within the system."[28]

Crucial to the success of desegregation efforts everywhere in the Deep South was the degree to which economic considerations influenced the thinking and actions of white leaders.[29] In South Carolina, "enlightened economic self-interest" showed itself early in the war and postwar years, sparked, ironically, by concern among a handful of perceptive whites about the drain of black labor from the state. In May 1948, for example, the prominent Charleston attorney and former circuit solicitor Robert M. Figg, Jr., addressed the integrated Charleston Welfare Council and called for a major effort to elevate the economic status of black people, so as to "increase their ability to produce, consume, and save"—*and* to dissuade them from leaving the state.[30]

Needless to say, there was no immediate rush by business and financial leaders to heed Figg's call at the time; yet, even during the 1950s, some whites worked quietly with blacks to effect some positive economic change. In a major study of the health of southern blacks and white mill workers from 1900 to 1963, Edward H. Beardsley has discovered that black physicians in South Carolina began to experience equal—or near to equal—professional opportunities in the early 1950s, sooner than their colleagues in other southern states. Although they continued to be victimized by segregation until the 1960s, they benefited during the years of massive resistance from the assistance of both northern black and southern white physicians.[31]

But the most significant economic breakthroughs for blacks took place in the early 1960s in the state's key industries of textiles and construction. These developments related directly to the changing perceptions among white leaders about race relations in general and, in particular, to their recognition that "social instability" was perhaps the major impediment to rapid, but controlled, economic development. Typical of the manner in which change has been generated historically in South Carolina, the new "economic realism" derived in large measure from the work of a few influential individuals. Charles E. Daniel and John K. Cauthen, in particular, stand out as prime movers in bringing the state's industrial, commercial, and, ultimately, political leaders to an acceptance of change.

Head of a giant international engineering and construction firm, Daniel was a tough-minded realist in all things relating to business. Rigidly conservative on such issues as unionism and government "intrusion" into the marketplace—and certainly not sympathetic by either upbringing or temperament to the notion of racial integration—he was nonetheless prepared, even during the 1950s, to accept measurable change in race relations. To a group of New York industrialists in 1958, a peak year in massive resistance, he predicted that "the South will solve its most touchy sociological problem long before most of the large metropolitan centers do so." In 1961 and 1962 he told large gatherings of South Carolina businessmen that "our Negro population is becoming an increasingly productive force in the state's economy. This is as it should be."[32] It was an echo of the advice Figg had offered some thirteen years earlier, but now Daniel's enjoinder conveyed a sense of urgency deriving from the changed climate of opinion nationally about race relations and civil rights.

Daniel spelled out his views in the most explicit terms, significantly, to a rural, heavily-black audience at the annual Hampton County Watermelon Festival in 1961: South Carolina must at once come to terms with its "race problem" in such a way as to insure the increased productivity and consequent well-being of all its citizens *and* the maintenance of civil order. "We must handle this ourselves, more realistically than heretofore, or it will be forced upon us in the harshest way," he warned. "Either we act on our own terms, or we forfeit the right to act." To underscore his plain-spoken views, Daniel integrated his own large work force, to the point where it quickly became some 26 percent black.[33] Whether it arose out of sheer expediency or from an honest acceptance of a changing world, Daniel's example was one that no business or political leader in the state could ignore.

Daniel was aggressive and impatient of impediments to achieving what he had decided must be achieved. By contrast, John Cauthen was preeminently a man of compromise and conciliation. A journalist and publicist by trade, he moved into a position of great power and influence in 1945, when he became executive vice-president—and chief legislative lobbyist—of the South Carolina Textile Manufacturers Association. Later he helped to found the South Carolina Educational Television Network, an immensely successful state-supported operation, in which he exerted a strong influence until his death in 1974. Deceptively mild-mannered, Cauthen worked quietly and carefully, but with dogged persistence, behind the scenes to persuade politicians and businessmen to accept a number of changes, including improved race relations, designed to bring South Carolina at last into the mainstream of economic and social development.

No more an integrationist than Daniel, Cauthen nonetheless recognized injustices in the old order and understood that change, aside from making good economic sense, had become as well a powerful moral imperative. Probably no member of the establishment better combined expediency and conscience in approaching the problem, and this posture made him an authoritative force in bringing about racial accommodation in the state. Indeed, Cauthen provided the "spark" that persuaded Daniel and other economic leaders to take the lead in bringing about change.

Well before the passage of the Civil Rights Act of 1964, for example, Cauthen saw the need for the textile industry to drop its color bar. White workers were leaving the mills and their replacements could only be blacks: in practical terms it was as simple as that. But Cauthen was also sufficiently sensitive to the changing moral temper of the country on the race question to recognize that blacks had an ethical claim to economic opportunities that mill owners and other major employers of labor could continue to deny only at the risk of doing serious damage to their own interests. In a steady, deliberate manner, he spread the message of accommodation among his employers and then into the larger community. His toughest problem was persuading white workers to accept the fact that blacks would soon be standing beside them in the mills, and he solved it in a typically systematic manner. First, he arranged for the personnel directors of the mills to meet with a group of experts to discuss all legal and labor relations aspects of the situation. Next, he put the experts on the ETV network to explain to the workers themselves (and their bosses, the mill owners) just what they could expect, and followed through thereafter with orientation sessions in the mills. When integration of the textile work force actually took place in the mid-sixties, some observers predicted a violent reaction from white workers; but the transition proved instead to be both peaceful and remarkably successful. Indeed, to the delight of the mill owners, within a short time black and white workers were competing with each other to see which group could outproduce the other.[34]

Because of his close association with most of the state's business, financial, educational, and political leaders, Cauthen was the natural leader of the "conspiracy for peace," the covert operations that ultimately facilitated the peaceful desegregation of the state's universities and other public facilities. The colorful term itself was coined by Edgar A. Brown, powerful leader of the state senate at the time, and it aptly described the undercover, highly informal, activities of Cauthen, Daniel, and other key individuals, in persuading people in positions of authority that it was their civic duty to help insure orderly change in race relations. Of the peaceful integration of Clemson in 1963, Brown recalled a few years later that

Johnny Cauthen came to see me. He said he thought peace could be preserved if business people would take the lead at the right time, taking politicians "off the spot." Johnny summed it up by saying that politicians and educators were in a "hell-if-you-do, hell-if-you-don't predicament," but that business people might take a public position when the time came with the help of newspapers, building up sentiment for law and order and breaking the ice so that South Carolina could do the right thing. Johnny and I agreed on this general premise.[35]

The "conspiracy for peace" worked well at Clemson and established a precedent subsequently used, in one form or another, in the desegregation of such cities as Columbia, Florence, Greenville, and Sumter. At the outset the "conspiracies" were composed entirely of whites, although contacts were quickly established with officials of the NAACP, the Urban League, the Councils on Human Relations, and other representatives of the black community. And as accommodation became a reality, some of the "conspiracies" came into the open as genuinely biracial groups, even in small rural towns where racism had long been endemic. A combination of resignation and relief, the attitude of white participants in the "conspiracies for peace" was perhaps expressed best by one Columbia businessman: "Well, if this is the law, then we're going to live by the law, and we're going to make it work, and we're going to do whatever we can for the children of this state and for this state."[36]

Economic expedience, political realism, traditions of deference and paternalism, the basic conservatism of both blacks and whites in the state—all of these factors came together in the 1960s to direct South Carolina away from massive resistance to peaceful accommodation. Little progress would have been made without the persistent pressure of the federal courts and other "outsiders" or unless black leaders locally had held firmly to their goals. Yet, the outside pressures were oddly selective in nature, and white political and economic leaders benefited enormously, in terms of time and opportunities to adjust, from the NAACP's strategy of "watchful waiting" and the failure of such activist organizations as SNCC (Student Nonviolent Coordinating Committee) and CORE (Congress of Racial Equality) to make appreciable headway in the state. South Carolina's accommodation to a new order in race relations had its dramatic moments, to be sure; but the spotlight of national and international publicity never focused on the state's "ordeal" as it did on the traumatic experiences of Mississippi and Alabama.

Moreover, the responses to both the external and internal pressures—ranging from the initial massive resistance to the accommodation that followed—reflected the unique character of the state's history, demography, and sociology. It is not enough to conclude that South Carolina really had no choice except to conform, that it held out until the last possible moment before giving way to inevitable change. Even at the "last possible moment," the potential for violent defiance lurked visibly beneath the surface in public affairs; and as late as the gubernatorial election of 1970, demagogues did their best to stir up trouble for the accommodationists. Although the Orangeburg tragedy of 1968 resulted essentially from a momentary, unexpected breakdown of "control," it sears the history of the entire period with an immutable reminder of the savagery with which South Carolinians were capable of treating each other in certain circumstances.

But it was more than a matter of luck that such circumstances did not prevail—many times over—in the two decades preceding Orangeburg. Few whites had the foresight and calm good sense of James McBride Dabbs, who counseled his fellow South Carolinians in 1956 that they were "today waging a fight which they will lose as surely as the sun will rise tomorrow, and about which, when they have lost it, they will wonder why they fought so hard to stave off so small a change."[37] Most people were slow to change and clearly reluctant to do so; but change they did, for all the complex and varied individual reasons that characterize any human experience. To the genuine surprise of many people elsewhere in the nation, the one state that seemed most surely to be wracked by violence during those years weathered the period remarkably unscathed; and within an unexpectedly short period of time, relations between the races in South Carolina had been altered in a decisive, positive way. That the change was an incomplete one in need of constant buttressing in no way diminished its significance at the time or later.

Viewed in this context, desegregation in South Carolina was entirely in accord with the tradition of pragmatic accommodationism in American history. Reform ordinarily is generated by small groups of dedicated activists who perceive a "wrong" and set out single-mindedly to correct it. But reform becomes acceptable in the larger society only as pressure mounts, often out of considerations relating only tenuously to the reform itself, sufficient to persuade political and other leaders of a need to accept *some* change if only to deflect demands for more extensive tampering with the status quo. The rhetoric of accommodation may ring with references to the justice of the change; and, indeed, some high moral purpose may be advanced by whatever change occurs. Moreover, the practical needs of society may be addressed, so that people enduring misfortune may enjoy a measure of relief, if not a remedy. But the change itself comes because leaders of the established order perceive its practical necessity and make a conscious decision to accept it. As Elizabeth Jacoway has remarked with respect to businessmen and desegregation, "Southerners did not abandon racism, but they did choose, for the first time, to place other considerations above the maintenance of white supremacy."[38] Moreover, they did so in a conscious, rational manner, in which they assessed the probable political, economic, social, and international consequences of their actions.

American history abounds with examples of such pragmatic accommodationism at work. In human relations, it has been especially evident in effecting adjustments among ethnic groups sufficient to keep the general social peace. If the process discourages Americans from confronting their most fundamental problems in a systematic manner, it is nonetheless central to the effective functioning of the political system and social order. It serves to defuse explosive issues and to meliorate social and political irritants. It explains the phenomenon of the "great American sponge"—that extraordinary capacity of American society to receive and absorb an infinite diversity of people, ideas, interests, and institutions, many of which are in profound basic conflict with each other. It is, in short, the mainstay of that consensual balance without which the viability of the United States as a nation is problematical.

1. William D. Workman, *The Case for the South* (New York, 1960), 229.

2. At about the time he entered politics, Byrnes abandoned Catholicism in favor of the Episcopal faith.

3. Cyril B. Busbee, interview with C. Blease Graham, May 15, 1979, in the Governor Robert E. McNair Oral History Collection, South Carolina Department of Archives and History.

4. David W. Robinson and Robert McCormick Figg, Jr., both of whom served as counsels to the committee (Robinson as Chief Counsel from 1955 to 1961), discussed the committee's work with me in taped interviews on Aug. 9 and 10, 1983. See also Papers of the South Carolina School Committee, South Carolina Department of Archives and History.

5. *Columbia State,* Jan. 17, 1951.

6. Several important political figures expressed this view to me in "off-the-record" conversations. Evidence of Byrnes's continuing inflexibility can be found, for example, in his article "The Supreme Court Must Be Curbed," *U.S. News and World Report,* May 18, 1956.

7. *The Rise of Massive Resistance: Race and Politics in the South During the 1950s* (Baton Rouge, 1969), 58-66. Footnote 11 of the *Brown* decision (347 U.S. 483 [1954]) was a "red flag" to segregationists, because it cited such psychological and sociological authorities as Gunnar Myrdal and Kenneth Clark. Robert M. Figg, Jr., recalls that Leander Perez, the notorious Louisiana racist leader, tried unsuccessfully to persuade him to file for a rehearing on the grounds that footnote 11 was "outrageously communistic" (interview with Figg, Aug. 16, 1983).

8. Busbee, interview, May 15, 1979, McNair Oral History Collection.

9. See Thomas L. Johnson, "James McBride Dabbs: A Life History" (PhD. diss., University of South Carolina, 1980), for indications of the effect this aspect of the ruling had on moderates in the South.

10. William D. Workman, Jr., in *Charleston News and Courier,* July 26, 1959.

11. The most explicit treatment of the period is Howard H. Quint, *Profile in Black and White: A Frank Portrait of South Carolina* (Washington, 1958).

12. Ernest F. Hollings, quoted in George McMillan, "Integration With Dignity: The Inside Story of How South Carolina Kept the Peace," *Saturday Evening Post* (March 16, 1963), 16-17; interview with McMillan, Aug. 13, 1981.

13. Ibid.; also letter from Sen. Ernest F. Hollings to author, Aug. 5, 1983, and interview with William E. Mahoney (South Carolina correspondent for the Associated Press in the 1960s), Aug. 8, 1983.

14. Mahoney, quoted in *Southern School News,* Sept. 1962, 9; and interview, Aug. 8, 1983.

15. Hollings, quoted in *Southern School News,* Jan. 1963, 15. See also William Bagwell, *School Desegregation in the Carolinas: Two Case Studies* (Columbia, S.C., 1972), 164-65, and Neil R. Peirce, *The Deep South States of America: People, Politics, and Power in the Seven States of the Deep South* (New York, 1972), 393-94.

16. The most important recent study of black community dynamics in South Carolina is Leon Fink, "Union Power, Soul Power: The Story of 1199B and Labor's Search for a Southern Strategy," *Southern Changes* 5, no. 2 (March-April 1983), 9-20, which deals with the Charleston hospital workers' strike of 1969 and is part of a larger, forthcoming history of the hospital workers' union. I. A. Newby, *Black Carolinians: A History of Blacks in South Carolina from 1895 to 1968* (Columbia, S.C., 1968), is an important and highly-informative study; but it does not address the question of how the conservatism of South Carolina blacks has affected both the historic and the more recent inter-relationships between blacks and whites in the state.

17. Dabbs, *Who Speaks For the South?* (New York, 1964), 367-68; see also Johnson, "Dabbs."

18. McNair and Newman, quoted in Philip R. Grose, Jr., "Activist Spirit Still Burns in Rev. Newman," *Columbia State*, Oct. 4, 1981.

19. Some indication of this problem's complexity is revealed in Grace Jordan McFadden's videotaped oral history collection, "The Quest for Human Rights: Oral Recollections of Black South Carolinians," University of South Carolina Instructional Services Center, 1976-80.

20. Newby, *Black Carolinians,* 193-201.

21. J. Preston Strom and J. Leon Gasque, interview with John J. Duffy and Steven Gietscher, March 10, 1979, McNair Oral History Collection.

22. Ibid.; McMillan, "Integration With Dignity," 18; telephone interview with Harry Walker (legal counsel to the governor during Hollings's administration), April 26, 1981.

23. An exception was Hollings, who came out of a Charleston Republican background and in 1940 was a member of the integrated South Carolina delegation to the Republican National Convention in Philadelphia.

24. Peirce, *Deep South States,* 380-434; Jack Bass and Walter DeVries, *The Transformation of Southern Politics: Social Change and Political Consequence Since 1945* (New York, 1976), 248-83; Quint, *Profile in Black and White,* 128-44; Ernest F. Lander, Jr., *A History of South Carolina, 1865-1960,* 2d ed. (updated to 1968) (Columbia, S.C., 1970), xvi-xxi, 169-206.

25. John J. Duffy discussed with me at length his informed observations on Thurmond's early career and insights into his extraordinary political "survivability." David Bruck, correctly emphasizes the influence on Thurmond's life of his Edgefield County background, but fails to explain his ability to ride the political tides over a long period of time to a virtually unassailable position among many black voters as well as most whites in the state ("Strom Thurmond's Roots," *New Republic,* March 3, 1982, 15-30). Far more than ideology or party affiliation, it is constituent service—at which he is a master—that explains Thurmond's popularity among South Carolinians.

26. Robert McCormick Figg, Jr., recalls that as a young member of the state House of Representatives in the 1930s, he (and many of his colleagues) considered then state Sen. J. Strom Thurmond the "wildest liberal we had . . . he was a populist, he really was. Everybody was afraid he might introduce this, that, and the other thing" (interview with Figg, Aug. 9, 1983).

27. *Columbia Record,* May 19, 1948; R. Beverley Herbert, quoted in *Columbia State,* June 3, 1948; see also Herbert's privately-published pamphlet, *What We Can Do About the Race Problem* (Columbia, S.C., 1948).

28. Bass and DeVries, *Transformation of Southern Politics,* 249.

29. Two important recent works on economics and desegregation are James C. Cobb, *The Selling of the South: The Southern Crusade for Industrial Development,*

1936-1980 (Baton Rouge, 1982), and Elizabeth Jacoway and David R. Colburn, eds., *Southern Businessmen and Desegregation* (Baton Rouge, 1982).

30. Interview with Figg, Aug. 16, 1983; *Charleston News and Courier,* May 27, 1948.

31. Beardsley has discussed his findings with me at some length.

32. Charles E. Daniel, quoted in C.R. Canup and W.D. Workman, Jr., *Charles E. Daniel: His Philosophy and Legacy* (Columbia, S.C., 1981), 164.

33. Ibid., 182-86. Daniel and John Cauthen were close friends, and there is little question but that Cauthen's "enlightened conservatism" on the race issue strongly influenced Daniel's thinking and actions. According to people who knew both men well, Cauthen wrote—or at least sketched out in detail—most of Daniel's speeches.

34. Mrs. John K. Cauthen kindly made available many of her late husband's personal papers, including some correspondence with Daniel. *The Journal of John K. Cauthen* is an unusual series of twenty-one videotaped interviews with Cauthen on a wide range of subjects, conducted in the last months of his life by the South Carolina ETV Network. My views on Cauthen derive from these sources, as well as extended conversations with Mrs. Cauthen, her son Henry J. Cauthen, and several of John Cauthen's erstwhile associates. See also a perceptive report on the integration of the textile work force by Hugh E. Gibson, in *Charleston News and Courier,* March 6, 1969.

35. Brown, quoted in William D. Workman, Jr., *The Bishop from Barnwell: The Political Life and Times of Senator Edgar A. Brown* (Columbia, S.C., 1963), 299; and author interview with Workman, Aug. 18, 1983.

36. Robert S. Davis, interview with C. Blease Graham, Sept. 25, 1979, McNair Oral History Collection; Paul S. Lofton, Jr., "Calm and Exemplary: Desegregation in Columbia, South Carolina," in Jacoway and Colburn, eds., *Southern Businessmen and Desegregation,* 70-81; McMillan, "Integration With Dignity," 17-18; Jack Bass, in *Charlotte Observer,* June 7, 1976.

37. *Charleston News and Courier,* Feb. 5, 1956.

38. "Introduction," Jacoway and Colburn, eds., *Southern Businessmen and Desegregation,* 14.

10

The Soul Is Fled

JOEL WILLIAMSON

"The soul is fled," declared one southerner in contemplating the passage of the world the slaveholders had made. It was after the Civil War, and he had just viewed the remains of a plantation that had once flourished.[1] All over the South, paint was peeling from plantation houses, shutters sagged, and gardens grew weeds. With emancipation, the soul had indeed fled the Old South, but the body lived on. The great fact about southern history since emancipation is that the body lived on, and the body must somehow be sustained—first with bread, and then with spirit. Bread came, but the spirit required a new fabrication beyond slavery. To provide a soul to legitimate the presence of our bodies upon this American earth is what we "thinking" southerners are all about and have been about since 1865. It is the essence of William Faulkner, Wilbur Cash, C. Vann Woodward, and all the numerous rest.

The problem is made especially difficult by the fact that until 1865 we in the South were so vastly sure not only of our material and moral rightness but also of our absolute superiority as a social order. With defeat we were suddenly and roughly pulled down, and the cornerstone of our rightness and superiority— slavery—was destroyed. In Reconstruction we had difficulty in understanding how we could have felt we were so right when we were apparantly so terribly wrong. "It does seem strange that so lovely a climate, and country, with a people in every way superior to the Yankees, should be overrun and destroyed by them" wrote a Carolina aristocrat, William Heyward, in 1868. "But I believe that God has ordered it all," he concluded, as punishment for having mixed "the human and brute blood" under slavery.[2]

Heyward was at least partially correct, it had begun with slavery. Southern-ers in the early 1800s realized that with slavery they were riding the tiger, and they decided that either they must master the beast or be eaten by him. They chose to try for mastery. Southerners made that decision most significantly in the 1830s in the wake of Nat Turner's rebellion. The choices that came after the commitment to slavery multiplied, and southerners elaborated around that theme until in the end they were making decisions about themselves that, ostensibly, had little to do with slavery. In the end, in order to manage slavery and black people, southerners had to manage themselves. On the eve of the Civil

War they were weaving out a peculiar culture that was based on black, but it featured white.

Threatened at home by their own slaves and embattled internationally by a western world that was tilting rapidly against the institution, southerners put together a lengthy argument to defend slavery, and they chose to base their argument upon race. They need not have gone that way. In the long span of written history southerners well knew that slavery had been aracial. In ancient Greece and Rome slavery was not tied to color. But in the South, of course, it was already racial, and they made a virtue out of a necessity by discovering that Negroes were natural slaves. The "peculiar institution" of Negro slavery, as they sometimes rather proudly called it, was not only peculiar for its persistence in the South when it was dying elsewhere in the world, it was also peculiar for its color. What they needed for their slavery was a certain kind of person to be a slave, and they created one . . . almost out of thin air.

Their creature was Sambo, the white child with a black skin and an adult body. Sambo possessed all the virtues and vices of the white child. Like a child he could know love and loyalty to the parent. He was a physical person, often comical, energetic, playful, fun-loving, and innocent. But like a child he could also be careless, improvident, animal, and thoughtlessly cruel. Without white guidance he would destroy not only others but himself as well. With enlightened white guidance, he would survive, be made useful, and flourish. The proper white attitude was to be as a parent to these sable children. "Paternalism," in brief, was the saving idea that God gave to southern white slaveholders to redeem His black children. And it was more. Beginning with that providential idea, southerners spun out a whole society.

If one created Sambo, one had to create Sambo's keepers, people made to care for the careless creature. In constituting a black world, southerners were constrained to reconstitute the white world as its complement. In the ideal world, men of the slaveholding class became fathers to their slaves. White women, correspondingly, became mothers. Caring intimately for so many people by so many people was no less than a giant task. As always there were some who failed, utterly and totally failed, either in management, discipline, or simply in caring. These the system condemned, took their slaves, and, metaphorically, put them up for adoption. But those who succeeded, those who managed, who disciplined, who even loved their slaves, undertook gigantic works. With such large and difficult families, they were pressed to become gargantuan fathers and supermothers. Motion picture images of Burl Ives as "Big Daddy" with 28,000 flat black acres holding together a large brood tightly constrained and often badly damaged by the system itself are not inappropriate. The South in late slavery generated Big Daddies by the hundreds, perhaps by the thousands. It was a tough, tight, imperious system, and it bred hundreds of thousands of "cats" on hot tin roofs.

Big Daddy's origins and persistence seem clear. Would that we could so easily straight line up from the plantation woman. The southern belle is not the plantation woman, nor even the plantation lady, even though each is in each somewhere. If plantation women had been bells, they would have rung like brass; southern belles tinkle pleasantly, like silver. There is worth in each— indeed, great worth. But it would be difficult to describe the true value of the southern belle of the twentieth century, and one is at a loss to describe her origins. Somehow it all began with Negro slaves, masses of Negro slaves. And somehow, perhaps, it began to end in 1957, 1959, and 1960 in Atlantic City, New Jersey, on the ramp of the Miss America Pageant with Burt Parks singing, "Here she comes, Miss America . . . " and three Deep South women winning that tinsel crown. Whatever cruelty it was that made the southern belle—and it was cruel—southern men were responsible. Clearly, southern white men of the slaveholding class had difficulty meshing their women into the system. Planta- tion women assumed the female version of the "paternalistic" role dutifully enough but with less enthusiasm than their men. As a whole they were always smolderingly rebellious against slavery, and the smoldering had something to do with the mulatto children who continued to spring up in and around the big house. Sometimes, down South, the tin got blistering hot.

Planter men also had trouble with nonslaveholding whites—but not much. The great mass of these people were farmers, others were laborers, artisans, and small to middling merchants. An insignificant few were the "poor whites" so often stereotyped in print and film. The role of this mass of white people was not clearly set on the eve of war. The thinking elite was working toward a role for them that would be something like that of squire to knight, a perpetual squire who would intuitively value the same things that the knight valued but never quite know why. He would carry lances and in a pinch he would wield a pike, but he would never rule. In return for his fealty, he would get maintenance and protection, and, unlike the slave, a steady respect for his women. The plain folk of the Old South bought what the slaveholders sold, and their women aspired to emulate their ladies. They *were* well enough integrated into the system, and they never gave the system much trouble—nor have they yet.

The great middle class was in the system, economically, politically, reli- giously, and even by kinship. But they were also directly and physically involved in the enforcement of Negro slavery. Every white male of military capacity was made a policeman in the presence of blacks. Beyond the slaveholder as a controller of slaves there stood, ultimately, the state. The state made its power over the slave manifest most immediately in the "patrol" system. The patrol took over at day's end when the master retired. The patrol beat up and down the highways and byways of the slave South at night to make sure that the slaves were in their places. They were, literally, citizen police, and they had the power to arrest, to question, to try, convict, sentence, and punish on the spot slaves who were caught out of place. They were not stupid, fat-bellied, lust-filled, drunken rapists and sadists. They were everybody. They were a part of riding the tiger, and it was not all sadistic fun in living color. It was an institution as creditable as the courts, the police, and the militia, and its purpose was very much the same as those. The problem of slave control was so central to the concerns of white people in the black-belt states that the very term used to designate the area for which a patrol was responsible—the "beat"—came to be applied to the most local area of civil administration. To this day, what is a "township" in New England is a "beat" in Mississippi and Alabama. And there are no town meetings in beats.

The militant South, the military South prone to shoot first and answer questions later, did and still does exist. It sprang primarily from the necessity of controlling a potentially explosive black population. The military personality that we call Spartan arose in an ancient society where an elite group confronted a slave population some twenty times its size. The South was not another Sparta, but it was Sparta-like and from a comparable necessity. The price of slavery, as of freedom, is eternal vigilance. The white South was alert and it was vigilant. In the nineteenth century the key to control lay in possessing all the guns and the mobility for that fire power that mounted men afforded. Given blacks with only knives and hoes, it was very possible that the armed and mounted patroller could match twenty of them. Negro slaves were well aware of the facts of life—and death. Every important insurrection and every insurrectionary plot aimed for arms and an arsenal. When John Brown struck at the federal arsenal at Harper's Ferry in October 1859, both he and the white South knew full well what he had in mind.

White southerners on the eve of the Civil War were a tension-laden, often self-contradictory people. They kept insisting that blacks were naturally built for slavery, while, at the same time, their behavior argued otherwise. Of course, the two things could be reconciled if blacks only became terrible when tampered with by outsiders, by abolitionists. But that led to another tension. The South developed a great fear of the alien, and they tended to see him even when he was not there. To see the invisible is a talent not without value, especially when the invisible is real. Nat Turner was real and his reality was horrible. John Brown was real, and he was not alone. The South grew extremely fearful, perhaps overly fearful, even paranoid about outsiders. It tightened itself up, it became the closed society, and suspicion lavished on the outsider was not spared the domestic dissident. The South came to watch its own as intently as it watched others.

The South on the eve of the war was a high-tension culture, coiled like a spring. It was wound up to overreact by a trigger that none could easily describe. No one, then or later, could explain exactly why it did what it did. Like a frightened, back-to-the-wall society it would overreact to any threat or any imagined threat. The South by 1860 needed assurances without end—there could hardly be Munichs enough to keep the spring coiled. Any northern stiffness would be too stiff, and the South would respond extravagantly and with overwhelming violence as it had learned to do in slavery. The rubble of Fort Sumter in April 1861, a response to an effort simply to feed the troops there, was the appropriate symbol for southern psychology. "Overkill" became a southern syndrome.

The South was ready for the war. The message to its young men in the last decades of slavery was to be more Spartan than the Spartans. It was probably true that most young southerners conditioned to martial postures by the travail of slavery really believed, in 1861, that one of them could lick ten Yankees. When one is told early and late that he is the transcendent warrior, a veritable Mars on earth, and when he is rewarded in every way for striking the military posture, he is liable to strike the pose and take the role. And if he steadily plays the role, without relief, he and his sons too will become what they play.

When the war came, the South showed amazing strength. If there had been no South before, there was one then, and it had spirit. In the contest, however, it soon became evident that the North had spirit too. One southerner, it developed, could not lick ten Yankees. Other things being equal and excepting draws, he could beat one Yankee half the time. But other things were not equal. The essential military fact of the war was that when a southern soldier was killed, he was gone; when a northern soldier was killed, he was replaced.

Overkill is a spectacle awful enough. But what does it mean when a people "overdie"? Even in the days before the machine gun, prudent armies did not attack across open fields and in broad daylight other armies entrenched and superior in numbers and guns to themselves. Robert E. Lee must have known what he was doing at Gettysburg, but he did it. The South passed up many excellent chances to surrender honorably, but they did not. Even at Appomattox, the southerners charged one last time, broke through a thin line hastily formed by Gen. George A. Custer's dismounting cavalry, only to find another stronger line rapidly filling in behind it. At last, they gave up the ghost. Southerners had shared slavery, race, and the war. Now they shared what became, tragically, their most valuable and lasting asset—defeat. Appomattox, Robert E. Lee, and the Lost Cause became the great shared experience of the South.

It is difficult to discern exactly what had been defeated, surrendered, and lost at Appomattox. Quite literally, only an army had surrendered. Slavery had already been so badly damaged by marauding northern armies, by emancipation as a war measure, by the enlistment of freedmen as Union soldiers, and by the Confederate government itself in attempts to use the slaves to win the war, that the keystone of southern society was already shattered beyond repair. If the Confederacy was willing to destroy slavery itself to win independence, for what, indeed, had it stood? In actuality, over time the Lost Cause was an array and sequence of things. It was an empty box that the South could fill retroactively with what it pleased. Moreover, it could empty the box out at will and fill it again. The Lost Cause became the South's great renewable resource.

What the North had won was only slightly less vague than what the South had lost. Rather clearly, the Union was saved, but beyond that, specifics were lacking. Lincoln at Gettysburg chose to attempt to explain what the war was about. He said, in essence, that it was for republicanism; government of, by, and for the people. Unionism at Gettysburg had no specific economic, class, or caste content, and it was only vaguely religious. Southern society as built upon slavery, in contrast, had a strikingly clear economics, a vividly explicit hierarchical and caste structure, as well as a politics and a religion. Whatever else southern society had been, it was defining itself starkly well. Southern society built upon slavery was a very solid pyramid; Unionism was at best a sphinx—it was visibly, unmoveably there, but it was grossly unwilling to say what it meant.

The North could hardly define itself beyond a vague republicanism; one could hardly expect it to force a much more elaborate definition upon the South during Reconstruction. Indeed, it did not. Lincoln gingerly tapped out a sort of "union as it was" message of civil restoration. Johnson amended Lincoln's plan by defining any southerner with $20,000 or more as a special kind of traitor, and he soon decided that even any of those who would shake his hand was exempt from the definition. Among congressmen and senators, as always, each had his separate plan. Some of these breathed fire, but the fire of Washington solons, as usual, seldom burned. There was no program to compare with American occupation forces carefully democratizing Japan while geiger counters were still clicking like runaway clocks at Hiroshima, or the total dismantling of Germany. There was no Marshall Plan for white southerners and, the Freedmen's Bureau notwithstanding, not much of one for the freedmen.

Even that part of Reconstruction that was planned was planned piecemeal and similarly executed. There was no totality to the pattern. Once free labor was established, economic Reconstruction (as contained, for instance, in the promise of "forty acres and a mule") faded rapidly; slave property would end in the South but all other property would remain sacred, as it was in the North. The religious Reconstruction of the South planned by the northern churches was soon diverted to the blacks because the white South simply would not submit to a reformation in the northern image. Political Reconstruction proceeded by fits, and one could not have told from one fit to another what the ultimate course would be.

Ironically, it was the South that initiated the fits that led to jumps in Reconstruction. A pattern emerged in which the South acted—not defiantly or even irrationally—but simply unawares, and the North reacted pointedly. In the late spring of 1865, there was a period of a few weeks in which the South was truly plastic. It was thoroughly beaten and submissive, waiting to be shaped by northern hands. Shortly, however, they understood from the Johnson administration that not much was wanted of them. An end of slavery and loyalty to the union seemed to be the essential conditions of reentry. The South took heart. Some masters were even slow to recognize the freedom of their slaves. Most were realistic enough to know that slavery was at an end. But the blacks did remain, and the leadership naturally set about drawing up codes for the regulation of, as they saw them, these childlike people. Southerners were surprised when Congress, interpreting the codes as southern defiance, denied seats to their representatives and, among other things, passed the Civil Rights Act of 1866 giving federal protection to federal citizens. When the South broke out with violence designed to put the blacks in their place again and began to join hands with the Democrats in the North as in the days of old, a Republican Congress laboriously bestirred itself and offered the Fourteenth Amendment. By this time southerners felt so powerful that they turned the proposed amendment down, abruptly, with a shake of the head. In response an irate Congress finally moved yet another step to enfranchise all black men and to use those voters to overthrow the governments in the southern states and install more or less Republican regimes. All this last they did in barely a year. Then, almost as if they could not wait to relieve themselves of the nuisance, they turned on their heels and walked away. One can not avoid wondering what would have happened if the North had had a plan of reconstruction at the end of the war, or if the South had continued submissive.

In any event, with the exception of some fulminating laws and a few forays by the United States Army, political and civil Reconstruction in the South as directed by Washington was over. After 1868 even those few forays were largely ineffectual. There were not many soldiers, and they were almost always infantry. While the Ku Klux rode, the infantry walked. When they did move, they usually got to the scene of the disturbance just in time to count the bodies. In the last great struggle in 1876, the army again proved a paper tiger. The military posts of the east were denuded, and especially so of cavalry, because the army was all in the West trying to save its face after Custer's final embarrassment at the Little Big Horn.

The real reconstruction, the long-run reconstruction in the South was unplanned, unrehearsed, and unthought out, and it is still in progress. It sprang from that primal event—emancipation. The death of slavery meant that two great adjustments had to be made—one in race and the other in economics.

It is ironic that when the nation freed the slave in the South it also freed racism. In a sense white thinking about black people in mid-century America was a slave to slavery just as was the Negro. Because the South had chosen to rest its case for slavery on race, southern thought in the slave period was constrained to conserve the Negro. High racist thought in the antebellum South, then, was the running dog of slavery. Once slavery was dead, however, racism in the South was no longer confined by that stern master. Southern whites were now free to think anything they chose about black people and even to contemplate their demise. The latent extravagance in southern character, built up in the prewar years, fell upon race and ran to the wildest kinds of thinking about black people, often with violent results.

Of course, white southerners were much disturbed by black people moving into political and civil realms in Reconstruction. In the lower South it sometimes seemed as if black power would never end. However, once Reconstruction was over, southern whites were quick to convince themselves that it was not the fault of the blacks that things had gone wrong, but rather of the carpetbaggers and scalawags. Blacks were, after all, only children. If left to us, they were saying in the 1880s, our people were good people. Reconstruction in the white mind of the South soon became another evidence in the case for local autonomy.

Emancipation also forced an economic adjustment. Emancipation was a revolutionary equalizer among whites in the South. Slavery had raised some men extravagantly above others. Slavery gave the master dominion, power of an absolute kind not even present in the theory of feudalism, and certainly not present in the wage labor society of the North. The exercise of dominion over all those people and all those broad acres must have been a heady thing for masters, an ego booster perhaps unparalleled in the American experience. Masters were also elevated economically. Slavery on good lands under a hard-driving and astute manager was very profitable. New men could rise fast in the slave system. The classic new planter was the young lawyer on the slave-plantation frontier who turned windfall fees into lands and slaves. When the price of cotton was up—as it was in the 1850s—and lands were available, one slave might buy another for a master in a few year's time, and two might buy two more, and so on. In a short generation slaves would breed slaves, and the master would be slave-rich. Slavery, by its very nature, raised some men suddenly high. Compared to the North where the masses were plain farmers and a few were great merchants, slavery raised a lot of men high. Moreover, it raised them very high, not just head and shoulders above their fellows, but, because they stood upon the heads of their sturdy slaves, backs, hands, and feet above as well. Finally, it bred an elite of large slaveholders that was monolithic in its sense of mastery if in nothing else.

The end of slavery brought slaveholders suddenly and dramatically low. The land was still there, but land that had sold at $50 an acre when slaves had sold for $1,000 was now of little value. Slaveholders kept the land that the slaves had worked, but that left them with only a fragment of the wealth and control they had had over the economic life of the South before the war. With emancipation, the former slaveholder felt not only a poverty relative to what he had enjoyed before, he felt an absolute poverty. One who reads the correspondence and diaries of plantation people immediately after the war is struck most of all by the grinding poverty, the threat of actual starvation that touched nearly every house. The great problem was literally getting enough food to survive. Margaret Mitchell, when she wrote that brilliant revelation of southern culture, *Gone with the Wind*, not only chose the perfect title for Civil War and Reconstruction in the South, but also offered the perfect image of the result when she had Scarlett O'Hara come back from burning Atlanta to plantations ruined and survivors nearly starving. In the early morning, desperately hungry, Scarlett went into what had been a slave's vegetable garden on one of the plantations, fell to her knees and scrambled about in the dirt until she found an unharvested radish. In the film, Scarlett, played by Vivien Leigh, digs in the earth with her finely tapered fingers, draws the root out of the soil, and gnaws hungrily at it with her perfectly even white teeth. She retches and falls face forward on the ground, sobbing, defeated. Ever so slowly she recovers. She rises, grim determination in her face. Scarlett looks to the sky and raises her fist. "As God is my witness," she swears, "as God is my witness. . . . They're not going to lick me! . . . I'm going to live through this and when it's over I'll never be hungry again . . . no, nor any of my folks! . . . If I have to lie—or steal—or cheat—or *kill*! As God is my witness, I'll never be hungry again!"[3] Like Scarlett, the great slaveholders of the South were determined never to be hungry again. After 1865 they turned their interests in this world toward material things, and for a time, again like Scarlett, they neglected the soul.

Avoiding hunger in the postwar generations was a much more difficult task than it had been under slavery. Planters had the land, and there was plenty of unlanded labor about, white as well as black. What they did not have was capital. Soon, that was supplied from the North, through bankers in towns like Richmond, Charleston, Atlanta, and New Orleans, under what came to be called the "lien system." In the lien system the prospective crop was mortgaged to gain capital. Interest rates on crop loans ran high, ranging from 12 percent to 35 percent a year. In addition, there were often hidden costs. Planters and others who became storekeepers borrowed money to stock the goods necessary for making the crop—from mules and harness, through seed and fertilizer, to flour and canned peaches for the tenant and his family. When the crop was harvested and sold, the books would be "toted up." In the end the tenant made a bare subsistence. Altogether, the South fell further and further into debt. Creditors came to insist upon the planting of cash crops, such as cotton, before extending financing for another year. More and more acreage was devoted to cotton and less food until southern farmers were growing cotton and buying food. When farmers in those times had to buy their food in the country store at credit prices and sell vast amounts of cotton at bottom prices, obviously they had lost control of their economic world. The planter was the man in the middle. What he made was squeezed out between tenant and banker. The banker was least vulnerable, and so it was the tenant whom the planter squeezed. The planter and the tenant were in the same boat, but somebody had to row and somebody else had to steer.

The real benefits of the system were going to the sources of credit—to New York, Boston, London, Paris, and Brussels. The profits, ultimately, went where the cotton went, and the profits of the crop were vastly multiplied by the textile mills of Lowell and Manchester. Because the North controlled the politics and the tariffs and because it controlled the money supply and the railroads and virtually everything else worth controlling, more and more of the fruits of southern agriculture flowed northward. Where mansions had once flourished in Pineville and Demopolis, they now rose five times as large and ten times as splendid on Riverside Drive and Beacon Hill. The truth was, in fact, the incipient American Empire had found her first real colony in the conquered South.

That the South became a colonial territory involved a kind of poetic justice. In a sense she had reaped precisely as she had sown. If she had not opted for slavery, and instead settled her land with a hardy yeomanry, for instance, like that of Illinois, she would not have been nearly so vulnerable to imperialization. But, rather deliberately, her leaders gambled for the spectacular win, and they lost. The planter South in its last years was a skater society, gliding swiftly and agilely across ice dangerously thin. Southern leaders were, indeed, often somehow suggestive of riverboat gamblers. William Lowndes Yancy, Robert Barnwell Rhett, even Jefferson Davis all had something of a racy air about them. Perhaps Margaret Mitchell lost a historical point when she did not make Rhett Butler a general. The charges, the gambles, the bloody losing long-shots that southern leaders often attempted are suggestive of a plunger mentality.

In truth, southern leaders had a long and relatively independent history of seizing other people's lands on the bet that they could keep them. They took the Floridas, East and West, almost before the federal government could decently negotiate to accept them virtually as Spanish gifts. Jefferson might have legitimately bought Louisiana, regardless of what the Spanish said about Napoleon's duplicity in selling it, but the same could not be said for Texas and the Mexican cession. In 1853, two southern diplomats in Europe, in the so-called Ostend Manifesto, insisted that the United States either buy Cuba or seize it in order to make secure the southernmost frontier of slavery. For two years in the same decade, Mississippian William Walker, leading a rag-tag cadre of mostly southerners, took possession of the entire country of Nicaragua and as president opened it to slavery. The South was undeniably imperialistic, and it clearly had no compunctions about seizing other people's lands. In a sense it pulled off its most important imperialistic venture in 1861 when it simply seized itself from the United States government by the use of force. It could hardly complain in 1865 when it lost itself in the same way.

Crustly old Thad Stevens in Congress argued the case for a Radical

Reconstruction precisely upon the ground that the South was conquered territory. "Conquered" meant that the conquerors could do with it as they pleased. Ironically, for a few weeks after Appomattox, southerners expected precisely that; more than most Americans they could understand a total expropriation of territory by force. What they could not understand was the North's halting clumsiness. In the end the North pleased to make of the South a dependent colony. They did not do it by any grand plan, they did it piecemeal and by giving full license to individual self-interest. They used a few conventional political tools, and day by day they followed the invisible hand of Adam Smith. There was no conspiracy. There was no smoke-filled room, not even a dozen or a hundred of them, but more like a thousand and not even always smoke-filled. Yankee "Captains of Industry" by following their purses, for simple profit, for simple dollars and cents, brought the planters low. Before the war, many of the richest men in America had been southerners. Immediately after the war very few southerners were rich and the count was heading down. Subsequently, southerners who made it big made it in New York. And they still do.

Yankee entrepreneurs did not aim specifically to bring the plantation colonel down. Beyond the matter of slavery, they really had little against him, and it was evident shortly that they rather liked him. He was often threadbare, but always elegant, with his drawl and easy small talk, with a ready battery of well turned phrases and classical allusions, with a truly warm and genteel manner, with, in short, an abundance of grace in an American era that afforded less and less of that commodity. The colonel had learned in slavery, ironically, to care about people. He marked the sparrow that fell, if only because he owned it. His obvious caring was, of course, his charm, and that had not ended with slavery. In a way his paternalism saved things in the postwar South. Each planter-become-colonel disciplined and used his own people in the captive island that was the South. He took a lot of what little they had, to be sure, but in the end he would not do without them even if he could, and he made provisions for their preservation. If he could barely do for his own people vis-à-vis the North, he did well enough by them at home. A good worker need never worry about what was being served for dinner in the county jail on Monday, and a worthy person would not starve. The colonel adjusted, and he led his people, white and black, to adjust. In the "real reconstruction" that occurred mostly after Redemption, they put together communities where there was a place for everybody and everybody was in his place.

The colonels did their best. They had played the game and lost. They lived in occupied territory, and they knew it. They controlled their people locally, and they sent their diplomats to Washington routinely to see what might be done. The diplomats sent back word that nothing could be done, that if they got too restive down there, the Yankee captains would let the blacks loose again. So they waited. Now and again some southerners led by some colonels broke out, but it was always the other colonels who beat down the rebels. It was, after all, southerners who beat the Southern Populists, and Southern Bryanites and New Dealers, too. The colonels kept a low profile when it came to rebellion.

Emancipation, as we have said, was the great leveller. The planters were indeed brought low. No longer rich and isolated on their plantations surrounded by their slaves, they were within sight, sound, and a handshake of the white mass. But let no one suffer illusions. The South was not democratized in Reconstruction and afterward, even on the white side of the line. The forms of hierarchy that had been created in slavery persisted, and it still persists in a degree rivalled in America only in New England. The South is not democratic and does not much pretend to be so. Practically every southerner consciously knows that the hierarchy exists and in some way accepts it. Also, it is more a personal ordering across and up and down than it is a class ordering. There are dozens of layers if layers there be, few are labelled, and one strata merges imperceptibly into the other. Communication runs easily all the way up, down, and across the system. Everybody votes every day, and there is "upward mobility." Poor boys, and poor girls too, do rise. But it is not democratic. In every community in the South there is a bottom, and there is a top, and everybody who is anybody knows who fits where.

The pyramid was flattened considerably in Reconstruction, the top came nearer the bottom, and the whole structure slipped downward, but what changed primarily was what the hierarchy was supposed to do. In the antebellum South it was to control the blacks, work the slaves, and set the tone for the great society. In the postwar world it was there to win survival for those who continued to exist. With slavery gone, with only the poor pale god of white supremacy to worship, the earthly concerns of southerners often declined from the ideal to the real, from the spiritual to the material.

The change was evidenced strikingly in the southern church. Before the war one could hardly imagine a church more engaged in the total earthly life of its people. The church was slow to support slavery, but when it did it was a tower of strength. In the mood of what later came to be called the "social gospel," it carried the message directly to where the people were. Not only did it press in among the slaves and preach diligently the Christian message, including "servants obey your masters," it also collared the masters and told them that they were responsible to God for the stewardship of their slaves. In the generations after the war the southern church fled this material and social world. It became very much a church of the hereafter. "This world is not my home, I have no mansion here" runs a song favored in southern churches. The words ring true in the churches of the laboring people in the union-free South, and it has a happy, hand-clapping, liberated beat. Before the war, there was no Billy Graham in the South, and no one accused the South of being the "Bible Belt." Afterward they did so, and with good cause.

Southern religion left this world during Reconstruction, and southern politics went into it. Gone was dedication to the natural rights of man as advocated by Thomas Jefferson. Gone too was its sometimes opposite of devotion to an aristocratic society based on slavery. Politics became not loyalty to principles, but loyalty to people. Politics lost idealism, and it descended to The Man. The Political chief became the recipient of loyalties that had previously flowed elsewhere. Local chiefs gave way to big chiefs, and the big chiefs gave way to the North. Usually, there was one big chief per state. At first, the big chiefs were colonels. Recently, they are almost never colonels, with the exception of a few like Sam Ervin who somehow slip away to Washington. In the beginning the big chief was colorful. In Reconstruction and Redemption he was the great war leader, a colonel or a general. Around the turn of the century he had only one eye and spoke extravagantly, or he wore all white and spoke extravagantly. In the mid-twentieth century he came down pretty far to be less colorful: he wore red galluses (suspenders), or silver shirts, or had white hair, or, in his late middle age, stood on his head on capitol steps for the cameramen of national magazines for reasons that stymie the imagination. More recently still, some simply are there without much color and hardly speak at all. Reconstruction ushered in the age of the chief in the South—first the Hamptons and Vances to end Reconstruction. Then came the Tillmans and the Vardamans, and after these in our own times the long-lasting, the seemingly almost forever living, the unretiring Thurmonds, Stennises, and Longs. The new chiefs stand at the end of a long line of trading off high principle for local power, a line so long that it must have become difficult for them to tell where it all began.

By a curious half circle, these political sons of former rebels are also the *ultra* Americans, the knee-jerk Americans, traveling beyond America first into America only. They are a sort of final mutation in a declining idealism in southern politics. They are as unintrospective, as un-self-critical as Scarlett O'Hara herself. They seem to have no life significant for society outside of politics, the Congress, and Washington, D.C. Moreover, they have only half-a-life there. Their names are not associated with any ideal cause—medicine, education, peace, conservation, or environment—foolish or otherwise. Their names appear in the press most often in connection with national "defense," banking, and business as usual. True to the new role of the South in national affairs, they are programmed to do nothing at home and almost anything abroad. In foreign affairs they take their orders from Washington and march—racing to be, if possible, at the head of the column. With lusty voices the southern chiefs sing "America" while their feet tap "Dixie." Being real men, they see, of course, that they are courageously meeting a savage world, and it seems to be the world they love to meet.

Back home, for instance, in the Jenrettes' South Carolina or Elizabeth Ray's Canton, North Carolina, the colonels are more complex. Taken all together, they have a bigger, a more subtle, a more important job than the chiefs, and they know it. They would probably rapidly admit that Washington is unreal and of limited relevance; that the Jenrettes and Miss Ray mean a little money wasted and that the Thurmonds, Stennises, and Longs mean a lot gained—money in appropriations for internal improvements and military bases for the home state and keeping the Yankees off our backs. The Jenrettes and Miss Ray are merely unfortunate, the chiefs are survival and possible prosperity. The colonels are a cautious crew and very good at their job. They are always smart, many well-educated, and some even cosmopolitan. Many have gone to Princeton and Yale but you have to ask them for the fact after you conceive the suspicion. They seem, often, to have avoided Harvard, except they do sometimes slip quietly through the School of Law. At home they watch the egg and they preach its beauty. The "good old boys" take up the chorus. "Everything is beautiful," they sing, and sway in unison. The harmony is rarely broken. When it is broken, as in the 1960s on race, it is because of some outside and markedly alien influence— the Yankees did it, or the Communists, or both. Breaks are usually local, and, thus far, all have proved temporary. Down South, when Humpty Dumpty falls, horses and men do rush in, and they have always put him together again. The white South remains intact, and, surface appearances to the contrary notwithstanding, relatively unmoved and unmoving, America's anchorman.

The South is still, in the most fundamental way, unreconstructed. We in the South have stitched together a body, and its functions. It has a society, an ecnomics, a politics, a religion, and it survives. But the soul, it grieves me to say, is still fled. We once had a universe, with stars and horizons. It was a wrong universe, and it is good that we lost it. But we have not found another. The wind that blew our universe away still drives us, across this dark and shoreless ocean, flat without horizons and under a starless sky. What we have is each other, what we are is together, and we are still alive.

1. George W. Bagby, *The Old Virginia Gentleman and Other Sketches,* ed. Thomas Nelson Page (New York: Scribner's, 1911), 6, cited in James L. Roark, *Masters Without Slaves, Southern Planters in the Civil War and Reconstruction* (New York: Norton, 1977), 156, 209.

2. Joel Williamson, *After Slavery: The Negro in South Carolina during Reconstruction, 1861-1877* (Chapel Hill: University of North Carolina Press, 1965), 296.

3. Sidney Howard, *GWTW, The Screenplay*, ed. Richard Harwell (New York: Collier Books, 1980), 243.

The Contributors

Robert H. Abzug, University of Texas at Austin. Author of *Inside the Vicious Heart: Americans and the Liberation of Nazi Concentration Camps* and *Passionate Liberator: Theodore Dwight Weld and the Dilemma of Reform.*

William W. Freehling, the Johns Hopkins University. Author of *Prelude to Civil War: The Nullification Controversy in South Carolina, 1816-1836*, which was awarded the Allan Nevins Prize and the Bancroft Prize in American History.

William E. Gienapp, University of Wyoming. Author of *The Origins of the Republican Party, 1852-1856.*

Leon F. Litwack, University of California at Berkeley. Author of *North of Slavery: The Negro in the Free States, 1790-1860* and *Been in the Storm So Long: The Aftermath of Slavery.* The latter work won the Francis Parkman Prize, the Pulitzer Prize in History, and the American Book Award.

Robert McColley, University of Illinois. Author of *Slavery and Jeffersonian Virginia.*

Stephen E. Maizlish, University of Texas at Arlington. Author of *The Triumph of Sectionalism: The Transformation of Ohio Politics, 1844-1856* and co-editor of *Essays on American Antebellum Politics, 1840-1860* and *Essays on Walter Prescott Webb and the Teaching of History.*

Reid Mitchell, Rutgers University. Recently completed his dissertation, "The Civil War Soldier: Ideology and Experience."

James Oakes, Princeton University. Author of *The Ruling Race: A History of American Slaveholders.*

John G. Sproat, University of South Carolina. Author of *"The Best Men": Liberal Reformers in the Gilded Age.*

Joel Williamson, University of North Carolina. Author of *After Slavery: The Negro in South Carolina during Reconstruction, 1861-1877; New People: Miscegenation and Mulattoes in the United States;* and *The Crucible of Race: Black-White Relations in the American South since Emancipation,* which won the Francis Parkman Prize, a Robert F. Kennedy Book Award, the Mayflower Cup, the Frank L. and Harriet C. Owsley Award, and the Ralph Waldo Emerson Award.

Arthur Zilversmit, Lake Forest College. Author of *The First Emancipation: The Abolition of Slavery in the North* and editor of *Lincoln on Black and White.*

Index